S268 Physical Resources and Environment
Science: a second level course

D1324675

BLOCK

PHYSICAL RESOURCES

AN INTRODUCTION

Prepared for the Course Team by Peter Sheldon

S268 Physical Resources and Environment

Course Team

Dave Williams (Course Chair)
Andrew Bell
Geoff Brown
Steve Drury
Chris Hawkesworth
Ian Nuttall (Editor)
Janice Robertson (Editor)
Peter Sheldon
Sandy Smith
Peter Webb
Chris Wilson
John Wright
Annemarie Hedges (Course Manager)
Charlie Bendall (Course Coordinator)

Production

Jane Sheppard (Graphic Designer)
Steve Best (Graphic Artist)
David Jackson (Series Producer, BBC)
Nicholas Watson (BBC Producer)
John Greenwood (Liaison Librarian)
Eira Parker (Course Secretary)
Marilyn Leggett (Secretary)
Lynn Tilbury (Secretary)

Course assessor

Professor Peter W. Scott, Camborne School of Mines.

Dedication

Professor Geoff Brown was a member of the Course Team when he was killed on the Galeras Volcano, Colombia, in January 1993. The Course Team dedicates S268 to his memory.

Acknowledgements

The Course Team gratefully acknowledges the contributions of members of the S238 course team (S238 *The Earth's Physical Resources*, 1984).

The Course Team also wishes to thank Sheila Dellow for careful reading of early drafts of the course material.

This text has been printed on Savannah Natural Art™ paper. At least 60% of the fibre used in the production of this paper is bagasse (fibrous residue of sugarcane, a waste by-poduct of sugar processing), and the balance is softwood fibre that has undergone an oxygen bleaching process.

The Open University, Walton Hall, Milton Keynes MK7 6AA.

First published 1995. Reprinted with corrections 2001.

Edited, designed and typeset by The Open University.

Printed in the United Kingdom by Henry Ling Limited, The Dorset Press, Dorchester.

ISBN 0 7492 5145 X

This publication forms part of an Open University second level course. Details of this and other Open University courses can be obtained from the Call Centre, PO Box 724, The Open University, Milton Keynes MK7 6ZS, United Kingdom: tel. +44 (0)1908 653231, e-mail ces-gen@open.ac.uk

Alternatively, you may visit the Open University website at http://www.open.ac.uk where you can learn more about the wide range of courses and packs offered at all levels by the Open University.

To purchase this publication or other components of Open University courses, contact Open University Worldwide Ltd, The Berrill Building, Walton Hall, Milton Keynes MK7 6AA, United Kingdom: tel. +44 (0)1908 858785; fax +44 (0)1908 858787; e-mail ouwenq@open.ac.uk; website http://www.ouw.co.uk

Edition 1.2

S268block1i1.2

CONTENTS

1 INTRODUCTION

1.1 Introducing the Course themes

Let's clarify straight away the meaning of our title 'Physical resources and environment'. Firstly, what are resources? The word has a variety of meanings in everyday speech, all of which have in common the notion of something that is useful or of value, especially to humans. It's probably most often applied to a source of economic wealth, especially of a country (its mineral resources, land resources, labour resources), or of a business enterprise (its capital resources, equipment resources, personnel resources). Without resources, life in all societies would grind to a halt. A resource is often seen as the means of doing something, especially in time of need, such as having a fleet of lorries to spread salt on roads in freezing temperatures, or being able to supply medicines after an earthquake. 'Human resources' usually refers to the total of a group of people's intellectual and physical capabilities. Individuals are often said to possess particular resources such as stamina or strength.

Much of this Course is concerned with the type of resource that economists call **commodities**. All commodities possess two basic attributes: they are useful or of value because of certain physical and chemical properties, and they can be exchanged for other commodities. This exchange once took the form of barter, but now in almost all societies the exchange value of a commodity is expressed in money. In general usage, the term 'commodity' refers mainly to raw materials, such as iron ore or latex, or readily derived (primary) products, such as iron, steel or rubber – as opposed to complex objects such as cars or radios which are manufactured, often after much processing, from many different commodities. Such commodities are to a large extent the basic building blocks of trade and industry.

But what are *physical* resources? A simple definition is that **physical resources** are useful materials or energy extracted by humans from today's *inorganic* world, either at or beneath the Earth's surface.

○ Which of the following materials are classified as physical resources: milk, water, wood, salt, pepper, cotton?

○ Water and salt. Both are inorganic materials that have useful properties (not the least of which is that each is life-sustaining) and both can be exchanged (via money or by barter) for other useful materials. All the others are organic materials, i.e. products of modern biological systems, and, being biological resources, they are outside the scope of this Course.

The products of some *ancient* biological systems are, however, immensely important physical resources today: coal, oil and natural gas. The carbon in coal, for instance, was once in living plants. Today's organic material may become the future's rock. Limestone is mainly composed of the hard parts of ancient organisms, and although not a source of energy like coal or oil, it is an important physical resource. As we will see later, some of *today's* organic materials, while not being physical resources themselves, can provide alternative sources of energy to offset some of the energy demands otherwise met by physical resources such as oil and gas.

What about the term 'environment' in our title? In everyday usage, the word 'environment' is used in a variety of ways and contexts. Most generally, **environment** has come to mean total *surroundings*, such as in the phrase 'the global environment'. But environment can be applied to microscopic settings, such as to the chemicals in immediate contact with a bacterium, and to settings that lack life, such as the chemical environment surrounding a crystal that grows as molten rock solidifies in the neck of a volcano. A common definition of environment involving living things is:

> All the surroundings of an organism, including not only the physical, inorganic surroundings but also all the other organisms in the vicinity.

Increasingly, the word environment has been used for the things that *interact* in some way with whatever is being surrounded — whether those things are substances, individuals or processes — rather than the external things that just happen to be there passively. During this century, the perception of the human environment has evolved away from one which assumed that human beings were almost separate from nature, though surrounded by it, back to a much earlier view in which humans see themselves as an integral part of nature, dependent on external physical and biological processes for continued existence.

At one extreme is the environment of a single individual organism. An individual's environment is its life support system — everything that provides a setting for its growth and development. At the other extreme is the global environment of life on Earth as a whole. In the case of humans, our environment is much more extensive than that of any other individual species — consider for a moment the sum total of your own surroundings, inorganic and organic, since you were born. A world-wide system of agriculture, industry and trade sustains modern societies, most of which use technology along with elaborate economic and political arrangements to produce and distribute essential food, water, shelter, and so much else besides. This immensely complex global society can itself alter the environment for other organisms to an extent unprecedented in the 4 billion year history of life. In this Course we shall not only be attempting to understand the geological origin of physical resources, but we shall also see examples of how their extraction and use affects the environment of human societies and the living world in general.

Although in this Course we shall be considering physical resources as *extracted* materials or energy (as they are defined above), another important dimension links physical resources to the human environment. Physical resources are also a *cultural* resource. The beauty of the physical world — whether mountain crags, limestone cliffs, spectacular waterfalls or dazzling gemstones — is an inspirational and aesthetic resource. And the scientific study of physical resources yields a vast amount of knowledge, which is itself another cultural resource.

It's quite likely that you're reading this with a pencil in hand. Let's take the pencil in Figure 1. What resources have gone into it ?

Figure 1

The wood is Californian incense cedar, from managed forests where the average tree lives for about 80–100 years from seed to harvest. Pencil 'leads' contain no lead metal these days, but are a mixture of graphite and clay, with harder pencils having more clay; ordinary HB pencils have an approximately equal mixture of the two. (The HB stands for 'Hard' and 'Black', and is the conventional centre point for grading pencils.) Graphite is a very soft form of the element carbon. For this pencil the graphite comes from Sri Lanka, and the clay from Dorset. The baked clay and graphite mixture is impregnated with tallow (animal fat derived from cattle and sheep) to ensure the pencil is not scratchy in use. The lacquer on the pencil contains castor oil from tropical Africa. (Castor oil is a vegetable oil, as opposed to a 'mineral oil' such as petroleum, which is obtained from rocks.) The lettering is aluminium which is hot-stamped into the pencil from aluminium foil, derived from deposits in Russia. The eraser contains rubber and oil seed from Malaysia, a compound of sulphur and chlorine produced from inorganic sources by the chemicals industry, and pumice (an abrasive volcanic rock) from Italy. The brass holder for the eraser contains copper from Zambia, and zinc from Ireland. This ordinary pencil thus contains physical and biological resources from at least nine widely scattered countries.

⬤ Read through the previous paragraph again and note down or highlight the physical resources (or inorganic materials derived from them) that have contributed directly to the pencil, as opposed to resources of recent biological origin.

As with any product, fluctuations in market price and availability will influence the sources from which the pencil manufacturer obtains materials. Aluminium used for the lettering on the pencil should be suitable whether the minerals providing it are from Australia, Brazil, Russia or Surinam; the manufacturer normally buys whatever is cheapest, as long as it is known to be of adequate purity and is in the appropriate form. Chemicals, if absolutely pure, would be the same the world over, whatever their origin. But different producers will be able to achieve different levels of purity, and the precise level of purity may be an important issue. Often, materials from different sources are not precisely equivalent in their properties. Manufacturers may require very specific properties of raw materials: for example, one British pencil manufacturer favours clay from Germany rather than Dorset, because of its particular kiln firing characteristics, and so on.

If we take into account the materials and energy required to obtain the resources for the pencil, such as a saw to cut down the cedars or a machine to excavate the graphite, and then on through transport, processing, and manufacture, to the coins, plastic, or paper used in its sale, a vast number of countries will have contributed in some way, directly or indirectly, to the existence of the humble pencil. It's easy to imagine, but extremely difficult to analyse, the immensely complex global network of connections required to produce a more sophisticated object such as a video recorder or telephone. In addition to raw materials, two indirect resources are crucial to the manufacture of virtually anything: fuels (for energy) and water. And at any stage in all this, there may be consequences for the environment, beneficial or otherwise.

Throughout the rest of the Course, then, it's worth bearing in mind that the manufacture of virtually any item involves:

(a) a vast number of *indirect* physical resources, in addition to those of which the item is directly composed;

(b) an economic and social context, which usually involves complex financial, political and social factors;

(c) some degree of technological development;

(d) environmental consequences that can arise at any stage in the production of any manufactured item, from obtaining the raw materials right through to how the final product is used, and eventually disposed of.

Activity 1

Look around your kitchen (or perhaps another room, wherever you may be) and write down five countries that you can identify as having contributed directly to objects or substances in your immediate vicinity. (The word 'substance' here covers anything, whether it's a solid, liquid or gas.) This will be easier in some settings than others; in the kitchen, for example, many items are labelled with their country of origin. Try to choose items derived from physical resources rather than biological ones, but in any case classify each item appropriately as either one or the other.

1.2 The nature and use of physical resources

Let's consider the physical and chemical nature of physical resources. All matter — whether it is a solid, liquid or gas, and whether or not it is part of living things — is composed of a limited number of chemical **elements**. About 109 different elements are known, of which about 94 occur naturally, the rest having only been synthesized artificially in nuclear reactions. The majority of elements, however, don't occur separately but in various combinations. Chemical combinations of two or more elements are called **compounds**, and in compounds the elements are bonded together in fixed proportions. The only elements in solid form occurring uncombined (or 'native') on the Earth's surface in economically important amounts are gold (Au), platinum (Pt), sulphur (S) and carbon (C) (as diamond, graphite and, less purely, in coal). Copper (Cu), iron (Fe), mercury (Hg), silver (Ag) and a few other metals may also occur in their uncombined form, but are more commonly found in combination with other elements. Each element has its own unique set of physical and chemical properties, and these properties can vary enormously from element to element. The smallest particle into which an element can be subdivided while still retaining the chemical characteristics of that element is called an **atom**.

Chemical elements may be classified as either metals or non-metals, though a few elements, called *metalloids* (or *semi-metals*), are intermediate in their properties between metals and non-metals. About 75% of elements are metals, although not all metals possess all the typical metallic properties, such as being good at conducting heat and electricity, malleable (capable of being reshaped by hammering, rolling, etc., without breaking), and opaque but reflecting light well. Among the best known metalloids are silicon, germanium, arsenic and selenium. If you are unfamiliar with, or wish to revise, the use of symbols for chemical elements, read the boxed text below.

Table 1 gives an alphabetical list of element names and their symbols, together with each element's *unique atomic number* (explained in Section 3.3). Elements with atomic numbers over 94 have been omitted because they do not exist naturally in significant amounts, having been synthesized in particle accelerators or in nuclear explosions. Some elements in Table 1, such as the radioactive element plutonium, occur naturally only in very small quantities. From Table 1 you can also tell whether an element is a solid, liquid or gas in everyday conditions, i.e. at ordinary room temperature (20 °C) and pressure. Table 2 lists elements in alphabetical order of symbols, with names alongside. The tables are useful for quick reference; there is certainly no need to memorize them.

The use of symbols for chemical elements

Each element is given a standard abbreviation — a symbol — of one or two letters, which is a chemical shorthand, the same the world over. Most people probably recognize H_2O as the abbreviation for water. Thus, hydrogen is always indicated by H and oxygen by O, and the '2' in H_2O means that water is a compound of two hydrogen atoms for every one oxygen atom. In cases like hydrogen and oxygen, the abbreviation is simply the first letter of the element's name. Sometimes, as with silicon, Si, the abbreviation is the first two letters of the element's name. The symbol is always a capital letter, or starts with a capital letter. In some cases it may be the first letter of the element, followed by another letter that helps suggest the name; Cs is caesium, Zn is zinc. Sometimes, however, the symbols are less obvious, being derived from Latin or Greek. Lead, for example, is represented by Pb, from the Latin *plumbum*, from which we get plumber, plumb line and so on.

Table 1   The elements listed in alphabetical order with their symbols and atomic numbers

actinium	Ac	89	hydrogen[g]	H	1	radon[g]	Rn	86
aluminium	Al	13	indium	In	49	rhenium	Re	75
antimony	Sb	51	iodine	I	53	rhodium	Rh	45
argon[g]	Ar	18	iridium	Ir	77	rubidium	Rb	37
arsenic	As	33	iron	Fe	26	ruthenium	Ru	44
astatine	At	85	krypton[g]	Kr	36	samarium	Sm	62
barium	Ba	56	lanthanum	La	57	scandium	Sc	21
beryllium	Be	4	lead	Pb	82	selenium	Se	34
bismuth	Bi	83	lithium	Li	3	silicon	Si	14
boron	B	5	lutetium	Lu	71	silver	Ag	47
bromine[l]	Br	35	magnesium	Mg	12	sodium	Na	11
cadmium	Cd	48	manganese	Mn	25	strontium	Sr	38
caesium	Cs	55	mercury[l]	Hg	80	sulphur	S	16
calcium	Ca	20	molybdenum	Mo	42	tantalum	Ta	73
carbon	C	6	neodymium	Nd	60	technetium	Tc	43
cerium	Ce	58	neon[g]	Ne	10	tellurium	Te	52
chlorine[g]	Cl	17	neptunium	Np	93	terbium	Tb	65
chromium	Cr	24	nickel	Ni	28	thallium	Tl	81
cobalt	Co	27	niobium	Nb	41	thorium	Th	90
copper	Cu	29	nitrogen[g]	N	7	thulium	Tm	69
dysprosium	Dy	66	osmium	Os	76	tin	Sn	50
erbium	Er	68	oxygen[g]	O	8	titanium	Ti	22
europium	Eu	63	palladium	Pd	46	tungsten	W	74
fluorine[g]	F	9	phosphorus	P	15	uranium	U	92
francium	Fr	87	platinum	Pt	78	vanadium	V	23
gadolinium	Gd	64	plutonium	Pu	94	xenon[g]	Xe	54
gallium	Ga	31	polonium	Po	84	ytterbium	Yb	70
germanium	Ge	32	potassium	K	19	yttrium	Y	39
gold	Au	79	praseodymium	Pr	59	zinc	Zn	30
hafnium	Hf	72	promethium	Pm	61	zirconium	Zr	40
helium[g]	He	2	protactinium	Pa	91			
holmium	Ho	67	radium	Ra	88			

Liquids at ordinary room temperature (20 °C) and pressure are indicated by [l], and gases by [g]; the remainder are solids.

Table 2 The elements listed in alphabetical order of their symbols (atomic numbers 1–94)

Ac actinium	F fluorine^g	Nb niobium	Sc scandium
Ag silver	Fe iron	Nd neodymium	Se selenium
Al aluminium	Fr francium	Ne neon^g	Si silicon
Ar argon^g	Ga gallium	Ni nickel	Sm samarium
As arsenic	Gd gadolinium	Np neptunium	Sn tin
At astatine	Ge germanium	O oxygen^g	Sr strontium
Au gold	H hydrogen^g	Os osmium	Ta tantalum
B boron	He helium^g	P phosphorus	Tb terbium
Ba barium	Hf hafnium	Pa protactinium	Tc technetium
Be beryllium	Hg mercury^l	Pb lead	Te tellurium
Bi bismuth	Ho holmium	Pd palladium	Th thorium
Br bromine^l	I iodine	Pm promethium	Ti titanium
C carbon	In indium	Po polonium	Tl thallium
Ca calcium	Ir iridium	Pr praseodymium	Tm thulium
Cd cadmium	K potassium	Pt platinum	U uranium
Ce cerium	Kr krypton^g	Pu plutonium	V vanadium
Cl chlorine^g	La lanthanum	Ra radium	W tungsten
Co cobalt	Li lithium	Rb rubidium	Xe xenon^g
Cr chromium	Lu lutetium	Re rhenium	Y yttrium
Cs caesium	Mg magnesium	Rh rhodium	Yb ytterbium
Cu copper	Mn manganese	Rn radon^g	Zn zinc
Dy dysprosium	Mo molybdenum	Ru ruthenium	Zr zirconium
Er erbium	N nitrogen^g	S sulphur	
Eu europium	Na sodium	Sb antimony	

Liquids at ordinary room temperature (20 °C) and pressure are indicated by ^{l}, and gases by ^{g}; the remainder are solids.

Question 1

(a) Decipher the following silly message and then, using Table 2 where you need to, test and improve your knowledge of element symbols by working out the elements in the message:

GeT l U C K Y — Se Nd Th Eu Ni Co Rn S Al Ti Na W As Te B In.

(b) Fill in the element names:　　Ge ...., Tl ....
U ....,　C ....,　K ....,　Y ....,
Se ....,　Nd ....,　Th ....,　Eu ....,
Ni ....,　Co ....,　Rn ....,　S ....,
Al ....,　Ti ....,　Na ....,　W ....,
As ....,　Te ....,　B ....,　In ....,

(c) All these elements are solids in ordinary room conditions, except one. Which is it?

One way of assessing the significance of chemical elements as physical resources is to examine the amounts of individual elements that are produced and used in a year. Figure 2 enables you to get a feel for the contribution of different elements to the world economy. It is a bar chart showing the tonnage of an element produced in 1990 or 1991, with the length of each successive bar a factor of 10 greater (i.e. in increasing orders of magnitude). The quantities represent the weight of an individual element, whether it is actually extracted and used as the element itself, or remains as part of a compound. (An exception is silicon, which is shown only as the amount produced of the element itself, rather than its compounds, which are used in vastly larger quantities, for example in ceramics, glass and construction materials.) The majority of elements in Figure 2 are required both in elemental form and as compounds. The bars represent between 1 and 10 tonnes, between 10 and 100 tonnes, and so on, up to the tenth bar — between 1 billion (10^9) and 10 billion (10^{10}) tonnes. If you are uncertain how large numbers like 10 billion are described using powers of ten notation (e.g. 10^{10}), or if you wish to revise how to do so, then read the relevant text in Block 6 *Topics and Data*. Similarly, if you're not sure of the important distinction between weight and mass, read the boxed text below.

It will probably help you to appreciate the amounts if you write in at the right-hand end of at least some bars in Figure 2 the ranges for the interval, especially if you use a form you are more familiar with, e.g. 1000–10 000 instead of 10^3–10^4. Note that, in order to depict more clearly the different element symbols and names, the bar chart has been drafted rather unconventionally. The bars extend horizontally (as opposed to vertically), and elements produced in larger tonnages are situated *lower* in the diagram. For ease of reference, the bars have been labelled 1 to 10.

For every element, the amounts produced obviously differ from one year to the next, but rarely by more than about 10%. Although Figure 2 shows values for *production*, the values for consumption would be similar, because elements (and their useful compounds) are generally not stockpiled for long (unless they are being 'used' as an investment or for strategic purposes).

Within each bar of Figure 2, the elements are placed in approximate order of amount produced, the element with the smallest amount on the left and the largest on the right. (The relative position of elements within a bar can change from year to year.) It's important to realize that the amounts of two elements within a given bar could differ by almost as much as a factor of ten. For example, molybdenum (Mo), at 1.1×10^5 tonnes only just makes it into

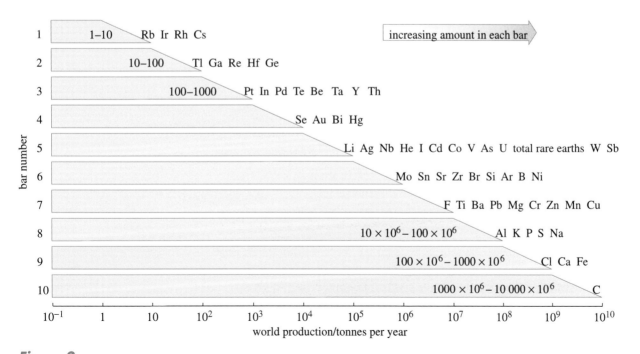

Figure 2 The world production of chemical elements in 1990 or 1991, in tonnes per year. Fill in the ranges at the ends of bars 4 to 7. See text for discussion.

Weight and mass

Scientifically, there is an important distinction between weight and mass. A kilogram and a tonne (1000 kg), are, strictly speaking, units of *mass* — the quantity of matter. The *weight* of anything is given by multiplying its mass by the local acceleration due to gravity; weight is therefore a force. A kilogram on the Moon weighs less than on Earth because the gravity on the Moon is about one-sixth that on Earth. And where there is virtually no gravity, as in some parts of space, a kilogram may be virtually weightless. In this Course, we will be talking about the weight of something using units such as kilograms, grams, or tonnes because the physical resources we are considering are located on the Earth. For most practical purposes, as long as we are comparing weights on the Earth (as opposed to elsewhere), it doesn't matter that we use units of mass for them; indeed, terms such as kilograms and tonnes are used in many situations as if they were units of weight.

Actually, in detail, the strength of the Earth's gravitational pull varies very slightly from place to place, so even on the Earth a kilogram will vary in weight in different geographical locations. But unless we need extremely precise measurements, we can assume that 'a tonne of lead' represents the same mass of lead whether it's in Chile, China or Chelsea.

The volume occupied by a tonne of material varies according to the material's density. A tonne of water (at 4 °C) occupies exactly a cubic metre (a cube measuring 100 cm on each side); whereas a tonne of lead, which is about 11 times denser, occupies less than a tenth of a cubic metre — in fact a cube measuring about 45 cm on each side. (Volumes can be deceptive: if a cube with these measurements sounds far too big to occupy only about a tenth of a cubic metre, try drawing it on paper.)

the 10^5–10^6 category (bar 6), while the value for nickel (Ni), which is placed in the same bar, is about 9.2×10^5 tonnes. There may be more difference between the amounts of two elements *within* one bar than between elements placed in adjacent bars, particularly if one element is at the top of the smaller category and the other is at the bottom of the larger category.

⬤ From the information in Figure 2 alone, what could be the maximum possible difference (in tonnes) in the amounts of lead (bar 7) and gold (bar 4) produced in 1990/1991?

◯ As lead is in bar 7, i.e. between 10^6 and 10^7 t, and gold is in bar 4, i.e. between 10^3 and 10^4 t, lead could be up to almost 10^7 t, and gold as low as about 10^3 t. The difference between them would then be about 10^7 minus 10^3 t, i.e. 10 million minus one thousand tonnes = 9 999 000 t. In fact, lead production in 1990 was about 3 400 000 t, and gold about 2050 t, so the real difference was roughly 3 398 000 t.

Some very important elements are omitted from Figure 2, mainly because we really do not know how much of them are produced or used. Two of these are the components of water — hydrogen and oxygen.

Question 2

Humans require a few litres of water per day for survival. Taking the world population (early 1990s) to be 5.5 billion, how many tonnes of water are needed per year simply for bodily survival alone, assuming each person requires a minimum daily intake of two litres? (1000 litres = 1 tonne)

Of course, water is also used in vast amounts for other purposes — washing, cooking, agriculture, industry, and so on — and its importance is such that it demands a whole Block in this Course for discussion — Block 3 *Water*

Resources. As we shall see, for many of its purposes, water is, in effect, 'borrowed' for a relatively short time from the complex natural cycle in which it is involved, and then returned. This contrasts with many other physical resources which, once extracted, are often modified chemically or physically, and removed from their geological setting permanently, at least as far as human timescales are concerned.

In addition to its presence in water, a vast amount of hydrogen is contained in fuels such as oil and natural gas. And oxygen, as well as forming 89% by weight of water, forms about 21% by volume of the atmosphere and about 45% by weight of Earth's crustal rocks, making it impractical to calculate the total amount used. (The Earth's crust is the outermost solid layer of the Earth, discussed in Section 3.) Oxygen, a very reactive substance, is obtained by separation from liquefied air, and is used in a huge variety of industries, especially in the manufacture of chemicals.

Another important element omitted from Figure 2 is nitrogen (N), a gas at ordinary temperatures and pressures, which forms about 78% by volume of the atmosphere. Again it is difficult to calculate its use; for example, industrial processes that require air simply for drying purposes are using mostly nitrogen. Nitrogen is present in a wide range of industrially useful compounds, ranging from nitric acid to nitroglycerine in dynamite. In 1991, about 85×10^6 tonnes of nitrogen (which, like oxygen, is obtained by separation from liquefied air) were required for ammonia production alone. Ammonia (NH_3) is a compound of nitrogen and hydrogen, and itself forms the starting point for the manufacture of fertilizers, the largest single use of nitrogen. Nitrogen is used in its own right in liquid form for applications demanding low temperatures (it boils at $-196\,°C$).

In addition to the gaseous elements H, O, and N, there are quite a few other elements that we do not discuss in detail because they are used in small amounts for highly specialized purposes, and their extraction relies more on chemistry or metallurgy than on employing the geological principles that form a significant part of this Course.

Many different elements make up the common rocks, gravels, sands and clays that are used for building purposes and road-making (Block 2 *Building Materials*). The tonnages of these elements have not been accounted for in Figure 2. In 1992, the consumption of sand, gravel and crushed rock in Britain alone was about 250 million tonnes. Elements such as silicon, aluminium and calcium are abundant in such materials, although in each case they are present in the combined state, as compounds with other elements.

○ Why do you think carbon (C) appears on Figure 2 as the most sought-after element in the world economy?

○ This reflects our use of coal (mainly carbon) and of hydrocarbons — oil and natural gas (essentially compounds of hydrogen and carbon) — to provide energy. These **fossil fuels** (i.e. combustible resources derived from ancient organisms) are featured in Block 4 *Energy 1 – Fossil Fuels*. Hydrocarbons are also a very important feedstock for the chemicals industry (feedstocks are raw materials used in the manufacture of a product).

From bars 8 and 9 in Figure 2 it is possible to pick out various groupings of other elements used in very large quantities. One group includes phosphorus (P), sulphur (S), calcium (Ca) and potassium (K), which, along with nitrogen (N), will be recognized by gardeners and farmers as the key components of fertilizers. Another, albeit small, grouping would be sodium (Na) and chlorine (Cl), found together simply as common salt (NaCl). Both sodium and chlorine are very important for the chemicals industry. As NaCl forms by far the largest source of these two elements, you may be surprised that they are not placed in the same bar. That is mainly because sodium is itself not quite as heavy as chlorine, and so forms a smaller proportion (39%) of the total weight of this compound. The net result is that sodium is placed in a lower category, though the amounts of both are not far off 100 million tonnes. This emphasizes an important general point: weights of different elements vary, even though the number of atoms they contribute to a particular compound may be the same. The chief source of lead, for example, is lead sulphide (PbS), a mineral called galena. Lead is so much heavier than sulphur that it forms about 87% of the weight of this compound, even though galena contains equal numbers of sulphur and lead atoms.

Many of the remaining elements in Figure 2 are metals, dominated by iron (Fe). Iron is the cheapest and most widely used metal; today most is converted into steel. Minor, though crucial, additives in steel include manganese (Mn), chromium (Cr), nickel (Ni), molybdenum (Mo) and tungsten (W). Other major metals include copper (Cu), lead (Pb), zinc (Zn), and aluminium (Al). These metals, and many other familiar ones which you will have spotted in Figure 2, are the subject of Block 5 *Metals*. There we shall look at the geological processes that lead to metals being concentrated into mineable ore deposits. An **ore** is a rock that can be worked economically for its metals, either at present or, with reasonable likelihood, in the near future. We also consider the fundamentals of exploration, extraction and the processing of ores.

You will have noticed the term 'rare earths' in Figure 2. This is used for a group of 15 metallic elements having atomic numbers between 57 and 71. Rare earths include cerium (Ce) and neodymium (Nd), and others with names that are even less well known, such as europium (Eu). (Sometimes yttrium and scandium are also considered as rare earths, but not here.) All rare earths have similar chemical properties, and their uses include specialized alloys, such as the 'flint' (or sparking pad) in cigarette lighters that emits sparks when rubbed against steel, and those used in the world's most powerful permanent magnets. (An **alloy** is a metallic material consisting of a mixture of metals, or a mixture of a metal with a non-metal in which the metal is the major component.) They are finding increasing use in high-tech devices such as lasers and catalytic converters. Most 'rare earths' are not quite as rare as their name suggests but they are seldom a major component in any mineral. This raises an important general point: even for elements like copper and lead that do tend to be highly concentrated in specific minerals, it is unusual for geological processes to enrich them to concentrations high enough to make their extraction from rocks economically viable. The natural processes by which chemical elements and compounds are concentrated is a topic we keep returning to in the Course.

In Figure 2, two other groupings of elements can be picked out from among those with lower production amounts. They include some of the best known metals, but ones that are produced only in small tonnages. One group includes the precious metals gold (Au), silver (Ag) and platinum (Pt). The other group includes uranium (U) and thorium (Th), which have naturally unstable, *radioactive* atoms that are the main sources of the Earth's internal heat. Their atoms release *radiation*, which, in controlled conditions, can be harnessed as a source of energy. Uranium is used for nuclear fuel, the basis of nuclear power, as discussed in Block 4 *Energy 2 – Nuclear and Alternatives*.

Some of the Earth's most important resources cannot be assigned a weight or volume like the elements discussed above, but they are nevertheless physical resources because they can be harnessed to generate energy. Examples include radiation from the Sun (solar radiation) and the converted solar energy 'bound up' in the movement of air and water over the Earth (in wind and waves), and the gravitational energy of tides. Another example is geothermal energy that derives from the heat released by the decay of radioactive elements such as uranium and thorium within the Earth itself. This heat is transferred from the Earth's interior to the surface in various ways, most spectacularly by volcanoes and hot springs. These various sources of energy which form alternatives to fossil and nuclear fuels are discussed in Block 4 *Energy 2*.

1.2.1 *The natural abundance of elements*

How does the pattern of production and use of physical resources revealed by Figure 2 compare with the natural abundance of elements? Study Figure 3, which has exactly the same form as Figure 2, except that it shows the approximate percentages by weight of chemical elements in the rocks of the Earth's continental crust, i.e. the type of crust that is most accessible to us. The values used are estimated averages for the whole of the continental crust, not just its upper part. (The nature of continental crust and the other type of crust, oceanic crust, are discussed further in Section 3.) The elements have been placed *within* each bar only in approximate order of relative abundance; estimates of average abundance may differ widely, especially for very rare elements.

Figure 3 could have been plotted as the actual tonnages of elements in the continental crust but the amounts concerned would have been enormous and rather difficult to deal with. So the scale in Figure 3 is in weight percentages, and this can easily be converted into grams per tonne of average rock.

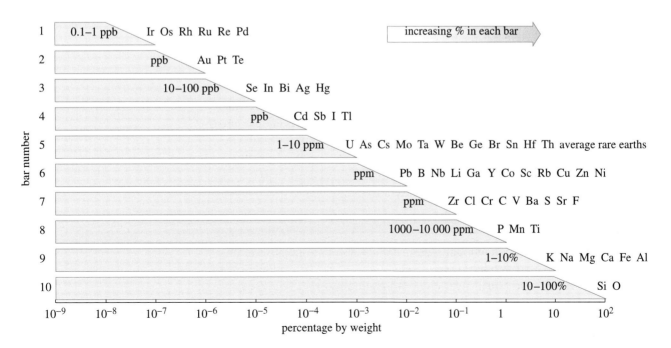

Figure 3 The percentage by weight of chemical elements in the Earth's continental crust. Fill in the ranges at the ends of bars 2, 4, 6 and 7. See text for discussion.

○ If a rock contains 10^{-4} per cent of an element, how many grams of that element are there in one tonne (10^6 g) of the rock?

○ 1 tonne contains one gram of the element (1% is 10^{-2}, so 10^{-4} per cent of a tonne is $10^{-4} \times 10^{-2} = 10^{-6}$, a millionth of a tonne, i.e. one gram).

This amount of 1 part per million (10^{-6}) (by weight) is often abbreviated as 1 ppm, and an amount of 1 part per billion (10^{-9}) is abbreviated as 1 ppb.

At one end of this bar chart lie oxygen (45%) and silicon (27%), which together form about 72% of the continental crust. At the opposite end, elements such as rhenium (Re) and osmium (Os) are so rare that they average less than a tenth of one millionth of a per cent (i.e. $< 10^{-7}$ per cent or < 1 ppb). Again, bear in mind that two elements in the same category could differ by almost a factor of ten (or be very similar in abundance), while two elements in adjacent categories could differ by a lot less than a factor of ten (or differ by a factor of almost a hundred).

Some elements appear only in one or other of Figures 2 and 3. The noble gases helium (He) and argon (Ar), present in Figure 2, have been omitted from Figure 3, though they do occur trapped in the minerals of crustal rocks in tiny amounts; being chemically inert, these gases do not form compounds. Osmium (Os) and ruthenium (Ru) are both extremely rare in the crust (as shown in Figure 3) and do not appear in Figure 2 because their total global production was less than 1 tonne in 1991. Oxygen, the most abundant element in the crust, appears in Figure 3, but was omitted from Figure 2 for the reasons explained earlier.

Whereas Figure 2 shows the amounts (and relative proportions) in which elements are *produced* (or *used*), Figure 3 gives an idea of the relative proportions of elements *available*, at least in theory, in all the continental crust. A comparison of Figures 2 and 3 allows us to answer the question: What elements are produced (and used) in proportions that do not closely match their proportions in the Earth's crust? Note that both Figures have ten bars, and that successive bars in each Figure differ by a factor of ten. Although the units on the axes are different, we can compare the *relative* importance of an element in each bar chart, by looking at the lengths of the bars against which it is plotted or simply by comparing the bar numbers for the element in question. Note that this is an entirely arbitrary way of linking Figures 2 and 3 together, but one that is useful for comparative purposes.

Let's consider a few examples. Iron (Fe) is situated in bar 9 in Figure 2 and also in bar 9 in Figure 3. There is therefore no significant difference in the relative position of iron in both Figures. Exactly the same is true for calcium (Ca). Barium (Ba) in bar 7 is about ten times more abundant than nickel (Ni) (Figure 3), and in fact about ten times more barium is produced than nickel (Figure 2). Both barium and nickel plot in the same relative positions (bars 7 and 6) in Figures 2 and 3. So Fe, Ca, Ba, and Ni are among those elements that are used in amounts that roughly reflect their relative abundance.

Ag (silver), however, is in bar 5 in Figure 2 (production) but in bar 3 in Figure 3 (relative abundance), indicating that, in relation to many other elements (such as Fe and Ca), we use silver rather more than its relative abundance would suggest. By contrast, the element Be is in bar 3 for production and bar 5 for relative abundance, so rather less beryllium is therefore used than might be expected from its relative abundance. The most extreme discrepancy is that of scandium (Sc), which is in bar 6 in Figure 3 but is absent from Figure 2 because it is produced in amounts of less than one tonne. Scandium is a metal found in rather small amounts in many rocks, being about as abundant overall as lead, copper and zinc, but it is very rarely concentrated in minerals and so is difficult and expensive to extract, and to date it has very few practical applications.

Question 3

Sort the elements below into the two following categories, referring to Figures 2 and 3. In your answer give the element symbols.

Caesium, carbon, chlorine, gallium, germanium, gold, magnesium, rubidium, vanadium, and yttrium

(a) those that are used in relatively *small* amounts compared with their relative abundance in the crust;

(b) those that are used in relatively *large* amounts compared with their relative abundance in the crust.

What are the principal factors that influence the relative amounts of elements used as physical resources, and how do these amounts compare with their relative abundance; i.e. why are there the similarities and discrepancies in element positions between Figures 2 and 3? About two-thirds of the elements in Figures 2 and 3 show such a close correspondence between the relative amount produced and their relative abundance in the continental crust that they differ by no more than one bar between the Figures. In other words, about two-thirds of the elements are produced in amounts that fairly closely reflect their relative abundance in the crust. For the other third, the amounts used are not in the same relative proportions as the amounts available.

Clearly, the proportions of elements we use relate in some way to their different physical and chemical properties, and to how useful these properties are to society. Thus, the elements and their compounds with the most appropriate properties for a particular use, or the greatest range of useful properties, have generally come to dominate the world economy. This is, for instance, undoubtedly true of oil (C) and fertilizers (P, S, Ca, K) (Figure 4a). In general, the rarer the element, the more special and desirable some of its properties have got to be for that element to be used in preference to a more abundant one.

Figure 4 (a) Fertilizer containing nitrogen, phosphorus and potassium being used on an English farm.

Many rare elements have a whole variety of potentially useful properties, but these cannot be fully employed because supplies are severely limited by the scarcity of the elements themselves and/or their high cost. Consider the development of gas-filled balloons. For a while, early this century, it seemed that air transport would involve balloons filled with hydrogen, which, being light and readily available, supplied buoyancy so that the balloons required a minimum of fuel. Fatal accidents showing that hydrogen was too readily explosive and flammable soon put a stop to that. The gas helium (He) (Figure 4b) is much more suitable: it is almost as buoyant, and is far safer, being chemically inert. Helium, however, is a very rare element in the Earth, and our supplies are by-products from only a few natural gas wells and from the extraction of other gases from air. Global production of helium is only about 17 000 tonnes per year.

Helium has another application based on one extraordinary property: it has the lowest freezing point of any element and can be used to achieve temperatures within one degree of absolute zero on the temperature scale.*

Metals immersed in liquid helium (which boils at 4 K) acquire superconducting and unusual magnetic properties: they offer virtually no resistance to the transmission of electricity and can have extremely high magnetizations induced in them. If more helium was available, all sorts of technical applications, both known and as yet unforeseen, might have already been developed. But as more materials are discovered that can be superconducting at temperatures far higher than 4 K, this particular need for liquid helium is reduced. Some helium is also mixed with oxygen in deep-sea breathing systems.

Figure 4   (b) Helium-filled balloon carrying research apparatus being launched at a British Antarctic Survey station, Antarctica.

In general, irrespective of an element's average crustal abundance, the costs of extraction may limit any potential economic benefit. As in the case of scandium (above), an element may be widely distributed and *on average* reasonably abundant, but high abundances may not occur locally in the crust. Presumably, had scandium been more readily accessible, we would have found many more potential uses for it.

In summary, the simple statistics for the production and use of elements in Figure 2 conceal a complex set of factors. The most important factors influencing the relative use of an element as a physical resource are:

1   its physical and chemical properties, from which arise the potential uses of — and demand for — an element and its compounds;

2   its abundance and distribution in the Earth;

3   its ease of extraction and hence cost of production;

4   the fact that physical resources are subject to immensely complex political, economic and environmental factors, including competition from other materials to fulfil the same function.

These are four important strands running through the Course, and the significance of each factor varies from element to element. We shall often

---

* Absolute zero is the lowest possible theoretically attainable temperature, −273.15 °C or 0 K; helium freezes at 0.95 K. 'K' is the abbreviation for degrees kelvin, a temperature scale which begins at −273.15 °C, and increases by the same degree intervals as the Celsius or centigrade scale; i.e. 0 °C is 273 K and 100 °C is 373 K. The degree symbol ° is omitted from Kelvin scale values.

place emphasis on the second factor, especially the causes of differences in the abundance and distribution of individual elements in the Earth. These differences necessarily depend on the physical and chemical properties of elements, which influence the way that they behave in geological settings. A time aspect will also be a recurrent theme, not only when considering how long it takes to generate physical resources naturally or to nullify some damaging environmental effect of human activity, but for understanding how yesterday's resource can become tomorrow's waste, and, with careful recycling, vice versa.

Titanium

Titanium is a metal that is lighter, stronger, and far less prone to corrosion than iron; indeed it is used in aircraft engines, aeroplane and missile frames, military hardware, helicopter rotor blades, and top-of-the-range bicycles, tennis rackets and golf clubs. Increasingly, titanium (with minor additions of alloying metals) is used in pipework for the supply of offshore oil and gas, and in the chemical industry, where long-term corrosion resistance offsets its high initial cost. As it is non-toxic, bonds to bone and is not rejected by the human body, it is used in hip and knee replacements, heart pacemakers, and for plates and screws in repairs to fractured bones.

So why is titanium not used far more widely as a construction material, instead of iron and steel, for example? After all, titanium is the ninth most abundant element in the Earth's crust and more abundant than tin, lead, zinc, nickel, chromium, and mercury combined. However, whereas these metals form easily mined ore deposits, the overall more plentiful titanium tends to be widely dispersed in low concentrations, and few geological settings have sufficiently high concentrations of titanium-bearing minerals for titanium production in commercial quantities. But most important, it is technically very difficult and expensive to convert the titanium oxide ores to titanium metal—far more so than, for example, it is to obtain iron from its oxide form. In 1993, the price of titanium metal was around £8000 per tonne, whereas steel was about £200 per tonne.

Only 5% of the titanium in titanium-bearing minerals mined in the early 1990s ended up as titanium metal and its alloys — the other 95% was used to manufacture titanium dioxide (TiO_2), probably the world's most important pigment. In 1993 titanium dioxide was a £3.5 billion-a-year industry, and its price was around £1500 per tonne. Titanium dioxide absorbs very little light and scatters it even more widely than a diamond does. In the form of a very fine powder, it is a brilliant white, and without this pigment much of our manufactured world would be dull and grey. For instance, the whiteness of domestic appliances such as fridges and washers is due to titanium dioxide. It does not discolour, is virtually inert, and is non-toxic. More than half the titanium dioxide produced ends up in paint, where it enhances the brilliance of any colour, not only white. It is used, for example, to brighten up the yellow lines on roads (as well as being a minor but important constituent in the white lines, for which the dominant pigment is actually chalk). Typing correction fluid contains titanium dioxide. A quarter of production is incorporated into plastics. The rest is used to whiten paper and to make it opaque, to whiten synthetic fibres, and, being non-toxic, titanium dioxide finds many uses in cosmetics, medical products, food additives and colorants, and children's toys.

Figure 5 In a typical kitchen, white objects such as the plug, socket, lead, kettle, mug, saucepan, as well as the white wall paint, all contain titanium dioxide.

1.3 A brief history of physical resources

The development of human society has gone hand in hand with the increasing use of physical resources. Here we review some of the important stages leading up to our present dependence on physical resources, the extent of which is at least partly revealed by Figure 2.

Of all physical resources, water is the one that has been essential from the very earliest stages in the evolution of our species, indeed of life itself. After air, water is the primary need of all terrestrial animal life; without it death comes much sooner than through starvation. Increasing populations of hominids (the family of primates to which humans belong) and the growing diversity of uses for water eventually necessitated a conscious, systematic search for it — exploration — in addition to simply following around canny animals like elephants.

Our distant ancestor, a species of *Australopithecus,* was probably using stone tools in Africa by at least about 2.5 million years (Ma) ago. The first use of tools, at the start of the Old Stone Age or Palaeolithic times, marked a revolutionary leap in hominid evolution. Natural selection quickly favoured individuals capable of manipulating existing types of tools, inventing new ones, and transmitting skills to the next generation. An expansion of consciousness seems to have been linked with an increase in social organization associated with the emergence of systematic hunting. The earliest fossils of our genus *Homo* are about 2.4 Ma old, although such dates are subject to frequent revision as new evidence comes to light. Precisely when true modern humans (our own subspecies *Homo sapiens sapiens*) appeared is contentious but it seems likely to have been as recently as 150 000–200 000 years ago.

From early in hominid evolution, the need for shelter would have led to the making of crude wind-breaks from piles of stones, as well as from biological resources such as tree branches and grasses. Later, there would have been more extensive excavations, either to deepen caves or to provide stone for simple dwellings, especially after hominids had left Africa and migrated to slightly colder climates in Asia and Europe. Geological thinking in its most rudimentary form had to develop at an early stage in human history.

The earliest known mine is in Belgium and dates from at least 41 000 BC. The quest was for ochre — various red, brown and yellow iron oxides probably used as pigments for painting, cosmetics and rituals. The best types of stone for tool-making were eventually sought methodically, leading to the mining of flints and natural volcanic glass. During the New Stone Age or Neolithic times, humans set up a wide-ranging pattern of trade in Europe and the Mediterranean. All the postulated trade routes shown in Figure 6 were set up by about 3000 BC, though some had started as early as 8000 BC.

Natural but unpredictable sources of fire such as lightning or volcanoes were probably available in several areas where very early hominids dwelt. No one is certain when our ancestors first used fire systematically, but it was at least by 700 000 years ago, and may have been much earlier. The harnessing of fire eventually supported the technological revolution based on metals that followed the Stone Age. Oxides of metals such as lead, zinc, copper and tin can be reduced to the metal at moderately low temperatures in the presence of carbon (charcoal) in a wood fire. Although direct evidence is lacking, it is thought that accidental smelting in fire-places produced not only these metals but their impure alloys such as bronze (copper + tin). Obviously, accidents

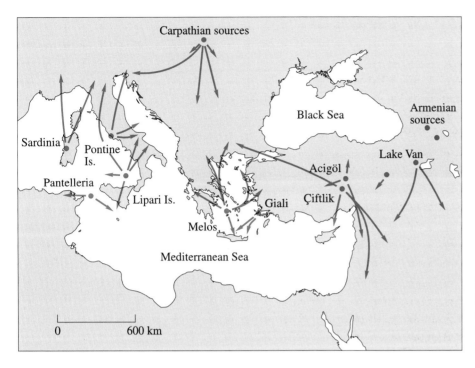

Figure 6 The distribution of Neolithic implements made from natural volcanic glass. The stars indicate volcanic sources, the arrows directions of trade and not exact trade routes.

like this could occur only in areas such as Cornwall where easily reduced metallic compounds were often present at the surface. Once the usefulness of metals — especially their malleability and ease of sharpening — was exploited, further supplies depended on success in exploring for and mining these compounds. Copper and bronze working spread from a few centres in the Far and Middle East, starting about 6000 BC, but in Europe at least, bronze was uncommon until after 2000 BC, the date often regarded as the start of the Bronze Age. The Iron Age followed once it was discovered that iron could be obtained from iron oxides. A few iron objects were used as early as 1500 BC, although 500 BC marks the more general start of the Iron Age.

Initially, metals required much effort to produce and were consequently materials of great value. Their use was mainly restricted to essentials, such as metal tools and weapons, which had many advantages over non-metallic ones. They therefore became important in barter for other resources, such as cloth, food and salt, and because of this some metals began to circulate as coins. Pre-eminent among these money metals was gold which, though attractive and much sought after as an ornament (even in the Stone Age, when gold nuggets may have been less difficult to find than today), had no other uses until quite recently.

Oxidation and reduction

An **oxide** is a compound of oxygen with another element, such as titanium dioxide (TiO_2) or potassium oxide (K_2O). **Oxidation** is a chemical process that typically involves the *addition* of oxygen to an element or compound. That element or compound is then said to have been oxidized. Rusting is an example of oxidation: when an iron nail rusts, oxygen combines with the element iron, and the iron becomes oxidized. An **oxidizing agent** is a substance that is capable of bringing about oxidation, and itself becomes reduced in the reaction. **Reduction** is the opposite of oxidation.

Reduction is another chemical process that typically involves the *removal* of oxygen atoms. Reduction may therefore free a metal from its compounds, such as the liberation of titanium metal from its oxide by the removal of oxygen. The titanium dioxide is then said to have been reduced. A **reducing agent** is a substance that is capable of bringing about reduction, and is itself oxidized in the chemical reaction. Thus a chemical reaction involving oxidation always involves reduction as well.

Small-scale exploitation of a wide range of metals was well developed in a few places in Europe in the Middle Ages. One of the first illustrated books on mining and minerals, *De re metallica* by the German Georgius Agricola, was published in 1556 (Figure 7). The use of metals on a very large scale for a wide range of purposes was, however, delayed for over 8000 years after their discovery, until the Industrial Revolution, which took off around the mid eighteenth century. Many factors delayed the onset of industrialization, including the lack of energy resources any more effective than wood, wind or water power. The steam engine, first developed for pumping water out of Cornish tin mines, was an extremely important invention, which soon supplied the power that made the Industrial Revolution possible. Being able to harness the abundant energy contained in coal (used as a fuel since Roman times) via the steam engine, stimulated a rapid increase in the quantities and ways in which physical resources were exploited.

Figure 7 Illustration of vertical, lined mine shafts and gently sloping adits from *De re metallica* (1556). These then-sophisticated methods of mineral extraction changed little in the next 250 years.

Smelting, iron and steel

Smelting is the process by which metals are extracted from their ores (containing mainly oxide or sulphide minerals). The word 'smelt' is derived from an old German word for 'melt'. During large-scale smelting a metal is extracted by heating the ore in a furnace together with a reducing agent such as charcoal or coke and a **flux** such as limestone which enables impurities to be removed in liquid form. **Charcoal** is produced by heating wood in the absence of air. **Coke** is a solid material which, like charcoal, often contains over 95% carbon. It is produced when coal is heated (away from air) in furnaces to distil off the volatile constituents (i.e. substances that, when heated, readily form a vapour). The charcoal or coke has two purposes during smelting: it burns to provide heat to melt the ore and promote the chemical reactions required, and it supplies the reducing agent (carbon) needed to set free the metal. The carbon, in effect, drags off the oxygen from metallic oxides, or the sulphur from metallic sulphides. Smelting results in two molten layers in the furnace — a lighter **slag** of unwanted impurities on top, and a layer of molten metal below. The slag layer keeps the molten metal away from air, preventing chemical reaction of the metal with oxygen (oxidation).

The chemical reactions taking place during iron smelting are complex but the essential process involves reduction of iron ore (with simultaneous oxidation of carbon):

oxide of iron + carbon $\longrightarrow$ iron + oxide of carbon
(ore)   (coke or   (metal)   (CO_2 gas)
            charcoal)

The crude molten iron produced by a blast furnace is generally called **pig iron**; this may be further refined to produce cast iron, wrought iron, or steel.

Cast iron contains 5–10% of other elements, including 2.5–4.5% carbon, and some silicon and manganese. Casting involves the pouring of molten iron into a mould. **Wrought iron** is a tougher, purer form of iron that has been worked in a forge (where it is shaped by hammering or pressing, i.e. wrought) but is more costly to produce, and today is little used except for decorative purposes, such as ornate gates. The Eiffel Tower in Paris was built in 1889 of wrought iron, which was then still cheaper than steel.

Steel is essentially an alloy of iron with a small but crucial amount of carbon (less than 1.5%) for hardness and strength, and minor amounts of other elements, the proportions of which are more tightly controlled than in cast and wrought iron. Stainless steel typically contains about 12% chromium and 10% nickel. There are many different types of special steels that require a wide range of element additives, some of which were mentioned in Section 1.2.

The conditions for the siting of the Industrial Revolution in Britain are strongly related to the geology around Ironbridge in Shropshire, where iron was first smelted with coke in 1709. The successful use of coke by Abraham Darby did away with the need for large amounts of expensive charcoal, and the cost savings and other improvements he made were a starting point for the large-scale manufacture of iron rails, iron boats, iron aqueducts, and iron buildings. On New Year's Day, 1781, the first metal bridge in Europe (built by another Abraham Darby, grandson of the above) was opened at Ironbridge, using 400 tons of cast iron. Near Ironbridge a single mine shaft intersected thick coal seams, iron ore, fire-clay (a heat-resistant clay used for lining furnaces) and limestone — all the basic requirements for manufacturing iron, and later steel. Iron and steel made possible the development of an entirely new infrastructure for the country — a significant part of which was the railways — as well as many new types of machine. The first railway in the world to use locomotives on a public line was opened in England in 1825, carrying coal and passengers from near Darlington to Stockton (Figure 8). Today, there are over four million tonnes of steel in the rails that form Britain's total railway track length of nearly 23 500 miles.

Figure 8   The opening of the Stockton and Darlington railway in 1825.

Pre-industrial society was dominated by agriculture and the exploitation of biological rather than physical resources. European nation states occupied various colonies in Africa, Asia and the Americas, exploiting mainly biological resources, a notable exception being gold in southern and western Africa (e.g. Gold Coast, now called Ghana) and the Andes. However, the distribution of physical resources is not constrained by national or colonial boundaries. The dramatic increase in the use and diversity of physical resources that began during the Industrial Revolution highlighted the discrepancies between political and geological boundaries, and these discrepancies have played an important role in world politics and economics. Physical resources such as oil, water and strategically important metals are still today the focus of political conflict. Countries keen to claim territory containing physical resources are less keen to accept responsibility for any attendant impacts on the environment, such as pollution and habitat destruction, and disputes over these issues are escalating.

(a)

(b)

Figure 9 (a) Hadareb house, 1993, Eritrea, Ethiopia. (b) Hadareb household goods from the same house. Note that the only metal object is an axe. The owner also had a metal knife and a porcelain coffee cup.

The last couple of centuries have seen enormous changes in the ways that we explore for, extract, process, and use resources. Today's technologically advanced societies can choose the most appropriate resources, wherever they come from on the globe, unlike earlier or less technical societies which were, and still are, dependent on locally available resources (see Figure 9). Changes that continue to escalate include increased mechanization and scientific understanding, resulting, for example, in better extraction techniques and new types of materials; the increasing consumption of materials and energy per person; more rapid transport and communication; and stricter safety procedures. Recently, in the last quarter of the 20th century, increasing awareness of environmental issues has led to attempts to limit pollution, preserve endangered species, recycle waste, develop alternative energy sources to fossil fuels, and so on. All these developments have important implications for the extraction and use of physical resources.

This would be a suitable place to watch Video Band 1: *The Great Iron and Steel Rollercoaster*. Afterwards, test your understanding of some of the most important points of the programme by answering the following Questions (4 to 9). It will probably help you to read these through quickly and have them fresh in your mind before viewing the film. The questions and answers together will serve as a summary of the programme.

Video Band 1   The Great Iron and Steel Rollercoaster

Speakers

Andrew Bell and Peter Sheldon, The Open University

This programme, which was made in 1993, illustrates many aspects of iron and steel making, especially in Britain. It covers the historical development of the industry, and emphasizes the importance of technological developments and changes in manufacturing processes. It shows the significance of shifts in economic factors since the industry began.

Question 4

What was the main reason why iron production in the Weald of southern England eventually ceased?

Question 5

Fill in the gaps in the following account.

During the process called 'puddling', ... iron is remelted and agitated to .... out remaining impurities such as carbon, silicon and phosphorus. After running off some slag, and driving out further slag with a steam hammer, minute strands of slag still remain, resulting in a fibrous texture which .... the iron's strength and resistance to fracture. Iron produced in this way is called .... iron.

Question 6

Which of the following items (a) to (h) are correct, i.e. contain only correct information? Where an item contains an incorrect statement, correct any errors.

(a) Girders of wrought iron are more susceptible than those of cast iron to brittle fracture of the kind that caused the Tay Bridge Disaster.

(b) Henry Bessemer invented a process for making steel in which air is blown through molten iron to oxidize the impurities, which burn off during the blow. This procedure results in partial oxidation of the metal, so iron containing carbon is added at the end of the blow to reduce any oxidized iron back to the metal.

(c) In the nineteenth century, proximity to high-quality iron ore determined where industry expanded far more than local availability of coal.

(d) The ability to use scrap iron and steel, and iron ores relatively rich in phosphorus, are some of the advantages of the Bessemer process over the Siemens 'open hearth' process.

(e) In the 1930s, Britain introduced tariff barriers that reduced imports of foreign iron and steel by two-thirds in two years, boosting its own iron- and steel-making industries. However, as the extract of 1934 footage in the programme made clear, the belching of smoke from chimneys that had been smokeless for years was seen by many at the time as detrimental to a healthy local environment.

(f) The Basic Oxygen System (BOS), in which oxygen gas is introduced into the melt with a lance, was far cheaper than the 'open hearth' process which had dominated steel-making in the first part of the 20th century. As a result of this, and the collapse of demand and higher energy prices of the mid-1970s, many old British works, not on the BOS system, had to close.

(g) Reserves of the Northamptonshire Ironstone, worked around Corby, and of the Frodingham Ironstone, worked around Scunthorpe, eventually became exhausted, forcing the local steel makers to import ore from places as far afield as Australia.

(h) Instead of accumulating in unsightly heaps, slag today can be used as hard core for roads and buildings, and in making tarmacadam and concrete.

Question 7

In the following sentence about a blast furnace taken from the programme, replace four incorrect words with the correct ones (see also Figure 10):

> In chemical terms, the job of the blast furnace is to get enough oxygen and enough energy close to the iron carbide so that it can oxidize it from iron carbide to iron.

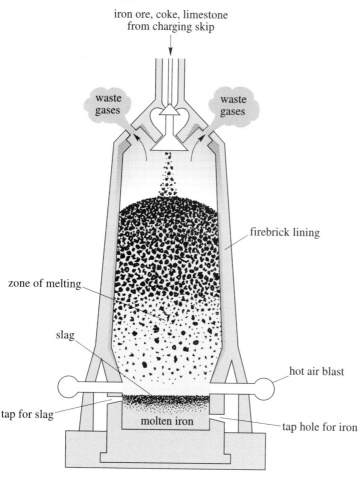

Figure 10 The main features of a blast furnace.

Question 8

Why is it important to quench coke quickly with water as it emerges from coke ovens?

Question 9

Fill in the gaps in the following account.

The response of the British Steel Corporation, formed in 19...7, to slackening demand was to imitate the style of successful industries abroad, notably .... Even the smallest blast furnace in that country made about .... times the tonnage of Britain's largest blast furnace. In 1973, BSC proposed that steel-making be organized into .... major works, the largest of which would be built at Redcar, on .... Deep water harbours were built to receive the cheapest ore from anywhere in the world. Steel works were constructed with everything on site, raw materials were bought in as needed, reducing stockpiling and wastage, and at least some recycling was built into the design — improvements that were all part of the process of ....

In addition to the spread of technology, an important influence in the rise in global consumption of physical resources has been the ever-increasing human population. Let's look at this in more detail.

Activity 2

To obtain a better perspective on the increase in world population, use the data in the following account to plot the appropriate values on Figure 11. Draw a smooth curve through them. (You may find it easier to make a table of the data first.)

From about 10 000 BC until about 3000 BC, the total world human population is estimated to have been no more than about 5 million, although earlier, of course, it had once been a minute fraction of this. The Neolithic Revolution, which for the first time allowed settled communities based on agriculture and domesticated animals, led to very rapid population growth in the last three millennia BC, and a population of 100 million is estimated for 500 BC. By about 1 AD, the population may have been about 200 million. Then, for a while the growth rate was slower, and by 1000 AD the population had probably reached about 250 million. When Columbus set sail for the New World in 1492, the population was about 500 million. By 1750, around the start of the Industrial Revolution, the total was about 750 million. By 1850, the population had soared to 1200 million. A hundred years later, by 1950, it was 2500 million, and by 1990 it was 5300 million. It's estimated that the current world population is about one-eleventh of the total of all humans who have ever lived. By 2032, if this exponential growth continues, world population is expected to exceed 9000 million. (If you're not sure what the term 'exponential' means, read the Box overleaf.)

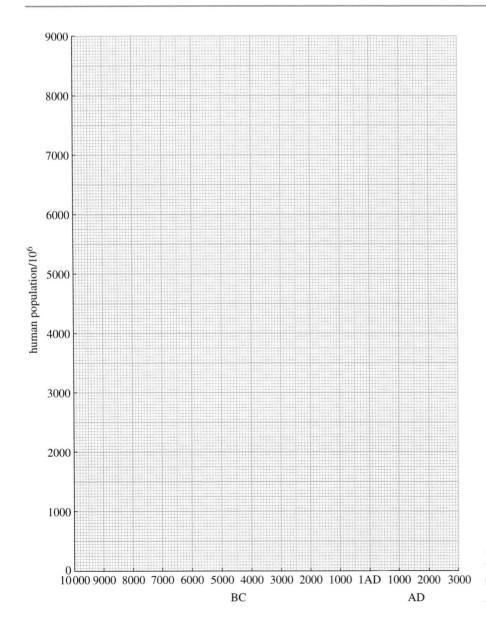

Figure 11   A graph on which to plot the values for the total human population in Activity 2.

The meaning of the term 'exponential'

The important term 'exponential' is often met in science, technology, population studies and the media, but what does it actually mean? In an **exponential** process, the rate of change of some quantity is proportional to the quantity itself. So, if a population is said to be growing exponentially, the rate of population increase itself becomes greater the more individuals there are in the population. Thus, in exponential change, the rate of change of some quantity (the actual amount of increase or decrease per unit time) is not constant, but the value of that quantity increases or decreases by a particular factor in successive time intervals. Compound interest on a sum deposited in a bank or building society is an example of an exponential process; the interest is calculated on the original sum *plus* the interest previously earned and reinvested. As a result, the actual amount of interest added to the account at regular intervals (when interest is due) increases with time, even if interest rates remain fixed.

If a population is growing exponentially, a graph of population size against time is not linear; that is, it is not a straight line, but is a curve with a changing gradient. The curve is relatively flat at first but after a while shoots rapidly upwards. Imagine a population of bacteria that doubles in number every hour, i.e. the **doubling time** is one hour. If there was initially one bacterium, at successive hourly intervals the numbers of bacteria would be 2, 4, 8, 16, 32, 64, 128 and so on. Were the population growth to continue at this rate, after just 24 hours there would be over 16 million bacteria! Similarly, if a population halves every hour, a graph of population size against time drops rapidly downwards at first but after a while tends to flatten out, i.e. the population shows an exponential decrease.

The rate of exponential change in the natural world may, of course, itself change with time. For example, the bacteria population might slow down its initial rate of exponential increase so that the population was taking twice as long to double, i.e. the doubling time was two hours instead of one hour. For example, if the new doubling time began after the population reached 128 bacteria, it would then take *two* hours rather than one hour to reach 256 bacteria. The rate of increase is still said to be exponential, because the increase is still proportional to the number of individuals. Question 10 asks you to consider changes in doubling time. (Exponential processes are discussed again later in Section 2.)

Question 10

Approximately how long did it take the world population to double from (a) its total in 1000 AD; (b) its total in 1850; (c) its total in 1950?

The main reason for the escalating rate of population increase, especially since about 1750, is not that people generally had more babies but that, on average, their children lived longer (particularly in western Europe) as food supplies increased, public health and medicine improved, and proper sanitation spread, among other changes. Birth rates (births per year per thousand of the population) initially stayed rather similar but death rates in some countries fell dramatically as life expectancies increased, causing populations to grow.

Eventually, as people in industrializing countries became more prosperous, the number of births per year in those countries fell until once again they virtually matched the number of deaths per year. By the early 1990s, the growth rates of most developed, industrialized countries were less than 1%, and the populations of a few countries, such as Germany, were actually declining. In 1990, however, only 23% of the world's population lived in industrialized countries, while the remaining 77% lived in developing countries. Many developing countries are now growing at over 3% per year; this may not sound much, but a population growing at 3% doubles in only 23 years. The average world population growth in the early 1990s was nearly 2%. Industrialized countries are typified by the USA, Canada, Australia, Japan and the countries of Europe. Developing countries are typified by China, India, and many countries in Africa and South America. The distinction between the two categories is, of course, blurred because some countries are developing very rapidly and before long will be regarded as industrialized; among these are Brazil, Chile and Mexico in Latin America, and Indonesia, Malaysia and Thailand in Asia.

This Course does not attempt to consider the complex factors influencing recent changes in birth and death rates. However, some key points are worth mentioning. Since 1945, death rates have fallen dramatically in developing countries, partly as a result of the battle against killer diseases such as smallpox and malaria. Infant mortality rates have generally fallen, although, in absolute terms, infant mortality is still shocking: in 1990 some 13 million children died in developing countries before their fifth birthday. In many developing countries, birth rates remain high, even when birth control is widely available. One reason is that children in such countries are often seen as economic assets, and as providers of security in old age, so it makes sense for individual families to have lots of children, even if this creates problems for society as a whole because of scarce resources. By contrast, lower infant mortality rates make parents more confident that even with a small family some of their children will grow to maturity. As a result, the rate of increase in the population of some countries eventually *diminishes* with lower infant mortality rates, rather than increases as one might initially expect.

As we shall see in Section 2, there are huge discrepancies between the average amount of physical resources consumed by someone in the industrialized world compared with someone in the developing world. To give one typical example, in 1990 the industrialized countries — 23% of the world's population — consumed about 80% of the world's production of copper. As consumption in the developing world catches up, are we in danger of exhausting vital resources or will humans have the ingenuity and technological skills to keep pace with the demands of an exponentially increasing population? These issues are discussed further in Section 2.

1.4 The substitution of physical resources

A very important role in the history of physical resources has been played by **substitution** — quite simply the use of an alternative resource for a particular purpose. A substitute is a material which, at least in part, replaces (or can replace) another material. Substitution may be partial or complete.

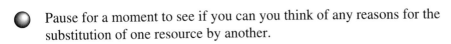 Pause for a moment to see if you can you think of any reasons for the substitution of one resource by another.

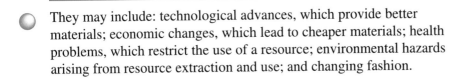 They may include: technological advances, which provide better materials; economic changes, which lead to cheaper materials; health problems, which restrict the use of a resource; environmental hazards arising from resource extraction and use; and changing fashion.

So there are several reasons for substitution.

1 Technological advances may lead to the discovery or invention of a more efficient or more desirable material for the purpose in hand. New techniques of extraction, production or manufacture may make an existing material more widely available, or a material available for the first time.

2   Economics is an important factor. Substitution may improve profitability. A manufacturer will often ask whether there is a cheaper material available that will do the job better, just as well, or adequately enough. Often economic considerations are interwoven with technological ones; for example, new techniques may push down the cost of extracting or processing raw materials. A vast array of economic factors may change the market price of a commodity, such as changes in supply and demand (discussed in Section 2).

3   Health problems or environmental hazards may emerge with prolonged use of a particular resource, in which case safer alternatives eventually replace the offending substance. For example, uranium ores were once used as green pigments in ceramics and glasses before their radioactivity was known to be dangerous. A similar example is given in the Box 'The strange case of Napoleon's wallpaper'. More recently, some forms of asbestos were extensively used for insulation against fire, heat and chemical attack until it became apparent that inhalation of the minute fibres was a common cause of cancer of the lungs and respiratory tract. Although still relatively rare compared with (1) and (2), awareness of health problems and other environmental hazards is becoming an increasingly frequent reason for substitution.

4   Fashion may influence or even override other factors. For example, when it was first available in significant quantities, the element aluminium became an expensive scientific novelty used by jewellers and craftsmen; aluminium teapots and cutlery were once status symbols for the very rich, including Napoleon III (the nephew of Napoleon I). Once aluminium became relatively easy to produce in quantity, it became a substitute for other metals, notably copper. In this case, a technological advance allowed an initially fashionable but expensive substitute to be more widely adopted.

The strange case of Napoleon's wallpaper

A poisonous compound of arsenic and copper was once commonly used as a green pigment in wallpapers. A celebrated case of chemical detective work revealed this as a plausible reason why the Emperor Napoleon I became very ill in a house to which he was increasingly confined during exile on the island of St Helena between 1815 and his death there in 1821. In the 1960s, analysis of a sample of Napoleon's hair revealed significant levels of arsenic, and for a while this was taken as evidence of the deliberate poisoning that Napoleon himself suspected. Later, however, a small surviving fragment of partially green wallpaper from the very damp house was revealed to contain arsenic in significant quantities, explaining Napoleon's symptoms and those of some other members of his household. It had been discovered in 1893 that, in damp conditions, mould converts the green compound into a highly poisonous gas (arsenic trimethyl) that disperses arsenic into the surroundings, accounting for many puzzling cases of illness or suspected deliberate poisoning. Sadly, the worse that patients became, the more likely they were to spend time in bed, which only increased their exposure to the poisonous gas emanating from the wallpaper. Not surprisingly, this knowledge led to substitution by other green pigments.

Figure 12   A fragment of wallpaper from the bedroom in which Napoleon died in St Helena in 1821. The pattern is mostly in green and brown.

Some or all of the above reasons for substitution may coincide, or they may shift from one to the other with time. A good example reflecting this typical complexity of substitution is the history of pipe materials used in domestic water supply, plumbing and drainage in Britain.

○   Spend a moment to write down what you think would be the most desirable properties of materials used for pipes that carry water.

○   Ideally, the pipes would be: impermeable (no water loss); strong; malleable (easy to shape and bend); insoluble and resistant to corrosion (decay by chemical attack) and, as a result, non-toxic; resistant to fracture, shrinkage and general physical decay; insensitive to changes in temperature; light (easy to transport or support above ground); easy to link together; and cheap to produce.

For some of their water supply systems in Britain, the Romans used lead piping, as can still be seen today at the Roman baths in Bath (Figure 13).

Figure 13   Roman lead pipe *in situ* beside the Great Bath, Bath. This pipe fed a fountain and a small immersion bath with hot spa water from a natural spring.

Britain's main water pipes ('mains') were made almost entirely of wood up to the eighteenth century, with lead pipes branching off to individual houses. The terms 'trunk line' and 'trunk call' derive from times when long-distance pipe and cable networks were carried mainly in hollowed-out tree trunks (Figure 14a). Wood (especially elm) and lead remained the only widely used materials for water supply and plumbing until the start of the Industrial Revolution, when cast iron started to be used, especially for large-diameter pipes. Edinburgh, for instance, replaced its lead mains water pipes with cast iron ones as early as 1755. Cast iron was not, however, generally used to replace wooden trunk pipes until the end of the nineteenth century. Today, many miles of cast iron water mains under London's streets are still in use

(a)   (b)

after 100 years. In the late 1950s and early 1960s a less brittle form of cast iron replaced ordinary cast iron, and in the 1970s a plastic, polyvinyl chloride (PVC), was introduced. Today, new mains are mostly polyethylene (which can now be extruded in large diameters) or PVC. Very large bore mains, such as the newly constructed London Ring Main (designed to distribute water around the metropolis), are made of concrete (Figure 14b).

Until this century, lead was used for virtually all underground supply pipes connecting houses to the mains. The materials substituting for lead in new mains connections have been successively iron and/or steel, copper coated with plastic, and, from the late 1950s, early plastics (mainly polyethylene). Today, pipes connecting to the mains are mostly polyethylene or PVC.

Lead was also virtually the sole material used in domestic plumbing systems. In the early twentieth century, cast iron started to replace lead, and is still used occasionally today, but only for relatively large diameter pipes. Copper began to be used for plumbing in the late 1930s and early 1940s, but only for heavy-duty pipes. In the 1950s, technological advances made available thinner, lightweight copper pipes, as a substitute for lead. Initially, plastics — unlike copper — were unsuitable for carrying hot water because they quickly became soft, and because the type of joints available could not cope with the expansion and contraction. With the invention of new polymers such as polypropylene in the early 1960s and, a little later, chlorinated polyvinyl chloride (CPVC), the properties of plastics gradually became more suitable for small diameter pipes carrying hot water. Today, special plastics, such as polybutylene, are widely used because they can be bent easily, soften little with hot water, and have effective joint systems. Copper, however, is still (1994) the dominant material for small diameter domestic pipes. Various other materials compete in pipe substitution, including heat-resistant, 'cross-linked' polyethylene, and a 5-layer composite pipe using aluminium, plastic and adhesive which combines the corrosion resistance of plastic and the malleability of copper and lead.

The history of domestic wastepipes (downpipes) and guttering also reflects the typical complexity of substitution. Plain wood, used in the earliest days of housing, led to wood lined with bitumen or lead, to cast iron, to asbestos (bound by cement, the asbestos fibres being used not for insulation but as reinforcement, enabling the cement to form strong pipe sections), to minor amounts of glass-reinforced polyester ('fibreglass') in the late 1950s, and

Figure 14 (a) A wooden 'trunk' water main at least 200 years old from near Piccadilly Circus, London. (b) The new concrete London Ring Main.

then, in the early 1960s, to unplasticized polyvinyl chloride (UPVC) which still remains the dominant material. (Unplasticized means that the material is relatively rigid, as opposed to plasticized materials which are more flexible, like anoraks or vinyl floor coverings.) Aluminium has also been used to a minor extent for gutters since about 1980. In older British properties that don't have modern replacement gutters, about half are still cast iron and about half are cement-bound asbestos.

Increasing medical evidence that lead could be poisonous eventually resulted in the passing of by-laws by every water company in Britain. By 1976, the use of lead in new installations had been banned throughout Britain. By then, its use in domestic plumbing had almost disappeared in favour of copper and plastics, both of which were not only safer and cheaper, but readily available in appropriate shapes and more suitable in various ways (e.g. lighter). Nevertheless, about 9 million households in Britain are believed to have lead somewhere in their water system. The cost of lead has fallen recently, and with that the incentive to collect and recycle it. Thus, plumbing lead is more likely to remain a potential hazard to health, especially from old buried pipes that are expensive to excavate. Lead is more easily dissolved from lead piping in soft water areas than in hard water areas, where water contains more dissolved calcium and magnesium. (Block 3 *Water Resources* looks at this in more detail.)

Not surprisingly, some of the various attempts at substitution in plumbing have tried and failed. When copper became relatively expensive in the late 1960s and early 1970s, the industry used steel tubes galvanized with zinc on the inside and coated with copper on the outside. These proved to be problematic, mainly because the steel rusted rapidly. Stainless steel was tried for a while, but was difficult to bend and hard to solder, although it is stronger and corrodes less easily than copper. Since 1986, when water by-laws allowed the use of mains water pressure for hot water supply systems in Britain, stainless steel has been increasingly used for domestic hot-water cylinders rather than copper. Attempts at making fibreglass cylinders failed because construction proved technically difficult.

As the above account shows, the rate of substitution of plumbing materials has increased enormously this century, as more and more possible materials became available. This pattern of rapidly accelerating substitution (paralleling technological development) is typical of most areas of resource use. In the second half of the twentieth century, many new materials have been invented, affecting a vast range of different objects and activities. Plastics have probably been involved in more substitution than any other material, as well as being employed for entirely new purposes. Plastics derive essentially from oil, coal or natural gas, and common salt. The salt (NaCl) provides chlorine for PVC (polyvinyl chloride) and certain other plastics.

But rapid change can produce unforeseen complications. For instance, some residents of the USA have filed successful claims that increased chlorine levels in the water supply have caused leaching of chemicals from some types of plastic piping, making it brittle. Inertia to substitute new materials is understandable: it's wise not to rush into a change based on price and *apparent* suitability alone. Prolonged field testing is essential to ensure materials perform at their best. Materials have often, in effect, been tried and tested for years in one country before being adopted elsewhere.

Inventing new ways of doing things has an obvious influence on substitution. For example, consider the capturing of moving images on film. Silver is a key part of the light-sensitive coatings on traditional photographic film, but with the ever-increasing use of video-tape — a plastic tape coated with iron or chromium oxide — this particular demand for silver may decline.

Flint as a physical resource

Flint occurs as hard lumps (nodules) in the Cretaceous chalk rocks of southern and eastern England, Europe and North America. Cretaceous rocks are coloured bright green on the Postcard Geological Map. Flint was a key physical resource of the Stone Age, providing the main material for tools and weapons. Indeed, the quarrying, manufacture and trade of flint were among the earliest of business ventures. The uniform texture, brittleness, and conchoidal fracture (i.e. curved fracture surfaces) made it possible (albeit with great skill) to shape it into sharp-sided objects such as arrowheads, axeheads, scrapers and knives. In Britain, flint tools date back to at least 250 000 years ago, and possibly twice that period. Flint became gradually obsolete for tools and weapons in the Bronze Age and the following Iron Age. It was discovered that sparks were produced when flint was struck against hard metals in tinderboxes. For a while flint made a brief comeback in the seventeenth and eighteenth centuries as a spark generator in muskets, including the flintlock firearm. Today flint is used in bulk as gravels for road and path construction and concrete aggregate, and sometimes as a facing stone in buildings or walls in southern and eastern England, for which *knapped* (deliberately fractured) flints are occasionally still used as an attractive alternative to flints with naturally weathered surfaces. Flint pebbles are also used to grind raw materials in the ceramic and paint industries instead of steel balls, in order to avoid contaminating the product with iron.

(a)

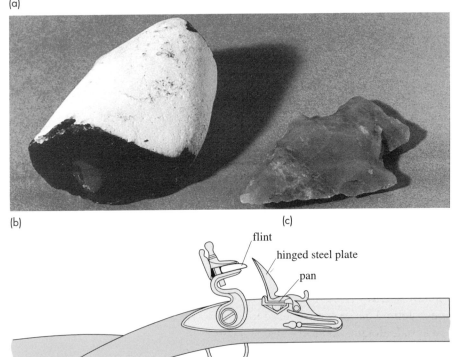

(b) (c)

flint
hinged steel plate
pan

(d)

Figure 15
(a) Neolithic flint mine at Grimes Graves, Norfolk; mining galleries run off from the base of the main shaft. (b) Block of flint. (c) A flint arrowhead. (d) A flintlock musket. Pressing the trigger caused the flint to strike a hinged steel plate, forcing it back to expose the powder in the pan to the sparks.

The extent to which a physical resource can be replaced is one of the many factors affecting its economics (Section 2). Some physical resources have unique or very unusual properties that make them essential for certain uses, so that they cannot readily be substituted. A good example is mercury, the only metal that is liquid over the range of ordinary room temperatures.

○ Recall Video Band 1: *The Great Iron and Steel Rollercoaster*. Is it true that one of the benefits of substitution, in addition to employing more efficient materials for particular jobs, is that it automatically makes recycling easier?

○ No. Substitution can often lead to the use of more efficient materials for particular jobs, but this can make recycling *harder*. The example given in Video Band 1 was the increased use in cars of a variety of plastics (as opposed to metals) that are difficult to separate out.

Every case of substitution has its complicating factors. For example, aluminium is the metal most frequently substituted for copper in electrical applications. Although aluminium has about two-thirds of the electrical conductivity of copper for the same cross-sectional area of wire, its density is only about one-third that of copper, resulting in its being a better conductor on a weight-for-weight basis. Largely for this reason, overhead conductors for the British National Grid are made of aluminium cable, strengthened with a thin core of galvanized steel. Aluminium smelting actually requires far more energy per tonne of metal than that required for copper, so to assess the overall success or otherwise of substitution in terms of 'energy accounting' one needs to consider the entire cost budget, though usually the energy required to produce a resource is directly reflected in its market price.

Activity 3

Can you find any examples of substitution involving a physical resource in your home? To get you started, try to answer the following questions.

1 When was your house built?
2 What materials are used for (a) the roof; (b) window frames; (c) hot water pipes; (d) guttering; (e) a fireplace, if any? Are they original? If not, what substitution has taken place?

The relative importance of a material as a resource — indeed, whether or not it is a resource at all — can obviously change with time, as has been the case with flint (see Box 'Flint as a physical resource'). Such shifts may occur because of substitution, with a new resource found to fulfil a continuing purpose, such as the element cerium which today is used for the 'flint' of a cigarette lighter. An entirely new use, sometimes even a first use, can be found for a substance, which may then become an important resource. For example, miners seeking lead, copper and zinc ores often left behind large tonnages of barite (barium sulphate), a heavy mineral for which there was little or no demand. Piles of pale-coloured barite crystals used to lie as waste around the mines. Today, this material, along with newly quarried barite, is ground up and used as drilling mud in the oil industry, where its high density ($4.5\,\mathrm{g\,cm^{-3}} = 4.5\,\mathrm{t\,m^{-3}}$) helps to prevent high-pressure blow-out from drill holes and to 'float up' chippings to the surface. (The majority of rocks, such as limestone and sandstone, have densities of 2.0 to $3.0\,\mathrm{g\,cm^{-3}}$.) Barite is also used as a filler for high-quality paper and textiles, and in paint manufacture.

Question 11

Study Figure 16, which shows a comparison of the materials used in the manufacture of a typical car in 1980 and in 1990.

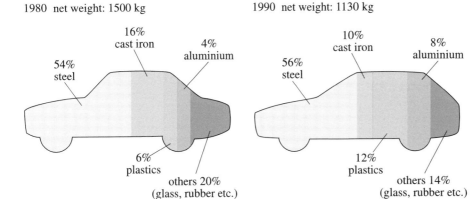

1980 net weight: 1500 kg

16% cast iron
4% aluminium
54% steel
6% plastics
others 20% (glass, rubber etc.)

1990 net weight: 1130 kg

10% cast iron
8% aluminium
56% steel
12% plastics
others 14% (glass, rubber etc.)

Figure 16 Comparison of materials used in the manufacture of a typical car in 1980 and 1990. Note also the change in net weight. Proportions not drawn to scale.

Fill in the missing parts of Table 3, calculating values to the nearest whole number. 'Change in percentage contribution' refers to the change in the percentage contributions of each material to the total (net) weight of the typical car between 1980 and 1990. 'Change in weight of materials' relates to the percentage change in the average weight of each material used in the typical car between 1980 and 1990. To make sure you understand what each column means, you could check first that you agree with the values already filled in for the 'Others' row.

Table 3

	Weight of materials in 1980 car/kg	Weight of materials in 1990 car/kg	Change in percentage contribution: % of 1980 value	Change in weight of materials: % of 1980 value
steel		633	+2	
cast iron	240			
plastics	90			
aluminium		90	+4	
others	300	158	−6	−47
totals	1500	1130	n/a	

Now answer the following questions.

(a) By what percentage did the average total (net) weight of a car change between 1980 and 1990?

(b) Was more or less steel needed to make the typical car in 1990 compared with 1980? By how many kilograms did the weight of steel change? What was this change in the weight of steel, as a percentage of its 1980 value?

(c) By what percentage did the weight of cast iron change in the typical car between 1980 and 1990?

(d) In terms of the actual weight of material used in a typical car, which category of materials increased most, and which category decreased most over the decade?

1.5 Summary of Section 1

1   Physical resources are useful materials or energy obtained by humans from today's inorganic world, either at or beneath the Earth's surface. Environment is a broad term, applying to all scales, and referring generally to the surroundings of whatever is being discussed. In practice, environment tends to mean the substances, individuals or processes that interact, or might interact, in some way with whatever is being surrounded.

2   Physical resources are either composed of one or more of the 94 or so chemical elements that occur naturally on Earth, or are certain forms of energy not composed of chemical elements, such as solar radiation and the converted solar energy in wind and waves, geothermal energy, and tidal (gravitational) energy. The quantities of different elements required globally by humans each year, whether the elements are used in their uncombined form or in compounds, range across 10 orders of magnitude — from less than 1 tonne to 10 billion (10^{10}) tonnes.

3   The most important factors influencing the relative use of particular elements are: their physical and chemical properties, which govern their uses; their abundance and distribution in the Earth's crust, which are similarly dependent on their physical and chemical properties; their ease of extraction and hence cost of production; and the fact that they are subject to complex political, economic, social and environmental factors.

4   Physical resources are enormously varied and include building and other constructional materials, water, sources of energy, metals and other inorganic raw materials used by humans. The products of some ancient biological systems form important physical resources today, including coal, oil and natural gas. Analysing the 'life history' of virtually any manufactured object reveals that a vast number of physical resources have contributed to it, either directly or indirectly.

5   Since the Industrial Revolution, begun in the mid-eighteenth century, exponential increases in the global consumption of materials and energy have occurred alongside technological advances and an exponential increase in the total population. Huge changes in the way we explore for, extract, process and use resources have meant that today's most industrialized societies can use the most appropriate resources, wherever they come from; less developed societies, however, remain more dependent on locally available resources.

6   Substitution — the use of an alternative resource for a particular purpose — has played an important role in the history of physical resources. The reasons for substitution include: technological advances, economic influences, the discovery of health problems associated with use of a particular resource, the generation of other environmental hazards, and changing fashion. A study of historical changes in the types of materials used for basic human requirements, such as water supply and drainage, usually reveals a pattern of rapidly escalating substitution, especially in the twentieth century, paralleling rates of technological development.

2 THE ECONOMICS AND AVAILABILITY OF PHYSICAL RESOURCES

2.1 The economics of physical resources

An essential aspect of most physical resources is that they are commodities which can be traded somewhere in the global economy. The economy is part of the whole 'outside world', not an isolated laboratory. It's far more complex than most scientific experiments, which are traditionally kept as simple as possible by minimizing the number of variables being investigated. Not surprisingly, the world economy, like British weather, is notoriously difficult to predict.

A feeling for the complexity of trade in physical resources can be gained from Figure 17, which shows the major trade flows of copper ores and concentrates in 1985. Note that the Figure does not show the copper produced *and* processed in the same country (e.g. almost all Zambia's copper), nor trade in refined copper, but only trade in copper ores and concentrates *between* countries. (Concentrates are the products of extraction operations in which ore minerals have been concentrated together ready for smelting or other chemical processing.) Japan dominates the picture as the major importer, with North and South America as the major exporters. In this case protectionism — the political regulation of trade — was a significant factor causing Japan to become the world's largest importer of copper ores and concentrates. Japan was protecting the markets for its smelters by making it financially more worthwhile for many countries to export ores and concentrates to Japan than to smelt the copper themselves. Japan did this by placing an import duty on refined copper, but not on copper ores and concentrates; as a result, about 90% of the world's traded amount of the latter went to Japan in 1985. Some copper-ore producing countries therefore import Japanese goods which contain copper that was mined in their own country but refined in Japan.

Figure 17 Major trade flows of copper ores and concentrates in 1985. The numbers represent copper content in 1000 tonnes. See text for discussion.

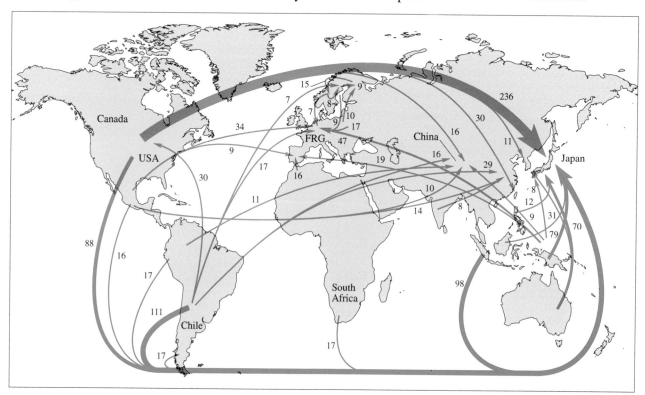

Table 4 lists the top two producing countries in 1991 for a selection of physical resources. The order is liable to change. For example, in 1991, some countries only just made it to second place: China just exceeded Chile's production of molybdenum, the USA just exceeded Peru's production of silver, and Indonesia just exceeded Brazil's production of tin.

Table 4   The top two major producing countries for some physical resources, 1991

Resource	Countries	Percentage share in world production
antimony	China	51
	Bolivia	14
asbestos	Former Soviet Union	59
	Canada	20
barite	China	34
	India	9
bauxite (aluminium ore)	Australia	37
	Guinea	16
beryllium	USA	54
	China	17
bromine	USA	43
	Israel	33
chromium	South Africa	38
	Former Soviet Union	29
coal	China	25
	USA	20
cobalt	Zaïre	37
	Zambia	26
copper	Chile	21
	USA	19
fluorspar (source of fluorine)	China	37
	Mongolia	12
gold	South Africa	28
	USA	14
gypsum	USA	15
	China	9
iodine	Japan	46
	Chile	26
iron ore	Former Soviet Union	24
	Brazil	18
kaolin (china clay)	USA	42
	United Kingdom	13
lead	Australia	16
	USA	15
manganese	Former Soviet Union	36
	China	15
mercury	Former Soviet Union	41
	Mexico	16
molybdenum	USA	48
	China	14
natural gas	Former Soviet Union	39
	USA	24
nickel	Former Soviet Union	27
	Canada	21
oil	Former Soviet Union	17
	Saudi Arabia	14
phosphate rock	USA	33
	Former Soviet Union	20

Resource	Countries	Percentage share in world production
platinum group metals	South Africa	50
	Former Soviet Union	42
potassium	Former Soviet Union	34
	Canada	27
rare earths	USA	31
	China	30
rhenium	USA	52
	Chile	14
salt	USA	20
	China	14
silver	Mexico	15
	USA	13
sulphur	USA	19
	Former Soviet Union	15
tin	China	22
	Indonesia	15
tungsten	China	58
	Former Soviet Union	19
vanadium	South Africa	50
	Former Soviet Union	30
zinc	Canada	16
	Australia	14
zirconium	Australia	37
	South Africa	29

⬤ Why should it be that countries with a large land area tend to feature prominently in the table, whether they have relatively large populations (as in China) or relatively small ones as in Australia)?

◯ Simply, the larger the land area, the greater chance there is, on average, of an appropriate geological setting for any given physical resource.

Let's choose just one of the physical resources mentioned in Table 4 and see how the total amounts extracted and used have changed during the twentieth century. Study Figure 18, which shows the world production and consumption of aluminium since 1900.

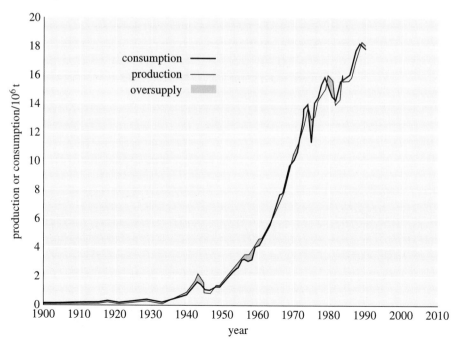

Figure 18 Global production and consumption of aluminium since 1900. Periods of oversupply, when production exceeded consumption, are shaded in colour.

○ When did production and consumption first start to increase rapidly?

○ About 1935, and then especially around 1940, shortly after the start of World War II, when aluminium was needed for aircraft. Notice how production and consumption fell towards the end of the war, after which followed a fairly rapid and sustained increase in production and consumption that continued until about 1974.

Between about 1945 and 1974, aluminium production increased exponentially, as can be judged from the fact that the curve not only goes up but over most of that period gets steeper upwards with time (i.e. it is non-linear).

In the period 1945–74 many other physical resources were being produced and consumed at an exponential rate, with a range of doubling times. Examples of average doubling times, in years, between 1945 and 1965 were: copper: 15; natural gas: 15; gold: 17; coal: 17; zinc: 24; lead: 35; cobalt: 47. The shorter the doubling time, the more rapid the rate of escalation.

Question 12

As Figure 18 shows, in 1955, aluminium production was about 3×10^6 t. Read off from Figure 18 in which years production reached 6×10^6 t and 12×10^6 t. Then estimate the average doubling time for aluminium production over that period from 1955, and calculate the average percentage rate of increase per year.

○ In general, have aluminium production and consumption been closely matched over the twentieth century?

○ Yes; it's striking how closely production and consumption generally coincide, with only relatively small deviations from each other.

More on exponential change and doubling times

In everyday language, the term 'exponential' tends to be applied to very rapid change. But even growth as little as 1% per year is exponential: if production was 100 units in one particular year, it would be exactly 101 the next year, and 102.01 (101 + 1% of 101) the next year, and so on.

As we saw in Section 1, in a period of exponential growth, the time taken for a quantity to double is known as the *doubling time*. For example, if production has a doubling time of 3 years, and starts in one year with 10 000 tonnes, 3 years later production would be 20 000 tonnes, and after another 3 years it would be 40 000 tonnes, and so on. There is a simple formula (the mathematical derivation of which need not concern us here) to estimate *approximately* what a doubling time means in terms of the percentage rate of increase per year:

70/doubling time ≈ % rate of increase

For example, if the doubling time is 20 years, the approximate rate of increase is 70/20 per cent per year, i.e. ≈ 3.5% per year. Similarly, if you know the rate of increase, the approximate doubling time is given by dividing 70 by the percentage rate of increase:

70/% rate of increase ≈ doubling time

The expression, however, breaks down for very large or very small rates. Remember, too, that the rate of any exponential change can itself change with time, so that the doubling time can vary. The formula assumes a constant percentage rate of increase.

○ To test your understanding of this formula, try these questions.

(a) If you invest £100 at 10% compound interest, how long will it take to reach £200?

(b) If an investment of £100 had grown to £200 in 16 years, what was the percentage rate of increase (i.e. the rate of compound interest)? (Assume the percentage rate of increase remains constant in each case.)

○ (a) 70/10 ≈ 7 years; (b) 70/16 ≈ 4.4%.

Notice, however, that the ups and downs of aluminium production and consumption have become larger since about 1973–75. This was the time of the first oil crisis when oil prices rose sharply, having restraining effects on the world economy, and subsequently times of oversupply (surplus) and undersupply (shortage) followed each other more rapidly. The same is true for many other metals. Probably the most common reason for this was that, in estimating demand, the previous high rates of increase in consumption were simply extrapolated, and as consumption fell, overcapacities developed. For a while, oversupply occurred as production exceeded consumption. As a result, smelters were not operated on full capacity, and some even had to close. As soon as consumption increased and became level with production again, additional production capacity was added in the vain hope that the previous high growth rates in consumption would return. However, consumption soon fell again, another period of overproduction began, and so the cycle started again.

These series of adjustments of production to consumption for aluminium are actually relatively rapid compared with some other commodities. One reason for this concerns the difference between fixed and variable costs. *Fixed* costs in this context are the costs of setting up quarries, processing plants, etc., and keeping them going. *Variable* costs are those that vary according to the volume of output, such as variations in the number of staff (salaries), the energy required per unit of production, and the cost of the consumables required to run the plant. A large amount of electricity is used in the production of aluminium metal, so the variable costs are high in proportion to fixed costs. It therefore does not make economic sense to produce large tonnages of aluminium that cannot soon be sold.

Over the long term, perhaps a decade or so, market forces ensure that production and consumption are balanced; there is no point in a producer amassing larger and larger stockpiles if they are never going to be sold. Sometimes, however, a producer will produce more of a commodity than the market demands and stockpile it if it is perceived that the market price is increasing and that selling at a later date will increase profit. This is particularly true with commodities used as investments, such as gold and diamonds. Equally, a consumer may purchase far more than their immediate needs if they perceive that the cost of the commodity is likely to go up faster than the cost of borrowing money. Production in the long term, however, is always cut back to meet consumption.

An increase in production does not itself necessarily lead to greater consumption in the short term, as witnessed by stockpiles of butter in the European Union, or the dumping of apples or tomatoes after a seasonal glut in the marketplace. Similarly, a fall in consumption may not immediately translate into a fall in production. For example, in the early 1990s, demand for bricks in the UK went down as house-building declined, and brick-making companies went on amassing huge stockpiles of bricks, which became cheaper. Consumption remained minimal, and therefore after a while production declined. We explore these fundamental relationships further in the next Section (2.2).

Two extremely important influences in the economies of individual countries and that of the world as a whole are (a) inflation and (b) major events such as wars, political upheavals and economic crises. Study Figure 19, which shows the price in US dollars for copper and zinc in **real** and **nominal** terms since 1900. The price in real terms means the price compared to the general purchasing power of money in a particular year, in this case 1900. Nominal price means the actual price paid. Because of inflation, it can be misleading to compare the nominal prices in different years. The price in subsequent years is adjusted for inflation over the period concerned. (Don't let the word 'real' mislead you here; it is *not* the actual price you have to pay when you buy something.)

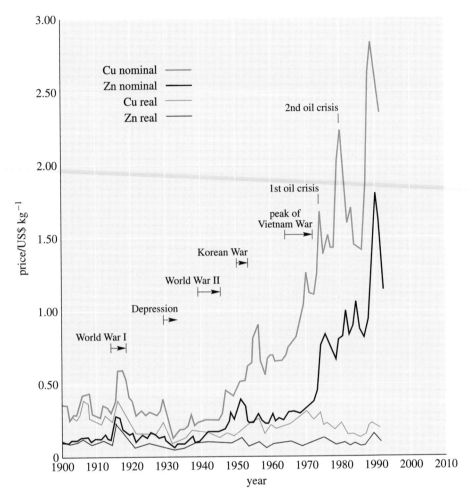

Figure 19 Prices (US$) for copper (Cu) and zinc (Zn) in real and nominal terms since 1900, with timing of major historical events indicated.

⬤ How do the prices of copper and zinc in 1991 compare with their prices in 1900 *in real terms* ?

◯ The price of copper in real terms has declined overall, such that it is about 40% cheaper than in 1900. The price of zinc, on the other hand, is about the same.

⬤ Study the curves showing changes in the nominal price of copper and zinc.

   (a) Has the price of zinc, in real or nominal terms, ever been more than that of copper since 1900?

   (b) Is there generally a close correspondence between the two curves?

   (c) Is there any evidence that the price of these metals has been influenced by the major historical events indicated?

◯ (a) The price of zinc has never been more than that of copper since 1900, though it came fairly close to it at times.

(b) There is quite a close correspondence between the two curves for much of the period since 1900. Sometimes the curves are slightly out of phase, i.e. there is a slight delay of a year or two between a change in one curve and a similar change in the other. Copper prices also tend to be a little more volatile, i.e. they go up and down by greater percentages; for example, compare the fall of copper and zinc prices during the early 1930s Depression.

(c) It's clear from Figure 19 that many of the major historical events indicated are coincident with changes in the price of both metals; and indeed the historical events are known (from other information) to be the primary cause of such coincidences. The two oil crises, for example, were clearly associated with a marked increase in nominal prices, and, less obviously, in real prices too. Notice, too, how prices sank to their lowest in real and nominal terms shortly after 1930 as the Depression hit hard, continuing a slide triggered by the Wall Street Crash in late 1929. The start of the world recession which began in 1989–90 can be made out in Figure 19 (and, incidentally, just discerned in Figure 18).

Free economies are those that generally allow the market forces of supply and demand to regulate prices. They contrast with 'planned' or 'command' economies, now very few, where prices are determined by state regulation ('interference'), government decree, etc. Cartels are, however, a common complicating feature of free economies. A **cartel** is an association of producers who have made a strict agreement to fix prices and/or to limit supplies, thus avoiding cut-price competition or overproduction. Restricting the supply often secures a higher price for members of the cartel. The tightest form of cartel would be where all the producers supplied their output through a central selling organization. Some might say that De Beers, which handles a large proportion of the world's supply of gem-quality diamonds, comes close to this. There are many other kinds of producer associations, which, even if not strictly cartels, try at least to ensure price stability.

The Organization of Petroleum Exporting Countries (OPEC) may be considered as a form of cartel. Formed in 1960, it consists of a group of thirteen major producers and exporters of crude petroleum. In the early 1970s, these countries accounted for about 60% of total world crude-oil production and about 90% of total world exports. The principle behind OPEC was to restrict the world supply with output *quotas* (limits to maximum output of each country) and so increase prices and profits. However, the high oil prices led to the expansion of oil supplies from non-OPEC producers (such as the United Kingdom) and to increasing substitution by other fuels (e.g. North Sea gas). The high price of OPEC oil greatly stimulated exploration for oil in the North Sea. Political hostilities also weakened the unity of OPEC, and several member countries exceeded their quotas. As a result, by 1991, the OPEC share of both world production and world exports had fallen to about 38%. It's easy to see that all cartels are inherently unstable; individual members have an interest in producing as much as they can to sell at an agreed price, or in cutting their own price to increase sales. Cartels are often considered to be undesirable as they do not allow market forces to operate freely; they are illegal in some countries.

Now look at Figure 20, which shows the price of aluminium in real and nominal terms since 1900. Until about 1970, the price of aluminium was determined by a cartel-like agreement among major producers. Aluminium then became quoted on the London Metal Exchange (LME), an important international forum where a number of major metals are traded in open market. The producers' agreement then started to dissolve, especially when the LME price (the 'free market price') dropped below the price set by those major producers. Note the overlap of free market price (coloured lines) and major producers' price until the latter petered out in about 1985.

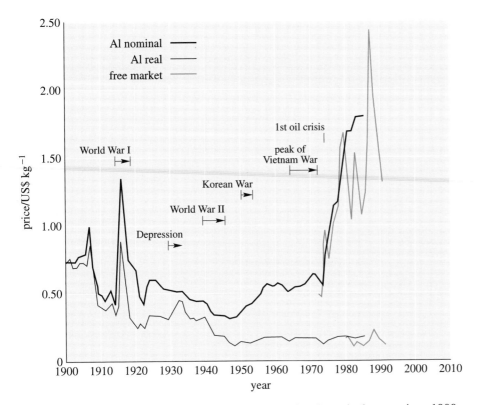

Figure 20   Price (US$) for aluminium (Al) in real and nominal terms since 1900, with timing of major historical events indicated. The coloured lines since 1970 are the free market price, as opposed to the price set by agreement between major producers.

⬤   Over the twentieth century, how has the real price of aluminium (Figure 20) compared generally with the prices of copper and zinc (Figure 19)?

◯   For the first part of the century, aluminium was more expensive than both copper and zinc, whereas since about 1950 its price has generally been *between* that of copper and zinc. For four decades, since about 1950, when the long-sustained increase in production and consumption began (Figure 18), the average *real* price of aluminium has been relatively low. Between 1950 and 1980 the real price was also relatively stable, in part due to the regulation by major aluminium producers referred to above. It is therefore mainly the influence of inflation that has caused the massive increase in the nominal price of aluminium, especially since about 1970.

As is the case with aluminium (Figure 20), copper and zinc (Figure 19), the real price of many commodities has not significantly increased over many decades. In fact, despite the impression gained from massive increases in nominal prices, the overriding trend of the real price of many non-fuel resources has been downward, with most of the plunge occurring during the 12 years following the first oil crisis in 1973. Real prices for many non-fuel resources recovered somewhat in the late 1980s but were in decline again by 1990.

2.1.1 Consumption in industrialized and developing countries

The consumption of most physical resources has, like aluminium (Figure 18), risen dramatically since the end of World War II. Since then more mineral resources have been consumed than in the whole previous history of human civilization.

The USA, Japan, and the countries of the European Union together typically consume between 50% and 95% of the total world production of mineral resources, depending on the individual commodity. Figure 21 compares the distribution of total world population and total world metal consumption between industrialized and developing countries over a forty-year period. In 1950, about a third of the world population (32%) lived in industrialized countries, which consumed at least 95% of the world's production of aluminium, copper, zinc, lead, nickel and steel.

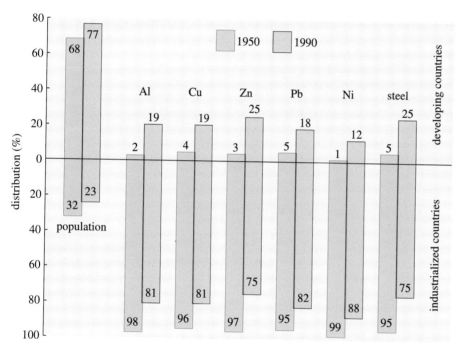

Figure 21 The distribution of total world population and total world metal consumption between industrialized and developing countries in 1950 (on the left of each pair) and in 1990 (on the right). The numbers given are percentages. See text for discussion.

○ How did the percentage of the total world's population in developing countries change from 1950 to 1990? By what percentage did the consumption of metals in developing countries change relative to industrialized countries in that period? Give the maximum and minimum percentage change for the range of metals shown, and in addition give the value for aluminium. (Assume that the same groupings of countries are being compared in 1950 and 1990.)

○ By 1990, the percentage of the total world's population in developing countries had gone up by 9%, from 68% to 77%. Relative to industrialized countries, the consumption of the metals shown rose in each case, by between 11% (Ni) and 22% (Zn). The value for aluminium was 17%.

Question 13

Use Figure 18, as well as Figure 21, to answer the following question. By what percentage did the *weight* of aluminium consumed by developing countries change between 1950 and 1990?

Question 13, like the comparison of materials used in the typical car between 1980 and 1990 (Figure 16), again shows how misleading it can be to compare percentages when the totals involved are not the same. In this case, it first appears from Figure 21 that the amount of aluminium used by developing countries went up by 17% (from 2% to 19%) — but that was the increase *relative to* industrialized countries. The amount actually consumed by developing countries went up by 11 300%.

- By what factor did the average amount of aluminium used *per person* increase in developing countries between 1950 and 1990? The population in developing countries was 1.7×10^9 in 1950 and 4.1×10^9 in 1990.

- If there had been no population increase, then the amount of aluminium used per person would have gone up by a factor of 113. But as the population rose by a factor of 2.4 (i.e. $4.1 \times 10^9/1.7 \times 10^9$), the amount per person must have been 113 divided by 2.4, giving 47. In other words, the average amount of aluminium consumed by an individual in the developing world increased by 47 times in 40 years.

- What was the average amount of aluminium used per person in the developing world in 1950 and in 1990?

- In 1950, the population in developing countries was 1.7×10^9, and the amount of aluminium they consumed was 3.0×10^4 t. The average amount per person was therefore

    $= 3.0 \times 10^4/1.7 \times 10^9$ t

    $= 1.76 \times 10^{-5}$ t

    $= 1.76 \times 10^{-2}$ kg

    $= 17.6$ g

    The average amount used per person in 1990 was, we know from the above, 47 times higher, i.e. 827 g.

    To check this, or as an alternative approach, divide the total amount consumed by the developing world in 1990 by its population; i.e. the average amount per person was therefore

    $= 3.4 \times 10^6/4.1 \times 10^9$ t

    $\approx 0.83 \times 10^{-3}$ t

    $= 0.83 \times 10^{-3} \times 10^3$ kg

    $= 0.83$ kg

    $= 830$ g

Question 14

Using similar logic, calculate and then fill in the six missing numbers in the following sentences. For this question you need to know that the population in industrialized countries was 0.8×10^9 in 1950 and 1.2×10^9 in 1990.

Between 1950 and 1990, the total weight of aluminium used by industrialized countries had increased by a factor of ...., compared with .... for developing countries. The average amount of aluminium used by *an individual* in the industrialized world had increased .... times.

In 1950, the average amount of aluminium used per person in the industrialized world was about .... times more than someone in the developing world used. By 1990, however, the average amount of aluminium used per person in the industrialized world was only about .... times more than someone in the developing world. In other words, over this period, the average consumption of aluminium per person in the developing world had increased .... times faster than for someone in the industrialized world.

It may have surprised you just how much aluminium is consumed, on average, by every man, woman and child in the industrialized world in a single year. This illustrates an important point: we use many physical resources every day of our lives that we never buy personally, nor are we conscious of their composition. This is particularly true of materials used for public buildings, roads, buses, trains, planes and so on. In the case of aluminium, about 45% of consumption in industrialized countries is used for transport and building construction, but we may only be aware of using aluminium in household items such as cooking foil, drink cans or saucepans. There are some physical resources, such as uranium, that most people not only never buy personally but never even *directly* use, although they benefit from them — such as electrical energy generated from uranium in a nuclear power station.

2.1.2 Future economic patterns

What are likely to be the major influences on future global patterns of production and consumption of physical resources? In general, as we have seen, consumption of physical resources is growing faster in developing regions than in nations that have long been industrialized. The increases are concentrated in countries like Mexico, Brazil, India and the newly industrialized countries of East Asia such as South Korea and Malaysia. The disparity in population growth between industrialized and developing regions, and the disproportionate increase in per person consumption in the latter (reducing slightly the long-standing inequality of consumption between industrialized and developing countries), are likely to continue.

Environmental issues are likely to influence production, consumption, prices and markets to an increasing degree. Steadily growing environmental awareness has, in some countries, already led to a range of restrictions and laws affecting extraction, production and usage of certain physical resources. Among the most important ways of reducing environmental impact are ceasing pollution, recycling, saving energy, and substitution.

Substitution can play a very important — if sometimes accidental — role in the conservation of specific raw materials. For example, in West Germany in 1988, it was decided to substitute glass optical fibre for copper in the telephone and telecommunications network, in order that messages could be coded more efficiently as pulses of light rather than as a fluctuating electric current. By 1991, this led to savings of copper of about 200 000 tonnes each year, about 18% of Germany's total annual consumption of copper. There has, however, been a corresponding increase in the consumption of the raw materials for glass. Glass optical fibres are replacing copper in many other telecommunications networks, including that of the UK. It seems likely that the demand for metals in general will slacken as high-technology materials such as new ceramics and composites compete with and substitute for them. (A **composite** material is produced by combining two or more materials with complementary properties into a composite form, e.g. carbon fibres set in a nylon matrix, as used in some tennis rackets.)

Another factor that has played a role in the past and may well continue to do so is political interference with the free flow of commodities that are concentrated in certain regions. Supplies may be vulnerable to local political events. Although *production* of physical resources is more evenly distributed through the world than consumption, many physical resources themselves, including some of strategic importance, are unequally distributed. For example, of the world's total reserves in 1993, China and Russia together had 62% of rare earths; South Africa had 89% of platinum group metals, and 69% of chromium; Zaïre had 50% of cobalt; Brazil had 95% of niobium, and so on. In general, many of the best reserves now lie in developing countries, partly because many industrial nations have a much longer history of mining so that their own resources have become depleted, and partly because many developing countries are relatively large.

One of the most important factors affecting the future pattern of resource consumption is that the industrialized nations have largely already built a basic infrastructure of roads, railways and buildings. Now, with relatively little population growth, such countries use physical resources more to *maintain* structures and equipment than to construct them, and to support a society where a high proportion of consumption relates to domestic (i.e. home-related) expenditure. As the major industrialized countries shift away from heavy industry towards services and high technology, fewer raw materials will be required to contribute to their gross national products, even if their economies boom. Among the fastest growing sectors in industrial economies are, for example, electronics and pharmaceuticals, which require far fewer materials and less energy than traditional extractive and manufacturing industries. Production too is declining in many countries that are major consumers. For example, since 1950, the percentage of the world's steel *produced* by the USA has decreased from 45% to 11%, and other decreases in the USA's share of world production include zinc, copper and aluminium.

As Table 5 shows, at least 14 countries get a third or more of their export revenues from non-fuel mineral resources. Many of these are developing nations, which are are hit especially hard by any general fall in price of these commodities. Reduced foreign earnings make it difficult or impossible to buy imported manufactured items and to repay international debts. The effects can be disastrous. As just one example, Zambia depends on copper for 86% of its export revenue, but the price of copper dropped sharply from 1980 to 1984 (although it later recovered after 1986). Consequently, Zambia's economy suffered severely in the early 1980s, no doubt contributing to the fact that twice as many Zambian children died of malnutrition in 1984 as in 1980.

This is not a comprehensive coverage of previous and potential influences on economic patterns. You may have spotted a major question that has not been mentioned yet — is the world going to run out of some physical resources altogether, and if so when? This is addressed in Section 2.5.

Table 5 Share of non-fuel mineral resources in the value of total exports for selected countries

Country	Resource(s)	Share in value of country's exports (%)
Botswana	diamonds, copper, nickel	87
Zambia	copper	86
Zaïre	copper, diamonds	71
Surinam	aluminium	69
Papua New Guinea	copper	62
Liberia	iron, diamonds	60
Jamaica	aluminium	58
Togo	phosphates	50
Central African Republic	diamonds	46
Mauritania	iron	41
Chile	copper	41
Peru	copper, zinc, iron, lead, silver	39
Bolivia	zinc, tin, silver, antimony, tungsten	35
Dominican Republic	nickel	33
Guyana	aluminium	31
South Africa	gold	29

Figures are for most recent year available; most are 1990 or 1991; earliest (Zaïre) is for 1986. Where more than one resource is given for a country, the resources are listed in decreasing order of export value.

2.1.3 Supply and demand

Physical resources are susceptible to market forces, just like other commodities. It's common to hear people talk of 'the market forces of supply and demand', as if they were common knowledge. But what exactly are these particular market forces — or, at least, what are the key concepts we need to know about them in order to place physical resources in their economic context? We will now look at the basic principles of supply and demand relationships, and initially take copper as our example.

Copper is almost always the metal used in electrical wiring, and it's present in virtually all electrical appliances involving motors, e.g. washing machines, and in appliances where strong magnetic fields are essential, e.g. television. Of course, the demand for domestic electrical goods varies in different societies; in most South American, African and Asian countries, fewer than 50% of dwellings have a supply of mains electricity. Items considered as more or less essential in highly industrialized societies — such as freezers, kettles, televisions, stereos, vacuum cleaners, hairdryers, etc. — are luxuries in many poorer societies.

Although about 15% of copper was being recycled globally in the early 1990s, most consumption is derived from newly mined material, produced from a wide range of mineral deposits. These range from immense open-pit mines of the western Americas, to underground operations in Zambia, to extremely rich but complex copper–zinc–silver mines of eastern Canada. The cost of producing copper depends on such variables as the location, the richness of the ore, the technical complexity of the processes needed to extract the copper minerals from unwanted rock, and the transport necessary to deliver the copper concentrates to refiners. Each copper mine will have its own unique set of production problems, which will be reflected in its production costs. Copper in household items is almost 100% pure. This contrasts with copper ores, the large majority of which contain only around 0.5% copper (mainly in sulphide minerals). The often costly processes by which metals are progressively concentrated and refined from their ores during production are briefly discussed in Block 5.

In times of general economic prosperity in industrialized countries, demand for household electrical equipment is strong, and so is the demand for copper. Further demand for copper arises from its use in the motors, generators and wiring used in the factories, and other systems (e.g. transport) needed to produce that equipment. Consumption may start to exceed production, and copper suppliers (and the mining companies themselves) will enjoy a seller's market; so prices will rise. Conversely, in leaner times, demand will fall below total mine capacity, and in a buyer's market, prices will fall. Higher cost producers will therefore be faced with low profits, or with losses, and may even be forced to shut down in an extended recession. Fluctuations in the market price of copper may not affect manufacturers equally because not all copper is sold on the open market. A substantial proportion of copper (like other metals) is sold on medium- or long-term contracts between a producer and manufacturer, an arrangement which may be tied to finance for a mining operation. The economic and social complexities arising from price fluctuations are such that at least a few people always gain as others lose. For example, repairers of electrical equipment may gain business in a recession because home-owners cannot afford to buy new appliances.

As will be clear from the above discussion, three particularly important variables are associated with any commodity such as a physical resource: its price, the demand for it, and the supply of it. We need to define supply and demand more clearly. Note that the following discussion applies to *any* commodity, but to emphasize its relevance to physical resources, the word 'resource' is used where an economist might use the general term 'commodity'.

> **Supply** is the quantity of a resource that suppliers are prepared to sell *at a given price*. **Demand** is the quantity of a resource that consumers are prepared to buy *at a given price*.

Note the emphasis on a given price. In economic theory there is no such thing as supply or demand *per se*; each is always linked to price. For example, in order to discuss the 'demand for copper' or the 'supply of apples' we need to know what price range is being considered. Supply in this sense is quite different from the quantity actually produced or the **output** (the quantity produced in a given period). For example, a glut of apples on apple trees in the autumn is an increase in output. It may well lead to an increase in supply, e.g. the quantity of apples that a supplier is prepared to sell at a given price (as long as the supplier has enough incentive to pick and market them), but an increase in output is not necessarily matched by an increase in supply, nor a decrease in output by a fall in supply. Output and supply are different concepts although the two often get used interchangeably in everyday speech. In the case of a physical resource such as copper, output is influenced by a great many factors from mine to market.

In a competitive, free economy, the relationship between price, demand and supply are completely interwoven. A change in one variable affects the other two. The market forces of supply and demand influence the market price, and changes in the market price influence supply and demand. Many factors are at work which can affect, and can be affected by, the three main variables. Examples include the purchasing power of consumers, which itself depends on a vast array of factors (including interest rates and taxation); technological developments; the discovery of new reserves of the resource; change in the price or availability of substitutes; change in government policies; change in social preferences; rumours of takeovers; workforce strikes; wars, and so on. Economists agonize over, and remain in dispute about, the relative importance of these factors in individual cases.

Let's now consider in more detail what usually happens to supply or to demand in the short term if the *price* of an established resource changes, while other variables are kept constant. You may find that the graphical treatment below reveals nothing unexpected and just displays pictorially what is common sense. You will *not*, however, be expected to use this theoretical analysis to solve *quantitative* problems.

Figure 22(a) shows a supply curve or 'S' curve, and is a hypothetical representation of what is generally expected to happen to supply if the price changes. The incentive to supply a resource will increase if the market price increases because a supplier stands to make more profit from selling a greater quantity. The curve therefore has a positive gradient (i.e. sloping upwards to the right), because the quantity supplied, Q (indicated along the horizontal axis), will tend to increase as price increases. The relationship is conventionally drawn as a curve, steepening up to the right, though this is not necessarily the case — the line may be straighter or more complicated. (Another limitation is that such curves are unlikely to represent accurately what might happen at extreme ends of the price range.)

Figure 22(b) shows a demand curve or 'D' curve, and depicts what is generally expected to happen to demand if the price changes. It has a negative gradient (sloping downwards to the right), reflecting the fact that, generally speaking, the higher the price of a resource, the less demand there is for it. If price rises, demand falls — i.e. the quantity demanded goes down. Conversely, if price falls, demand rises — the quantity demanded goes up. Again, the relationship is conventionally drawn as a curve, steepening up to the left, though this is not necessarily the case — the line may be straighter or more complicated. (An important, though temporary, exception to this price–demand relationship occurs if resources like precious metals are bought and stockpiled as investments when the price is rising or is expected to rise; demand is stimulated for a while — despite the price rise — in the hope that the stockpiles will be sold (or used) later at net profit.)

It's crucial to realize that the graphs in Figure 22 work only one way. They illustrate only how changes in price tend to affect the quantity supplied (Figure 22a) and the quantity demanded (Figure 22b). In other words, price is the *active* variable — the one that acts first — and quantity is the *reactive* variable — the one that reacts to the change. Individual S and D curves cannot be used to deduce the effect of changes in supply upon price, or changes in demand upon price. To depict changes in supply or demand, you have to move the curves themselves, as we shall see in a moment.

Figure 23 shows the S and D curves combined for a particular resource. This, like Figure 22, portrays what may happen in the actual market. At any particular time there is a price P_e, which would result in supply and demand being in balance. This price is called the **equilibrium price** and it will occur at an equilibrium quantity, Q_e. The equilibrium point is where the price and quantity that suppliers are willing and able to supply are the same as the price and quantity that consumers demand. It's a basic tenet of economics that the supply and demand of any commodity will always *tend* to move towards these equilibrium points, even if they are rarely reached.

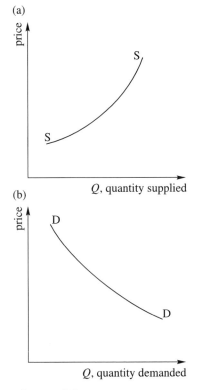

Figure 22 (a) A supply curve, showing how supply responds to a change in price. (b) A demand curve, showing how demand responds to a change in price.

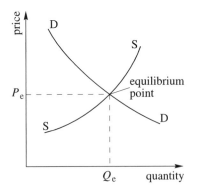

Figure 23 A supply curve (S–S) and a demand curve (D–D) for a particular resource. Supply and demand will be in balance at the equilibrium price (P_e), and the equilibrium quantity (Q_e).

Now let's consider how changes in demand may affect price. Several factors, not just a change in price, can increase the demand for a resource. Examples are: an increase in consumers' spending power or a change of priorities, and the availability of cheaper substitutes, e.g. an increase in the price of copper which may lead to greater demand for aluminium as a substitute in electrical apparatus. These factors will increase the demand at any particular price, resulting in a shift of the demand curve. Figure 24 depicts how the initial demand curve D_1–D_1 shifts to the right, giving curve D_2–D_2. Note the crucial distinction between shifts of the *whole curve*, as here, and shifts *along* a curve, as discussed for the curves in Figure 22. It's easy to see that, with this shift of the whole curve, there is now a greater demand at any given price. If the relationship between price and supply (the supply curve S–S) remains the same as before, i.e. if for any given price the same quantity would still be supplied, the new D curve and the old S curve will intersect at a different place, a new equilibrium point. Demand and supply will be in balance at a higher equilibrium price, P_2, and a higher equilibrium quantity, Q_2. The increased demand will thus have prompted an increase in the quantity supplied and a higher equilibrium price. Note too that if demand increased to give curve D_2–D_2, but the quantity supplied could not increase for some reason (as if the supply curve stopped beyond Q_1), then producers could get a higher price, well above P_1 (in fact above P_2).

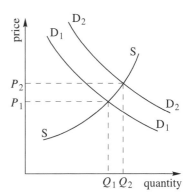

Figure 24 The effect on the equilibrium point if demand increases from D_1–D_1 to D_2–D_2 and the supply curve remains the same.

Question 15

What happens to the equilibrium price if demand falls, as in recession, and the relationship between price and supply (the supply curve) remains the same? Try sketching this on Figure 24.

In Figure 24, new equilibrium points were created because demand went up or down although the relationship between price and supply (the supply curve) remained the same. However, the relationship between price and supply may not remain the same. For example, the supply (i.e. the quantity that can be supplied at a given price) may increase independently for various reasons, without the initial stimulus of changes in price or demand; there may be increased output due to technological progress, discovery of new sources, the coming 'on-stream' of a new oilfield (for example), and so on. Investment typically causes a long-term increase in capacity, enabling an increase in supply at a given price, shifting the supply curve outwards to the right. How do such changes in supply affect price?

Figure 25 shows what happens to the equilibrium point when supply increases and the demand curve remains the same. An increase in supply shifts the initial supply curve S_1–S_1 to the right, giving curve S_2–S_2. If the relationship between price and demand (curve D–D) remains the same as before, the new S curve and the old D curve will intersect at a different place, a new equilibrium point. There is now a new lower equilibrium price P_2, which will stimulate more demand, so that supply and demand will be in balance at a new equilibrium quantity, Q_2. Conversely, if supply falls (for example because of higher costs, depletion of reserves, equipment failure, or workforce strikes), the supply curve shifts to the left, giving curve S_3–S_3 and another equilibrium point. This time, the new equilibrium price is higher (P_3) and so demand goes down to a new equilibrium quantity, Q_3.

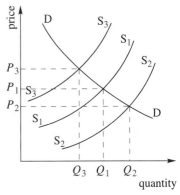

Figure 25 The effect on the equilibrium point if supply increases to S_2–S_2, or decreases to S_3–S_3, while the demand curve remains the same.

There is often a rapid succession of these various actions and reactions in the variables of price, supply and demand. In other words, the kind of changes depicted in Figures 24 and 25 are only part of the picture: they may be short-lived trends that start towards a new equilibrium point but get overtaken by other events. These complex short-term responses, often by *individual* suppliers or subgroups of consumers, can result in a variety of long-term outcomes to the overall picture. As an example, consider the increase in equilibrium price caused by an increase in demand shown in Figure 24. Figure 26 takes things further than Figure 24 by showing what can happen to the equilibrium price if the supply then increases, i.e. the supply curve shifts to the right. In other words, the quantity that can be supplied to sell at a given price has increased, perhaps because of new producers entering the market or a long-term increase in the capacity of existing ones. The new supply curve S′–S′ now intersects the new demand curve D_2–D_2, and the equilibrium price falls back to a lower level, although the equilibrium quantity has increased still further. The long-term result in this case is that the quantity demanded and supplied have both increased and the price has dropped slightly.

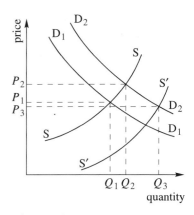

Figure 26 The effect of an increase in supply to S′–S′ following the increases in demand depicted in Figure 24. The result is another equilibrium point, at the equilibrium price (P_3) and the equilibrium quantity (Q_3).

It's relatively common for growth in the overall market to support a sustained increase in both production and consumption, with both keeping pace with each other in the long term, while overall the real price remains similar or drops slightly (as with copper and zinc, Figure 19). As we have seen, such a pattern is also generally true of aluminium, especially from about 1945 to 1973 (Figures 18 and 20), although in this case the pattern was influenced by producer regulation and by high variable costs.

It's worth emphasizing the distinction between *cost*, i.e. the expenses of producing a resource for the market, and *price*, i.e. the sum to be paid for that resource in the market. An immense number of factors can, of course, influence the price of a resource. In general, though, for any class of commodities, including physical resources, there are broad positive correlations between (a) price and the scarcity of a raw material in high demand, and (b) price and the costs incurred in extraction and processing to produce a saleable resource. For example, gold and platinum are many times the price of lead and copper, largely because they are much less abundant in the Earth's crust (Figure 3), more expensive to extract *and* they are in high demand. (Some metals are scarce and have remained in low demand, so their price is lower.) Over the long term, of course, prices must exceed costs for a resource to remain in production. The costs incurred in extraction and processing may bear little or no relation to abundance; for example, the element silicon is extremely abundant in the Earth's crust (Figure 3), but the cost of obtaining the element itself is very high. In 1993 the price of silicon 'metal' was about £1000 per tonne, more than lead and zinc, for example, which are about ten thousand times less abundant in the Earth's crust (Figure 3). However, another important factor concerns **economies of scale**. Generally, the bigger the operation, the lower the cost per unit of output. So, other things being equal, if a resource is produced in rather small quantities, the cost is likely to be relatively high per unit. Were elemented silicon to be produced in larger quantities, it would probably be cheaper per tonne.

2.1.4 Elasticity of supply and demand

As we have seen, changes in the price of a physical resource affect its supply and demand. But precisely how the quantity supplied or demanded changes in response to changes in price varies a great deal, depending on the type of resource and its context.

  Consider the demand for drinking water in a populated area with scarce freshwater supplies. Is it likely that demand for drinking water would fall off rapidly as its price increased?

○ No. Resources that are essential and scarce like drinking water in arid lands, and which have no substitute, usually have relatively steep demand curves; that is, the demand stays rather similar, decreasing only a little as price increases. For example, the price of drinking water in a dry area might rise by 20%, but demand might drop by only 1%, or not at all. Sometimes, the sudden price rise of a key resource such as water or oil can actually *increase* demand in the short term through panic buying and hoarding because of fears of shortages and even higher prices. Simply the *threat* of reduced supply can increase demand, even if the price has not yet changed, as may occur, for example, with the demand for oil following a political crisis in the Middle East.

Of course, in detail the pattern of demand for water varies a great deal between countries, and water in a dry area is an extreme case. Many of the uses to which water is put in a country with high rainfall like the UK, however, are certainly not essential, and, where supplies are metered, the quantity of water used would soon fall if prices greatly increased.

As a less dramatic example, the price of table salt can also rise significantly without much loss of demand (in the short term at least), because people who use salt tend to place it fairly high in their list of priorities. In detail, such relationships depend on price relative to income; the lower the income, the less likely that salt would remain a priority as price increased.

● Would you expect a *reduction* in the price of table salt to increase demand considerably?

○ The demand for table salt does not go up by much if the price drops since the quantity required for eating purposes is limited; demand in this case is far more likely to be influenced by changes in the perception of salt as a potential hazard to health.

In general, then, a relatively high-priority resource has a steep demand curve. When quite a large change in price has relatively little effect on demand, a resource is said to be in **inelastic demand**. The demand itself is said to be inelastic: the demand does not stretch or contract much as price changes.

● Now consider the demand for platinum earrings, marble ornaments, and similar non-essential items containing physical resources. Would demand be expected to fall off fairly rapidly as their price increased?

○ Yes. Inessential items and luxuries (and the resources involved) tend to have relatively shallow demand curves; the demand *decreases* rapidly as the price rises. This is particularly true if substitutes are available. For example, cheaper silver earrings might be just as attractive as platinum ones, and limestone or sandstone might become cheaper than marble and be just as appropriate.

If quite a small change in price leads to a relatively large change in demand, the resource is said to be in **elastic demand**. The demand itself is said to be elastic: it stretches or contracts markedly as price changes.

What about the way that supply can respond to changes in price? If a fairly small change in price leads to a relatively large change in supply, a resource is said to be in **elastic supply**. The supply itself is said to be elastic. If quite a large change in price leads to a relatively small change in supply, a resource is said to be in **inelastic supply**. The supply itself is said to be inelastic.

Where is the line drawn between elastic and inelastic? It's the *proportional* change in the variables that's important. If demand (or supply) responds *more* than proportionally to a change in price, the demand (or supply) is, by definition, elastic. For example, if the price of aluminium rises 10%, but demand drops by 30%, the demand is elastic. If demand (or supply) responds *less* than proportionally to a change in price, the demand (or supply) is inelastic. (Note: the concept of elasticity is a general one in economics; here we are referring to its most common application, *price* elasticity, which describes the response of demand and supply to changes in price.)

⬤ If the price of chromium rises 10%, and demand drops by 8%, is the demand elastic or inelastic?

◯ The demand is inelastic.

Normally, the higher the price becomes, the greater the incentive to supply a resource. Whether supply can increase usually depends on whether or not a producer has spare capacity (i.e. spare potential output). A mining company, for example, may already be operating at full capacity, and long-term investment may be needed before capacity can be increased. All sorts of other factors often limit supply in the short term: technological advances may be needed before resources can be extracted at lower concentrations; artificial quotas may be applied for economic or political reasons; there may be workforce problems; the supply infrastructure may be missing, as in war-torn countries or undeveloped regions; and so on.

⬤ Bearing in mind the above, for a given change in price, will resources tend to be (a) in inelastic supply in the short term and in elastic supply in the long term; or (b) in elastic supply in the short term and in inelastic supply in the long term?

◯ For a given change in price, resources tend to be in inelastic supply in the short term and in elastic supply in the long term (i.e. answer (a)). The generalization is particularly characteristic of primary commodities, such as many physical resources, as opposed to manufactured items.

A few resources are regarded as essential to the people that use them and are so rare that they are relatively inelastic in both supply and demand, whatever the price. An example is the noble gas helium (see Section 1.2). Large increases in price affect demand relatively little, because certain high-priority purposes (such as obtaining temperatures close to absolute zero) require helium, and for these purposes there is no substitute for it. Similarly, a large increase in price cannot translate through to much change in supply (at least in the short to mid term) because helium is very rare.

Substitution is clearly an extremely important factor in elasticity: above a certain price manufacturers will switch to another resource if it can do the job just as well, or well enough. Such a pattern fits the use of many additives in steel, such as vanadium, nickel and tungsten. If a metal additive becomes too expensive, a slight change in the mix of remaining metals, or addition of different ones, may compensate for its loss. Continued substitution eventually reduces demand to the level where a metal is irreplaceable for its remaining uses (i.e. cannot be substituted), at which point the demand is no longer elastic. The invention of new materials increases the probability of substitution. For example, one of the most important current uses of tungsten is as tungsten carbide in cutting tools, but some other newly developed engineering ceramics are proving relatively cheap and effective substitutes. Tungsten is, however, set to remain the preferred and essentially unsubstitutable material for filaments, electrodes and contacts in many lighting applications.

The demand for one resource is often sensitive to changes in the price of another — a phenomenon called **cross-elasticity of demand**. For example, the demand for electricity will tend to go up if its price comes down, which will also stimulate more demand for electric heating systems, cookers, and so on. Products such as these that are often bought together and whose demand changes in parallel, whether up or down, are known as **complementary goods**, or complements. Complements rarely occur just as pairs (such as cups and saucers, locks and keys); often many products are related together, with varying degrees of correlation. For example, the price of compact discs might come down, causing an increase in demand of CD players, of shelves to stack CDs on, of metal brackets to support the shelves, and so on — as well as, of course, CDs themselves. Similarly, more people might install electrically powered showers if they became much cheaper. This would also increase demand for electricity (and possibly water), and perhaps also other products such as shower curtains, sealants around the bath, solvents for removing perished sealant, etc. Next time you do a bit of DIY, notice the extent to which you have to use complementary goods (Figure 27).

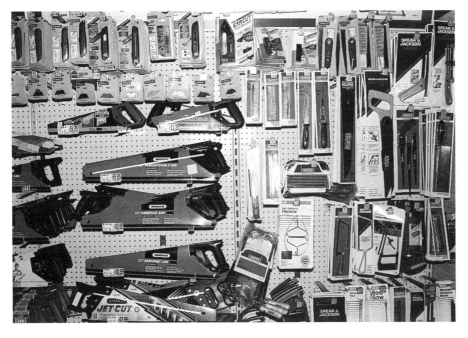

Figure 27 Typical complementary goods on offer in a DIY store: a range of blades to match a range of saws and knives.

Conversely, an increase in the price of one product may cause an increase in demand for another, especially if they are good substitutes for each other; for instance, if the price of electricity rises, there may be more demand for gas (and less demand for the complementary goods that go with electricity).

Activity 4

Try to find an example from your own life of: (a) cross-elasticity of demand; i.e. where a price change in one product caused you to buy more or less of another, and (b) complementary goods involving at least three products; i.e. where buying one product also led to you buying at least two others. Choose examples of products based on, or containing, physical resources.

2.2 The availability of physical resources

In assessing the availability of resources, we should consider only the parts of the Earth's crust that are economically and technically feasible to work. At present we can operate mines to depths of only about 4 km in the crust; in 1992 the deepest mine in the world, for gold, was at Carletonville, South Africa, at a depth of 3777 m (2.3 miles). At deeper levels the mine walls may explode inwards because of high pressures, causing rock bursts, and the high temperatures there cannot be regulated except at prohibitive cost. Exploratory boreholes can, however, go deeper; in April 1992 one in Arctic Russia exceeded a depth of 12 km, with an eventual target of 15 km.

Imagine for a moment, that it was possible to extract all the gold from, say, the top 5 km of the continental crust. How much gold, in theory, would that be? The total mass of the top 5 km of the Earth's continental crust is about 2×10^{18} tonnes. To work out the amount of gold in this mass of crust we need to know the average concentration of gold in it.

⬤ Using the information in Figure 3, calculate, very approximately, the total amount of gold in the top 5 km of the Earth's continental crust, i.e. the limit to mine depth in the foreseeable future.

○ From Figure 3, the *percentage* of gold in the Earth's continental crust is between 10^{-6} and 10^{-7} per cent, i.e. between 10^{-8} and 10^{-9} of that crust's total mass. Gold has the lowest percentage abundance of the three elements in that category, so, for the sake of the calculation, estimating its concentration as 3×10^{-9} throughout the continental crust, and multiplying by the total mass, 2×10^{18}, gives about 6×10^9 tonnes in the top 5 km of the continental crust.

To place this amount in perspective, look back at Figure 2. The world annual production of gold is about 2000 t, whereas 6×10^9 t is close to the annual production of carbon. If gold could continue to be extracted at its present annual rate, it would take 3 million years to extract all the gold in the top 5 km of continental crust. Platinum is present in a roughly similar amount to gold, and the total amounts of other, more abundant elements can easily be calculated by multiplying their percentage abundance shown in Figure 3 by 2×10^{18} t.

So even gold, silver and platinum are present in vast tonnages, but of course commercial mining has not the slightest chance of extracting these quantities. The cost of labour and energy required to win such tonnages of metals from common rocks would be utterly prohibitive, and the Earth's surface would become greatly scarred. Incidentally, there are about 4 kg of gold in a cubic kilometre of seawater, but the cost of extraction would, at present, be far higher than its value. Seawater is currently an important source for relatively few physical resources, including common salt (NaCl), bromine and magnesium, and sometimes, after desalination, fresh water.

Within a particular area the total mass of an element, in a mineral (or other form) from which it can be extracted economically, is known as the **total stock**. This is such an imprecise measure that it is rarely quantified. Total stock would be a lower quantity than the total mass of an element in a given part of the crust (as calculated above) because not all occurrences of an element are in extractable form. For example, aluminium metal can be obtained economically from only a few of its compounds because it is normally so tightly bound to other elements that isolating it by a process such as smelting would be far too expensive; the aluminium in clays, for instance, cannot be extracted economically.

In what sort of concentrations do metals have to be present in a rock before the rock is considered as being worth exploiting? To answer this we need to look at the concentrations of metals in rocks that are actually mined. **Grade** is the term for the concentration of an element, especially a metal, within a particular rock when the element is in a form suitable for extraction. For most elements grade is expressed as a percentage. The lowest grade in a particular deposit that can be mined for a profit is the **cut-off grade** and the **average minimum exploitable grade** is the average of cut-off grades for all mines, taking into account their individual contribution to world production. For example, the average minimum exploitable grade for gold today is 4 parts per million (by weight), i.e. 4 ppm or $4 \times 10^{-4}\%$; for mercury it is 0.2%; and for lead 5%. Local cut-off grades are subject to a host of factors that are considered in Block 5. In every case an element has to be more concentrated than its *average* crustal abundance, sometimes very much more. The **concentration factor** is the amount by which an element must be increased above its average crustal abundance to reach a particular concentration (such as a cut-off grade or the average minimum exploitable grade).

Question 16

The average abundance of mercury in the crust is 80 parts per billion. Given the above value for the average exploitable grade for mercury, what concentration factor does this represent?

Reserves are quantities of resources (e.g. ore minerals, coal, or petroleum) that can be extracted profitably and legally under existing conditions. To be a reserve, the resource must be at concentrations greater than the local cut-off grade, and a company or organization would have to have the necessary ownership and permissions to exploit the resource. In this classification, the category of **resources** contains concentrations of useful materials in such a form and amount that profitable extraction is either currently feasible (in the case of reserves) *or potentially* feasible, given reasonably foreseeable changes in techniques and/or price. Figure 28 expresses the typical relationship between reserves, resources and total stock in terms of concentration alone. The boundaries between the categories shift with time, and at any one time may not be clearly defined. Knowledge of each category is, of course, always incomplete. The relative and absolute size of the categories varies widely with different materials.

Note that 'total stock' in Figure 28 includes concentrations that are too low to be considered resources, but excludes occurrences in which the material is not in a form suitable for economic extraction. In practice, some very high concentrations may not be reserves because for some reason (such as a problematic location or legal restrictions) they cannot be extracted profitably at present.

To define the categories of resources and reserves more precisely we use two important parameters. First, there is the *degree of certainty that something exists*. This is a variable, because the crust is only partly explored, even in highly industrialized areas such as Europe and North America. The other parameter is *profitability*, which depends upon the price received, balanced against the operating costs. There are only two main divisions — profitable, or not profitable at present. The first parameter (degree of certainty that something exists) relates to scientific information concerning geological, physical and chemical characteristics — such as the grade, tonnage, location and depth of the material. It provides a relatively stable foundation upon which to assess the second, more subjective parameter, i.e. to make

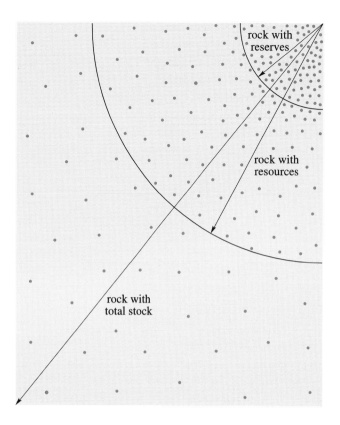

Figure 28 A diagrammatic summary of the typical relationship between reserves, resources and total stock, in terms of concentration alone. The dots represent the useful material, such as oil or a metal in an ore mineral, and the density of dots represents its concentration in the rock. See text for discussion.

profitability analyses based on the costs of extracting and marketing the material in a given economy at a given time.

When these two parameters are used as the axes of a simple box diagram (Figure 29), where the certainty of existence increases from right to left, and the price to cost ratio increases upwards, the top left segment of the diagram represents reserves. It is bounded at its base by a price : cost ratio of 1, and on the right by an arbitrary measure of how much is known about the existence of such rocks. Reserves must be materials that have been *identified* in or on the ground and would generate profit if worked under present economic, technical and legal conditions.

Those resources that have been identified in a well known area, but are uneconomic (or legally unavailable) at present, are termed **conditional**

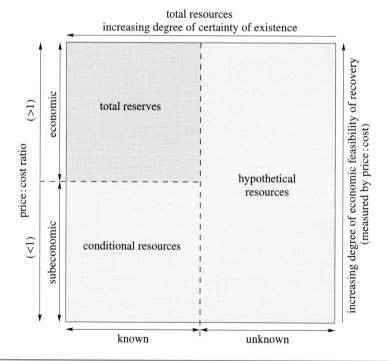

Figure 29 Criteria for separating reserves from resources. Note that the field of resources covers the *whole* box, reserves only the top left-hand corner.

resources; that is, they may become reserves if economic, technical, legal or political conditions change. Limited geological knowledge of a poorly known area may make it possible to estimate what valuable materials might be present, by comparing the area with similar ones that have been mined. Such estimates are termed **hypothetical resources**, i.e. they are as yet undiscovered. Thus hypothetical resources might eventually turn out to include both reserves and conditional resources.

What general factors could enable conditional or hypothetical resources to be reclassified as reserves and vice versa? The possibilities are summarized in Figure 30. Increased exploration and discovery could transfer some hypothetical resources from the top right area across into the reserves category (the *top* right because that is the area of high economic feasibility). An increase in reserves causes the lower boundary of the reserves box to expand downwards. Increases in the market price could transfer conditional resources in the lower left area up into the total reserves box. Conversely, decreases in price result in some reserves being reduced to conditional resources. When a price is static, a technological improvement such as increasing the efficiency of extraction decreases costs, increases the price : cost ratio and transfers conditional resources to reserves. The imposition of environmental or other restrictions may cause reserves to be relegated to conditional resources; conversely, the lifting of restrictions may cause conditional resources to be reclassified as reserves. Environmental restrictions are likely to increase costs, or they may even result in a total ban on extracting resources from certain places.

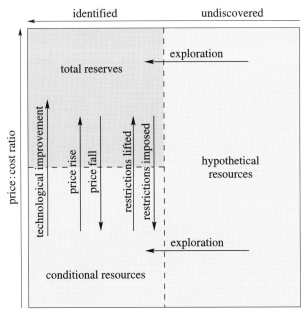

Figure 30 Diagram showing how estimates of reserves can be altered by exploration, technological advances, changes in price, and changes in environmental or other restrictions.

Although useful as a focus for discussion, classification schemes like this have their limitations. There are several problems to take into account:

1 Exploration is by no means complete, so estimates of undiscovered (hypothetical) resources are, by nature, extremely approximate and liable to be inaccurate, and are not often attempted.

2 The appearance of new technology may suddenly boost the demand for a hitherto ignored material, radically changing the amounts in various categories; this was true, for example, of uranium in the nuclear arms race of the 1940s and 1950s. Exploration for uranium was so intense in the 1950s, 1960s and 1970s that, compared with many other elements, a relatively small proportion of total uranium resources are now likely to lie in the undiscovered category.

3   New types of sources may sometimes be discovered, which contain vast tonnages, thereby transforming the total stock, resources and even reserves categories if they can be worked profitably more or less straight away. A well-known case is that of manganese nodules on the ocean floors, which contain high percentages of many metals (Block 5). For example, the resources of copper alone in deep-sea nodules are estimated at 700 million tonnes. However, until such nodules can be profitably (and legally) extracted, such discoveries will not increase the reserves of the metals concerned, only the conditional resources.

4   The classification schemes lag behind developments because data on resources are not always released quickly by companies and governments; indeed some data may be withheld for decades.

5   The guiding principle underlying the classification of resources and reserves is that of profit: reserves are classed as such only if they can be extracted profitably (and legally) at present. However, in some centrally planned economies, such as that of China, more emphasis is placed on the intrinsic usefulness of resources than on their strict financial profitability, and many of their deposits would not be worked by mining corporations of free market nations. Conversely, some potentially profitable deposits are not mined in centrally planned economies.

The classification is empirical, and provides a means of 'accounting', whereby deficiencies may be identified and the strategies needed to overcome them may be developed. At this simple level the classification can be applied to virtually any type of physical resource. Figure 31 gives an inventory for zinc.

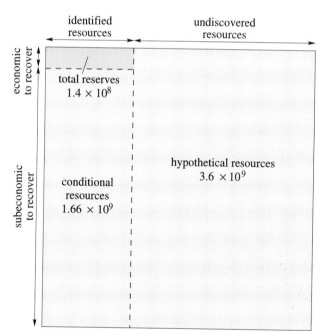

Figure 31   The estimated total world resources of zinc, in tonnes of zinc metal. The areas representing the various resource categories are drawn to scale.

What percentage do zinc reserves form of (a) identified zinc resources and (b) all zinc resources, i.e. identified and undiscovered?

(a) $1.40 \times 10^8/(1.66 \times 10^9 + 1.40 \times 10^8) = 1.40 \times 10^8/1.8 \times 10^9 = 7.8\%$;

(b) $1.40 \times 10^8/(1.66 \times 10^9 + 1.4 \times 10^8 + 3.6 \times 10^9) = 2.6\%$.

Should demand grow for materials with diminishing reserves but very large hypothetical resources, the easiest option could be to explore for rich deposits awaiting discovery, instead of improving mining techniques or waiting for the price to rise to a point where conditional resources become reserves. It often takes 10–20 years, however, before newly discovered deposits reach the market place; such a gap is called the **lead time**. Diagrams such as Figure 31 are always viewed in the light of other, more complex, considerations, such as the urgency of requirements set against the likely *rate* of new discoveries and the likely changes in price if rich new discoveries are not made. In any case, when national inventories are taken, political considerations often override the simple approach given here, as for example was the case with the UK coal industry in the early 1990s. In 1992, the government decided to support closure of a large number of mines, even though their coal was not exhausted. The main reason given was the diminishing market, partly because the privatized electricity-generating industry had decided to buy gas rather than coal to fuel many of the nation's power stations, and partly because existing coal-fired power stations were now allowed to import cheaper coal from abroad. Some people, however, suspected that the closure programme was driven by the wish to slim the industry down before privatization.

Now would be a good time to watch Video Band 2: *Copper – Resources and Reserves.* After watching the programme, test your understanding by answering Questions 17 and 18, which will also serve as a summary. It will probably help you to read these through first before viewing the film.

Video Band 2   Copper – Resources and Reserves

Speaker

John Wright   The Open University

The programme, which was filmed in 1984, illustrates many of the important concepts mentioned in Section 2, including:

(a) the effects of technological development on the demand for a resource;

(b) exponential growth and doubling time;

(c) the effects of demand, price and technological advances on the cut-off grade of ore and scale of mining;

(d) the uneven geographical distribution of physical resources and the problems experienced by the CIPEC producer association (International Council of Copper Exporting Countries);

(e) supply and demand curves;

(f) the effects of substitution;

(g) the relationships between reserves, conditional resources, and hypothetical resources;

(h) the problems and risks of exploration in remote areas and the advantages of re-evaluating old mining areas in politically stable regions.

The programme discusses in particular the fluctuating fortunes of the Parys Mountain mine on Anglesey, North Wales. Since 1984, exploratory drilling and evaluation continued, and small-scale mining by a Canadian based company began in 1986. The ore was milled and concentrated on site, before being sent by road for smelting in Swansea or Avonmouth. This phase of mining ended in 1991 because metal prices fell, and more capital was needed to develop the ore body underground. In 1994, the mine was being maintained, awaiting an upturn in metal prices before production could resume. The film also mentions the CIPEC producers, Chile, Peru, Zambia, and Zaïre: developing countries with relatively little consumption of copper, but heavily dependent on copper exports for their income (see Table 5). Since the film was made, CIPEC producers (the four countries above and a few associated members) have continued to have no influence in practice on the regulation of copper production and its price, mainly because there are so many other producers.

Figure 32 Parys Mine, Anglesey, in 1804.

Question 17

Four of the following items (a) to (k) are incorrect. Which four are they, and why are they wrong?

(a) After being used for centuries mainly for pots, pans, coins and ornaments, the demand for copper in the seventeenth century was stimulated by the need for bronze cannons and later for the sheathing of wooden-hulled warships.

(b) The Parys Mountain copper deposits were discovered and worked for the first time in 1768.

(c) After 1768, the Parys Mountain mines soon became the world's largest copper producer, reaching peak production in the early 1800s, but being virtually mined out by 1890, just as demand for copper really took off.

(d) The average grade of copper at Parys Mountain was about 5%, and its entire lifetime output (at least until 1984) was only 40 000 tonnes of copper. In contrast, by the mid-1980s, grades of 0.5% were economic to mine in some countries, and global production of copper was between 7 million and 8 million tonnes.

(e) Technological breakthroughs in the twentieth century included machinery to crush and grind ores on a large scale, and processes such as froth flotation to separate ore minerals from waste rock.

(f) Generally, cut-off grades have risen with increased global production.

(g) During recession, demand curves generally shift to the right.

(h) The threat of substitution is particularly serious to those countries whose economy largely relies on a single export such as copper.

(i) Only if the projected cost to price ratio is very high will a mine venture even be considered today.

(j) Between 1968 and 1983, the costs of copper production increased fairly steadily but prices fluctuated widely, such that the majority of mines by 1983 were losing money.

(k) Changes in price profoundly affect the boundary between reserves and conditional resources, but have little effect on hypothetical resources.

Question 18

Why, in a given year, are figures for global copper consumption higher than figures for global production of newly mined copper?

2.3 Cost and revenue factors, including place value

Whether or not a concentration of physical resources is classified as a reserve and eventually extracted depends on many factors, especially two: the cost of winning the resource and bringing it to market, and the revenue generated by its sale.

The *cost* factors are critical, and include:

- the geological nature of the concentration, which determines the techniques used to extract and liberate the resource from unwanted material;
- the size of the deposit, and the rate of extraction required to make it economic, both of which may influence the cost of the machinery involved;
- the geographic location, which determines the cost of transport, the ease of access, supply of services (e.g. electricity) and availability of labour;
- the cost of preventing environmental damage or of cleaning it up.

The *revenue* factors include:

- the size of the deposit;
- the maximum rate of extraction;
- how long the deposit will last;
- the local tax laws, which determine the proportion of revenues taken in taxes and royalties;
- the extent of planning permission for future extraction;
- the market price.

The market price, of course, depends on the supply–demand relationship and a host of underlying factors related to the economy as a whole. In addition to the above factors, unforeseen environmental, political and social factors may arise at any time, and may greatly affect the planned costs and revenues.

2.3.1 Place value

Let's look in more detail at one of the cost variables above: geographic location. Natural concentrations of elements and compounds occur where they do for purely geological reasons; geological processes and the boundaries between different rock types do not relate to national frontiers. Similarly, the locations of energy sources derived from wind, waves, tides, and high geothermal temperatures do not follow political boundaries. The location of physical resources in relation to where they or their products are used, however, often determines whether or not they are exploited.

Where water and building materials are very common, as they are in some countries, the maximum demand for them is less than the quantities available. Consequently, in such countries water and building materials generally command relatively low prices. The cost of extraction is low, so any transportation adds significantly to the total costs, especially because water and building materials tend to be used in large volumes. Consequently, they may only be marketable resources fairly close to where they occur; further away their cost — and thus their price — becomes too high. If the location of resources is an important factor in determining their price, they are said to have a high **place value**. If, however, water and building materials are needed but are very scarce because of climatic or geological reasons, these resources can sometimes command a high price, making long-distance transport economically viable. Water is, of course, an extreme case because it is the most essential of all the physical resources and it is rarely traded in the same way as other commodities. An example of international trade in water is its export from Britain to Saudi Arabia; fresh water is sometimes carried in oil tankers on their return journey to the Middle East.

High-value materials for which demand around the world remains buoyant irrespective of price (i.e. they are in relatively inelastic demand) tend to be sought and extracted more or less anywhere on the planet. Such resources are said to have a *low* place value. For this reason companies are, for example, prepared to extract oil and gas (but not building materials) out of inhospitable and relatively inaccessible places such as the bottom of the central North Sea or the frozen wastes of the Arctic Circle. The same is also true for most metals, with mine locations tending to be quite unrelated to where the metals are finally used. The higher the price of the metal, the more incentive to mine it in remote and difficult locations.

Increasingly, new technologies (e.g. huge ships) are, however, making place value far less significant than it was, especially where economies of scale in transport can be made, such as in the bulk carriage of coal, aggregates or iron ore. Nevertheless, for resources traditionally said to have a very high place value, such as gravel and rock used for general hard core, the size and proximity of the market may still override economies of scale *in production* because transport imposes very high costs.

2.4 Stages in resource exploitation

The exploitation of a physical resource may be on such a small and local scale that it can begin almost immediately, with little investment of time, money, machinery or human resources. Such a pattern would be true, for example, of a farmer digging up a cartload of gravel from a stream bed on the farm, or excavating a shallow well for water. But a major venture to extract large amounts of high-value resources like oil or gas requires massive investment of various kinds over a long period.

A large-scale project begins with a phase of *exploration* in an area that shows at least some economic or geological promise. Occasionally, though, exploration is undertaken just for political reasons, such as when a country or company simply wants to establish its presence somewhere — and this is almost certainly doomed to be fruitless without favourable geological indications. The incentive to discover a resource depends largely on its potential profit; a search for gold or oil is usually more expensive than a search for sand or gravel. Different financial outlays, exploration techniques, and degrees of effort will be needed to find different resources. The discovery of an important physical resource inevitably hits the headlines, but there are normally very long delays (lead times) between discovery and the first profitable operation.

Without exploration, a company would eventually run out of its reserves. Exploration is, however, usually costly and time-consuming. Advances in *remote sensing* techniques (such as airborne and satellite imagery) have greatly assisted exploration in relatively inaccessible, less well explored

Figure 33 Exploration geologists drilling for ores in Zimbabwe, Africa.

regions, but direct observation on the ground is always needed to collect samples of the resource, confirm its three-dimensional extent, and so on. There can be huge financial risks to investment in exploration, not only from the chance that physical resources will not be found in economic quantities, but also from political, social and environmental factors that may jeopardize progress at any time. In a recession, the first thing that usually gets cut is the exploration budget, and a project can be deferred or cancelled at any stage during the lead time from discovery to mine operation. If an established company, however, is making a reasonable profit, exploration is often undertaken to offset some of the tax that would otherwise have to be paid on that profit. Some of the financial risks can be reduced by exploring in areas where deposits are known to have been extracted in the past. Changes in prices, costs, demand patterns and technology may make it economic to extract some of the remaining deposits that were not worth extracting before. These same general principles apply to the exploitation of any physical resource, whether it be iron ore, oil, sand, water, or any other.

The discovery of a mineral deposit or an occurrence of oil is merely the beginning of what is often the most difficult stage of a project, its *evaluation*. What seems a bonanza when first discovered could prove to be worthless on further scrutiny. During evaluation all the geological attributes of a find have to be documented — how big is it, how rich is it, to what depth does it extend, what is its shape? Technical factors must also be considered: for example, whether the resource can be extracted by the means available, what type of working is required, what are the potential dangers from flooding or ground instability, what design of plant is needed to process the resource to a saleable commodity, what actions are needed to minimize environmental impact, and so on. The infrastructure (the geographical and social aspects of the area of discovery) also has to be carefully examined. Who actually owns the minerals? Often a time-consuming search is needed to establish legal rights. Will new road or rail links have to be constructed? Can advantage be taken of existing facilities such as pipelines or processing plants connected with other developments? Are workers with the necessary skills available, and what wages will have to be paid? Are there any adverse climatic factors? How stable is the political situation and what regulations are in force?

Because production still lies in the future, whether the project will prove profitable also depends on the future price of the resource, on costs over the lifetime of the project, on the degree of certainty that a customer will be found and on how other projects involving the same resource may affect price and marketability. Only after this evaluation stage is completed can a decision be made to go ahead with development, which involves a further commitment to increase expenditure on the project.

The *development* stage of the project means quite simply preparing for production on the basis of the information from the evaluation stage. It involves buying or leasing all the equipment required for both development and production, building the necessary processing installations and either drilling the production wells, in the case of oil and gas, or constructing the basic framework of the mine or quarry from which all production will stem. For surface-mining operations this requires laying bare the resource and setting up the system of roadways necessary for processing and waste disposal. For underground mining it may involve constructing a system of underground roadways in three dimensions, on the scale of a small town. This sort of preparation clearly provides more information about the resource, and evaluation continues not only into the development stage but throughout production too.

The *production* stage begins when the project 'comes on-stream', and both saleable product and revenues start to flow through the system. This can be anything up to twenty years from the first acquisition of rights to explore an area, and during this period the operator has had to go on seeking the means of financing the project. Once 'on-stream' the project can expect to face further problems, such as geological difficulties (e.g. hitherto unknown geological structures), and, as in any industry, wear and tear on equipment and possible labour strikes. These problems are surmountable, provided they do not drive down the price : cost ratio below the lower boundary of the reserves category (Figure 30). The one problem that eventually has to be addressed is that the project's reserves will sooner or later be exhausted. This aspect is one that distinguishes most extractive industries from others where production is not based on wasting assets (i.e. assets with a finite life). The main exceptions here are industries based on renewable energy resources and on water extraction, because in most cases water resources are mostly capable of renewal on timescales that allow continued supply as long as there is careful management.

In summary, the activities of a resource-based industry can be divided into four distinct stages: *exploration, evaluation, development* and *production*. The economics of extractive industries are dominated by three factors:

1   There are no immediate returns at the outset of a large-scale project because of the lead times between discovery and production. Lead times are often as much as ten or fifteen years for large and costly ventures such as a new oil field, but may be far shorter, as in the case of a small-scale gravel pit that may be doing business a few weeks after permission is granted.

2   Physical resources (other than renewable energy resources and water) are wasting assets that are removed from their source. After a finite time a particular operation cannot produce a marketable commodity.

3   In large-scale ventures, there tend to be high risks at every stage of a project, which is not necessarily true of some other types of industry.

2.5 The lifetimes of reserves

An important activity in any economy is to estimate the time by which currently proven reserves will become depleted and, where necessary, to react accordingly. Estimates based on current rates of production are simply made by dividing the reserves by the annual production to give the **reserves lifetime** starting from a given year. The lifetime changes from year to year according to current production and current reserve estimates. Depending on how far national or company economies are planned (rarely more than thirty years ahead), a strategy for enhanced production (or possibly conservation) may or may not be deemed necessary. If depletion in the short term seems likely, various options are open: either exploration can be increased deliberately and technical improvements can be sought, or the scarcities that eventually appear can be relied on to promote exploitation by driving up the price, raising the incentive to supply. Two other important ways of meeting supply problems are to find suitable substitutes from more abundant materials and to recycle used materials.

Question 19

Calculate the global reserves lifetimes in 1992 for the last seven elements listed in Table 6, based on their estimated reserves and production figures in that year. (Because of recession, many of the production values for 1992 were slightly lower than the values for 1990–91 plotted in Figure 2.)

Table 6   Global reserves and production figures in 1992 (for Question 19)

Element	Reserves/t	Production/t	Lifetime in 1992 (years)
antimony	4.2×10^6	8.4×10^4	50
cadmium	5.4×10^5	1.9×10^4	28
copper	3.1×10^8	9.3×10^6	33
lead	6.3×10^7	3.2×10^6	
mercury	1.3×10^5	3.0×10^3	
nickel	4.7×10^7	9.2×10^5	
rhenium	2.5×10^3	3.2×10^1	
silver	2.8×10^5	1.5×10^4	
sulphur	1.4×10^9	5.3×10^7	
tin	7.0×10^6	1.8×10^5	

Reserves lifetimes of over a century include aluminium (200 years), and iron ore (178 years). Eight out of ten of the reserves lifetimes of the elements in Table 6 are 50 years or less, and all are less than a century. Given that in 1992 zinc reserves were 1.4×10^8 t (Figure 31), and production was 7.4×10^6 t, the reserves lifetime of zinc, too, was only 19 years. Does this mean that we are likely to run out of, say, lead and zinc by the year 2012?

In the early 1970s, when global production and consumption of many physical resources were rising exponentially, there were many well publicized views that industrial society would soon run out of non-renewable raw materials and reach a limit to growth, possibly with doom-laden consequences. Calculations of lifetimes based on maintaining 1968 levels of production suggested that by 1990 reserves of several elements would have been totally depleted, including gold, lead, mercury, silver and zinc. In other words, the reserves lifetimes of all such elements were less than 22 years. Furthermore, had the exponential rate of increase in production from 1960 to 1968 continued after 1968, many reserves lifetimes would have shortened further, adding, for example, platinum and tin to the list of elements whose reserves would have been depleted by 1990.

In 1993, the reserve lifetimes of many of these elements are still similar to the reserve lifetimes calculated in 1968, and some are even a little longer. How can this be? There are several reasons. Many reserve lifetimes are still in the range 15 to 40 years simply because this reflects the usual pacing of exploration and evaluation to maintain reserves for the foreseeable future. Exploration constantly moves undiscovered resources into the reserves category. In addition, for some resources, price rises and improvements in efficiency have moved conditional resources into the reserves category; recycling has increased; and some inaccuracies in resource inventories have been corrected. Furthermore, for many resources the exponential growth of the 1960s and 1970s did not continue into the 1980s. An important reason for this was the emerging instability in the world economy, rather than limits to the availability of resources.

The term 'reserves' is often misunderstood to indicate a fixed quantity that necessarily reduces with every year's consumption — whereas in recent decades reserves have generally grown at least as fast as production. There is, nevertheless, an eventual limit to non-renewable resources. Recycling will certainly partially offset demand for some physical resources, especially metals. For example, in 1992, about 70% of lead consumption in the USA was supplied by recycling, although largely because the metal is so toxic that its use is now tightly regulated, and the cost of safe and legal disposal can sometimes exceed recycling costs. Other metals are as yet recycled less. Some non-metallic minerals are very difficult, i.e. prohibitively expensive, to recycle. It is *impossible* to recycle fuels such as coal, oil and natural gas in the same way that metals can be recycled: when burnt, the energy content of fuels is converted into other forms, and the fuel itself is, in effect, lost forever by being chemically converted to carbon dioxide (CO_2) and water, which are released to the environment.

There are some who argue that the question of scarcity is not, and was never, the most important consideration, and that the more urgent question remains: Can the world afford the general human and ecological cost of satisfying its appetite for physical resources? A market price does not, at least not yet, take into account the full costs of environmental damage — which may include the loss of forests, erosion of land, pollution of rivers, and the social upheaval of indigenous peoples living on valuable deposits, as well as less overt consequences such as global warming and the destruction of the ozone layer. In future, it seems probable that major environmental problems will arise from attempts to extract resources from lower and lower grades of material — problems relating to massive increases in energy requirements, land consumption, and disposal of rock waste and effluents produced during processing.

Human ingenuity may well end up solving some of the foreseen and unforeseen problems — but probably only as long as there is sufficient encouragement for research and development to tackle long-term problems that are not effectively accounted for by short-term market forces.

2.6 Summary of Section 2

1 In the long term, market forces ensure that production and consumption of physical resources remain in balance. Inflation and events such as wars and political upheavals are important influences in the economies of individual countries and commodities. Unlike the nominal price, the real price of many commodities has remained similar or even decreased over many decades during the twentieth century.

2 Future global patterns of production and consumption of physical resources are likely to be influenced especially by: the disparity in population growth between industrialized and developing regions, and the disproportionate increase in consumption in the latter; growing environmental awareness and regulations, with more policies for recycling, saving energy, and pollution control; increasing rates of substitution due to the invention of new materials; continued political interference with the free flow of commodities; and a shift away from heavy industry towards services and high technology in major industrialized countries. The complexity of the global economy is such that accurate predictions are difficult to make.

3 Supply is defined as the quantity of a resource that suppliers are prepared to sell at a given price, while demand is the quantity that consumers are prepared to buy at a given price. In a competitive, free economy, the relationship between price, demand and supply are completely interwoven. Many factors can affect, and be affected by, each of these variables. Cartels and other producer associations are a common complicating feature of 'free' economies.

4 Generally speaking, for any resource the quantity demanded increases as price falls, and the quantity supplied increases as price rises. Supply and demand tend to move towards an equilibrium point where the price and quantity that suppliers are willing and able to supply matches the price and quantity that consumers demand. Other things being equal, an increase in demand or a decrease in supply leads to a rise in price; similarly, a decrease in demand or an increase in supply leads to a fall in price.

5 If quite a large change in price has relatively little effect on demand, a resource is said to have a low price elasticity of demand. An inelastic demand is typical of resources that are considered more or less essential, and which have no substitute. Conversely, if quite a small change in price leads to a disproportionally large change in demand, the resource is said to have a high price elasticity of demand. An elastic demand is typical of non-essential items and luxuries. Substitution is an important factor affecting elasticity: above a certain price consumers may be able to switch to another resource. Physical resources tend to be in inelastic supply in the short term and in elastic supply in the long term. The demand of one resource is commonly sensitive to changes in the price of another (cross-elasticity of demand).

6 Reserves are quantities of resources that can be extracted profitably and legally under existing conditions. To be a reserve, the resource must be at concentrations greater than the average minimum exploitable grade or local cut-off grade, and a company or organization would have to have the necessary ownership and permissions to exploit the resource. The category of resources contains concentrations of useful materials in such a form and amount that profitable extraction is either currently feasible (in the case of reserves) *or potentially* feasible, given reasonably foreseeable changes in techniques and/or price. Total stock includes

concentrations that are too low to be considered resources, but excludes occurrences in which the material is not in a form suitable for economic extraction.

7   Two important parameters used to define the categories of resources and reserves are the degree of certainty that a resource exists and profitability. Conditional resources have been located, but are uneconomic at present, whereas hypothetical resources are as yet undiscovered but might well exist in a given area. Exploration and discoveries, technological improvements, changes in market price, and changes in environmental and other regulations, can cause reclassification of resources. The geographic location of physical resources in relation to where they or their products are used may determine whether or not they are exploited. Resources have a high 'place value' if their location strongly determines their price.

8   The activities of an extractive industry can be divided into four stages: exploration, evaluation, development and production. Three factors tend to dominate industries based on large-scale extraction, especially of high-value resources: very long lead times between discovery and profitable production; the fact that most physical resources, when exploited, are wasting assets; and high risks at every stage of a project.

9   The reserve lifetimes of many elements are currently similar to their lifetimes of a few decades ago, and some are even a little longer, reflecting the pacing of exploration and evaluation to maintain reserves for the foreseeable future. For many resources the exponential growth in production and consumption of the 1960s and 1970s did not continue into the 1980s. An important reason for this was the emerging instability in the world economy, rather than limits to the availability of resources.

10 An important question to address is: can the world afford the general human and ecological cost of satisfying its appetite for physical resources? In future, for example, it seems probable that major environmental problems will arise from attempting to extract resources from lower and lower grades of material. Human ingenuity, however, should be able to solve some of the foreseen and unforeseen problems.

3   THE GEOLOGICAL ORIGIN AND CHEMICAL NATURE OF PHYSICAL RESOURCES

One of the most important aims of this Course is to develop an understanding of the natural processes which provide physical resources. Almost all elements that occur naturally, whether uncombined or as part of compounds, have some industrial or commercial use, but in order to locate them efficiently we must have some idea of how they may be concentrated by natural processes. Two stages are particularly important: (1) gaining basic knowledge of the chemical characteristics of elements and the nature of minerals in the Earth's crust, and (2) understanding the geological processes responsible for chemical changes in the Earth and the local concentration of physical resources.

Most of the Earth's outer layer — its crust — consists of rocks in which individual elements and their compounds of interest to industry and commerce are present in concentrations too small to make it worth the effort and expense of extracting them. The occurrence of economic mineral deposits in the Earth's crust is a little like the distribution of currants in a bun. Much of the geology of physical resources is concerned with the 'currants', but their distribution can only be understood if you also know something of the 'bun' in which they are embedded, such as what type of bun it is and how it was made.

In this Section we turn our attention to the common rocks and minerals of the Earth's crust, some of which also happen to be resources in their own right. We shall briefly look at the overall structure of the Earth and then examine in more detail the chemical nature of elements and the minerals in which they occur, and the origin of the main types of rocks. Section 3.6 goes on to discuss the most important geological processes that concentrate physical resources. Finally, in Section 3.8, after an overview of these processes and their settings, we consider the implications of geological time and how the ages of rocks can be determined.

3.1   Rocks and minerals — an introduction

Look around you and see if you can find anything made of natural rock or mineral — perhaps something you identified in Activity 1, like a cheese board or chopping board, a stone collected on holiday, or a carved ornament. Whatever you choose, would you call it a rock or a mineral? And what's the difference?

Study Plate 1, which shows a piece of granite. You can see even at first glance a large number of discrete interlocking grains. Each grain is composed of a single mineral. In general usage, the term 'mineral' covers almost anything that comes out of the ground; but we must be more specific. A **mineral**, geologically speaking, is a naturally occurring substance that has a definite crystalline structure reflecting an ordered arrangement of atoms. Most minerals have a more or less fixed chemical composition that may vary only within certain limits. For example, quartz, which is a common mineral in granite (grey in Plate 1), can be represented by the chemical formula SiO_2, meaning that for every one silicon atom there are two oxygen atoms. Calcite, the most common mineral in limestones, is represented by the formula $CaCO_3$, meaning that for every calcium atom there is one carbon atom and three oxygen atoms. The minerals with the simplest formula are the native elements such as gold (Au) or sulphur (S). Many minerals, however, have more complicated compositions and therefore longer formulae. For example, orthoclase feldspar, another common mineral in granite (the large pink crystals in Plate 1), has the formula $KAlSi_3O_8$. The fact that there are many elements in a formula does not mean that the mineral is variable in composition, but that the mineral involves a relatively large number of elements combined together in particular proportions.

Coal is not a mineral in the scientific sense, as it lacks a crystalline structure, and neither is petroleum, for no liquid or gas, lacking crystalline structure, meets the definition. Thus, although the term 'mineral wealth' or 'mineral resources' may be used to include fossil fuels, these are not correctly classified as minerals in the geological sense.

A **rock** is simply a naturally occurring assemblage of mineral grains. The grains may all be of the same mineral, but more often a rock consists of an assemblage of different minerals. Granite is a rock composed of a particular combination of minerals.

All rocks are classified into three major types — igneous, sedimentary or metamorphic — according to how they were formed, rather than their chemical composition. Figure 34 and Plates 1 to 6 show typical examples of each of the three major rock types.

Igneous rocks, like the granite in Plate 1 and Figure 34(a), have formed by the solidification of **magma** (molten rock), either inside the Earth or on its surface. Magma erupted at the Earth's surface is called **lava**. As the liquid magma cools, it freezes to form a solid rock. When the rock is composed of crystals, which is usually the case, the process of solidification is called crystallization. The freezing characteristics of magmas differ according to their chemical composition, but all types of magma will have become solid rock once the temperature falls below about 550 °C; some are already completely solid at about 1000 °C. Note that in everyday speech, freezing usually applies to the freezing of water, and so 'freezing' suggests cold — whereas the freezing points of magmas are exceedingly hot by our everyday standards. For comparison, you cannot melt rocks in an ordinary kitchen oven, which typically reaches only about 250 °C. To melt completely a lump of **basalt**, which like granite is another very common igneous rock, you would need an oven that reached more than 1300 °C (a temperature that would melt an ordinary domestic oven). Basalt (Plate 2) is darker in colour than granite, denser, and finer grained, with smaller crystals.

Sedimentary rocks, like sandstone (Plate 3), conglomerate (Figure 34b), shale, and limestone (Plate 4), are formed by the deposition of material — sediment — that settles on the Earth's surface under gravity, usually from water or less commonly from air or ice. Most sediments have a *fragmental* texture because they consist of eroded fragments of pre-existing rocks and mineral grains, or parts of organisms such as their shells. Other sediments consist of chemical compounds precipitated from water. (In chemistry, *precipitation* occurs when a dissolved substance separates out from a solution to form solid particles. The resulting precipitate is often crystalline.) Eventually, loose sediments become compacted and cemented together to form sedimentary rocks.

Metamorphic rocks, like marble (Plate 5), slate, schist (Figure 34c) and gneiss (Plate 6), are rocks of any original type that have been changed by

(a)

(b)

(c)

Figure 34 (a) Granite, a typical igneous rock with a crystalline texture of interlocking, intergrown grains. Length of specimen is 15 cm. (b) Conglomerate, a typical sedimentary rock with a fragmental texture. The pebbles are mainly of quartz. Largest pebble is 4 cm across. (c) Schist, a typical metamorphic rock with a crystalline texture and alignment of minerals. Length of specimen is 12 cm.

heat and/or pressure, possibly accompanied by chemical activity. Usually, new crystals, often quite different from the original minerals, are formed during metamorphism. During this process, the overall chemical composition of the rock (its *bulk composition*) normally remains about the same, with elements just rearranging themselves into new minerals that are more stable under the prevailing conditions. The minerals in metamorphic rocks are often aligned, and may be segregated, in parallel bands. (Metamorphic rocks are discussed further in Section 3.5.3.)

3.2 The Earth's overall structure and plate tectonics

The study of rock sequences in different continents reveals some surprises. For example, the fossil remains of marine animals can be found thousands of metres above sea level in the South American Andes, and even rocks at the summit of Everest were once under the sea. Even more striking, there are rocks in Britain today that were formed in the southern hemisphere, rocks in Antarctica that were formed in the tropics, and there is clear evidence of ancient, widespread glaciation in some of today's low-lying tropical areas, such as Saharan Africa. Large-scale earth movements have transported rocks vertically to great heights and horizontally huge distances across the surface of the globe. How has this happened? To answer this, we first need to study the structure of the Earth.

The rocks that we see on the surface of the Earth are very varied, and, not surprisingly, the composition and physical properties of rocks also vary with depth. Figure 35 summarizes our knowledge of how the Earth's structure and composition varies from surface to core. This information was gained from studies of the Earth's physical properties using seismic waves (the waves produced from shocks such as earthquakes), and by analogy with the properties of meteorites of varying chemical compositions.

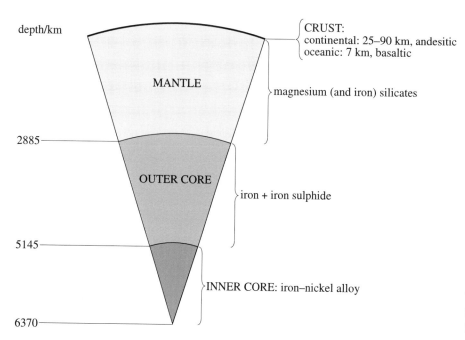

Figure 35 A schematic slice through the Earth, showing the major compositional features of the crust, mantle and core.

The **core** consists of iron, iron–nickel alloy, and some iron sulphide, whereas the **mantle** and **crust**, by contrast, contain huge quantities of oxygen and silicon, and most of their minerals are silicates (Section 3.4). There are therefore some interesting parallels between the differentiation of the Earth into a core with an overlying mantle and crust, and the smelting of iron ore in a blast furnace (Section 1.3): the melting of the solid mixture of iron ore, coke and limestone produces a dense layer of molten iron ($\approx$ core) below a layer of slag composed mostly of silicates ($\approx$ mantle and crust).

The mantle contains most of the Earth's magnesium. Crustal rocks, on average, have higher percentages of aluminium, calcium, sodium and potassium than mantle rocks. As explained shortly, this is because new crust consists of igneous rocks formed by melting part of the mantle, and one of the consequences of such melting has been (and still is) the movement of large quantities of elements such as Al, Ca, Na and K from the mantle to the crust.

Elements that *each* form more than 0.5% of common rocks are termed the **major elements** and between them they make up more than 99.5% of the crust. There are many other elements that occur, *on average*, in smaller amounts, and which *together* normally make up less than the remaining 0.5% of common rocks; they are called **trace elements**. Trace elements include, for example, chromium, zinc, gold and silver, and may be major resources where they have been concentrated into economically viable deposits. Trace elements are thus not rare everywhere; the term relates to abundances in the crust as a whole.

Question 20

Use Figure 3 to decide which of the following elements are trace elements, and which are major elements, in the continental crust: Al, As, Ba, Be, Ca, Cu, Fe, K, Mg, Mo, Si, Sr.

The crust, which comprises only 0.6% of the Earth by volume, is of two types: one forms the continents and continental shelves, and the other underlies the ocean basins (Figure 36). **Continental crust** is much thicker than **oceanic crust**, averaging 35 km but ranging from as little as 25 km in some places to as much as 90 km beneath mountain belts. In contrast, oceanic crust varies very little, and is everywhere about 7 km thick. To put these thicknesses into context, the maximum relief on the continents reaches nearly 9 km above sea level in the Himalayas and 11 km below sea level in the deepest ocean trench. Nowhere yet are we able to penetrate into the mantle, and, for the foreseeable future, extraction of physical resources from rocks will be limited to the upper parts of the crust.

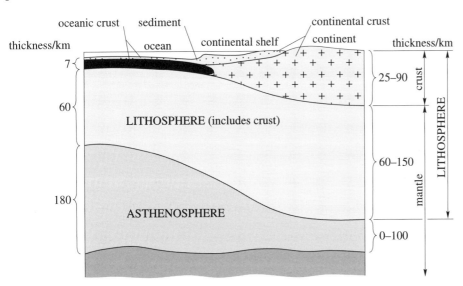

Figure 36   A cross-section through the outer part of the Earth to show the relationships between the crust, mantle, lithosphere and asthenosphere. The lithosphere, of which the plates are formed, includes both the crust (either continental or oceanic) *and* the topmost, more rigid part of the mantle.

The bulk of the continental crust is composed of igneous and metamorphic rocks, and while in many places it carries a cover of sediments, these have little influence on its overall composition because the sediments themselves are ultimately derived from igneous and metamorphic rocks. Only in a few places, such as in narrow strips near continental margins (Figure 36), does the sedimentary cover exceed 10 km in thickness. The continental crust as a whole has an average composition of a rock called diorite (or its finer grained equivalent, andesite), which, chemically speaking, is roughly between that of granite and basalt. (The chemistry of these igneous rocks is discussed in Section 3.6.) Oceanic crust is denser than continental crust, and chemically quite different. It consists of igneous and metamorphic rocks, covered by a thin veneer of sediments and sedimentary rocks, but the overwhelming bulk is igneous, with a chemical composition close to that of basalt. As about 70% of the Earth's surface is covered by water, much of which is underlain by oceanic crust, the part of the Earth we know best is not typical of the crust as a whole.

The crust and the uppermost mantle are relatively strong, and together they are known as the **lithosphere** (Figure 36). The lithosphere forms an irregular mosaic of more or less rigid segments or **plates** which move around the surface of the Earth. They move over the **asthenosphere**, a layer which is less rigid than the lithospheric plates, and which can move *en masse* very slowly, by convection. Note that the plates consist of the crust *and* the topmost more rigid part of the mantle.

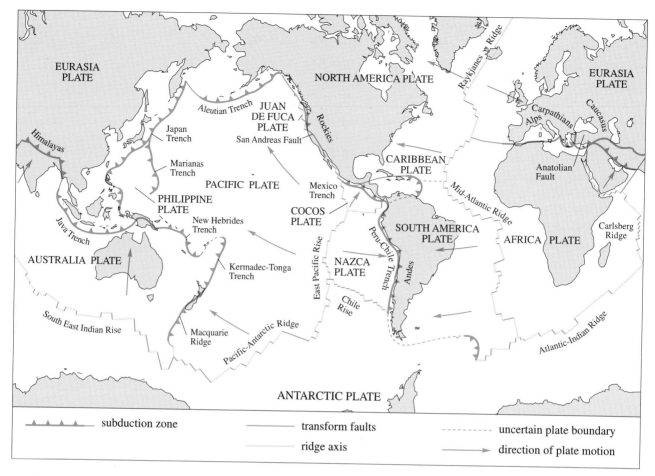

Figure 37 The distribution of lithospheric plates on the Earth's surface.

The boundaries between plates, shown in Figure 37, often correspond to long topographic features, particularly in the ocean basins. Some of the boundaries coincide with **ocean ridges** — mountain ridges running through the oceans — such as the Mid-Atlantic Ridge. Others are marked by deep **ocean trenches**, either along **active continental margins** such as that of western South America, or adjacent to slightly curved lines of islands called **island arcs**, such as the Japanese arc. On the continents, one plate boundary is marked by the Himalayan mountain range. Some individual plates (such as the Eurasia Plate to which the UK belongs) include regions of both continental and oceanic crust, which merge at a **passive continental margin**.

○ Going west from Britain, where is the boundary of the plate we are on, and if you flew over it would it be easy to recognize?

○ It is in the middle of the Atlantic ocean, at the Mid-Atlantic Ridge, and, generally being under the sea, the plate boundary is not at all noticeable. Only in a very few places, such as Iceland, does the ridge emerge above the ocean.

The principal cause of convection in the asthenosphere (and thereby also the ultimate cause of plate movements) is the heat continually being generated by the decay of radioactive elements in the Earth. (Radioactivity is discussed briefly in Section 3.3.) This radiogenic heat is dissipated by upward movement of hot material towards the surface. Some of the hot asthenosphere material melts on arriving at shallow depths and molten rock surges intermittently to the surface in submarine volcanoes along the ocean ridges (Figure 37). Because new crust is formed along ocean ridges, they are known as **constructive plate boundaries**. Either side of an ocean ridge the sea floor travels sideways, moving away at rates of a few centimetres a year in a process known as **sea-floor spreading**. The new oceanic crust is added to the trailing edges of each plate as they move away from each other.

Since new crust is continually being generated, and the diameter of the Earth is not continually expanding, there must also be places where crust is being destroyed. Where two plates converge, and if at least one of them includes oceanic crust, one plate sinks below the other and is eventually resorbed back into the upper mantle, which destroys its form. This process is called **subduction**. These regions are termed **destructive plate boundaries**, and they are marked at the surface by deep ocean trenches and, at a short distance from the trenches, by active volcanoes on the overlying plate. The friction at *subduction zones* (Figure 37) causes numerous earthquakes, the foci of which are located on the top of the subducting plate.

⬤   If two plates are moving towards one another, one with just oceanic crust and the other with just continental crust, which will tend to sink and hence be destroyed by subduction?

◯   It is the plate with oceanic crust that sinks, because it is more dense. Should two continents collide, they are both relatively buoyant, so neither is dragged down into the mantle. Instead the crust thickens, and spectacular mountain chains such as the Alps and the Himalayas are formed in a **collision zone**.

Sea-floor spreading at a constructive plate boundary and subduction along a destructive plate boundary are illustrated in Figure 38. In some areas, adjacent plates may move past one another along what are called **transform faults**, and here crust is neither generated nor destroyed, but conserved. Such plate boundaries are called **conservative plate boundaries**, and they occur in both the oceans and the continents. Because they are linear belts where rigid plates grind past one another along transform faults, they are often zones of major earthquakes; one of the best known is the San Andreas Fault System in California.

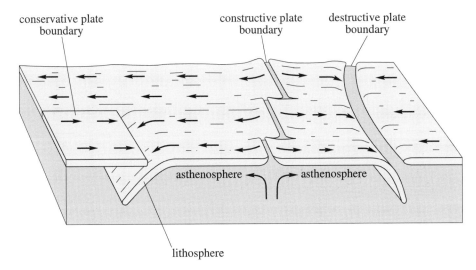

Figure 38   Diagram showing the basic features of plate tectonics.

In summary, then, the surface of the Earth consists of a mosaic of rigid plates, which are continually on the move, jostling against each other. Because the lithospheric plates are strong, most deformation, metamorphism and igneous activity generally takes place at the plate boundaries — the edges of the plates — where they interact with one another. Three types of plate boundary are recognized: constructive, destructive, and conservative

Figure 39 Mount St Helens erupting in May 1980. This volcano, in the Cascade Range, western USA, is situated above the subduction zone that forms a destructive plate boundary along the eastern margin of the small Juan de Fuca Plate.

(Figures 37 and 38). In oceanic areas, new crust is generated along oceanic ridges, and is basaltic in composition. The destruction of oceanic crust beneath destructive plate boundaries also results in melting and lines of active volcanoes (Figure 39). The igneous rocks generated above these subduction zones have the composition of continental crust, and it is largely the destruction of oceanic crust that leads to the generation of new continental crust.

So the Earth is far from static; there is ceaseless activity at its surface and within, but often at very slow rates. The motion of plates causes the continents they carry to drift slowly over the surface of the globe — a process called **continental drift**. Two plates may collide, pushing up huge mountain belts like the Himalayas, but such a collision takes place almost imperceptibly slowly — nothing like a collision between motor cars. Various analogies concerning rates of flow, growth or motion may help us to envisage slow rates. One analogy, based on flow, is exemplified by seemingly solid blocks of pitch, used in roofing, that slowly spread when left for a few months. The most popular growth analogy is the rate at which fingernails grow — just two or three centimetres per year — which is very similar to the average rate at which plates move around the Earth.

The term **plate tectonics** refers to the unifying concept by which the Earth's major structural features are seen as due to the relative motion of rigid lithospheric plates over a weaker asthenosphere. ('Tectonics' used on its own refers more narrowly to large-scale movements of the Earth's crust and the resulting structures.) Not surprisingly, the ideas of plate tectonics, first developed in the 1960s, revolutionized the earth sciences. Major geological features, such as high mountain ranges, deep ocean trenches, ocean ridges and island arcs were all explained in a single general model. As we will see, the distribution of plates, and, in particular, plate boundaries, determines to a large extent the location of appropriate geological settings for the concentration of physical resources.

3.3   Physical resources—the inside story

Nearly all physical resources are substances that owe their existence to — and can be destroyed by — large-scale geological processes, and, on a smaller scale, chemical reactions. To understand more of the chemical behaviour of different elements, we need to have a closer look at the internal structure of elements and compounds.

We know from Section 1.2 that elements differ greatly in their properties. There also tends to be a great difference between the physical and chemical properties of compounds and the individual elements that make them up. For example, quartz, one of the commonest minerals, is a compound of two elements — oxygen and silicon — as indicated by its formula, SiO_2. Quartz, when pure, forms transparent crystals (Plate 7). But at room temperature, oxygen is a colourless gas, while silicon is a grey, metallic-looking solid. Silicon never occurs naturally as the uncombined element, but is extremely common in combination with other elements, occurring in a vast number of different minerals. As we saw in Figure 3, oxygen and silicon are the most abundant elements in the Earth's crust.

○ What vitally important liquid resource is a compound of two elements that are colourless gases at room temperature?

○ Water, which is a compound of hydrogen and oxygen.

Another interesting example is common salt, sodium chloride. Sodium is a silvery metal, never found as the uncombined element because it is far too reactive, and chlorine is a poisonous green gas — yet sodium chloride forms colourless crystals that are very different from either element, and it is essential for animal life.

○ Recalling Section 1.2, what is the smallest particle into which an element can be subdivided while still retaining the chemical characteristics of that element?

○ An atom.

At the centre of each atom is a **nucleus** containing one or more **protons** which carry a positive electrical charge, and usually some **neutrons**, which have no charge. Negatively charged **electrons** surround the nucleus. By definition, atoms of the same element all have the same number of protons in the nucleus, i.e. they are said to have the same **atomic number**. For example, gold has the atomic number 79 (Table 1), meaning that every gold atom has 79 protons in its nucleus; an atom with any other number of protons would not be gold. The chemical and physical properties of elements vary enormously, but when placed in order of atomic number, elements display a periodic repetition of properties (discussed shortly).

An atom is electrically neutral when the number of electrons equals the number of protons. Most atoms, however, can gain or lose some electrons. When this happens, the atom has either a positive or a negative electrical charge, and it is then called an **ion** (pronounced 'eye-on').

⬤ If an atom loses electrons, will it become positively or negatively charged?

◯ Positively charged, because the number of positive protons then exceeds the number of negative electrons.

Conversely, if an atom gains electrons, it becomes negatively charged. Positive ions are called **cations** (pronounced 'cat eye-ons'); negative ions are called **anions** (pronounced 'an eye-ons'). If you're in doubt which is which, remember '*cat*ions are *puss*itive'. Metal ions tend to be positively charged, non-metals negatively charged. Iron, for example, tends to form cations which have either two or three missing electrons, represented by Fe^{2+} and Fe^{3+}, respectively. Fe^{2+} was traditionally called the *ferrous* ion, and Fe^{3+} the *ferric* ion, though now the terms iron(II) and iron(III) are used. By contrast, fluorine, for example, a non-metal, gains one electron, and forms simple anions represented by F^-.

In solids, ions do not exist freely as separate entities; the cations and anions are bonded together, often in complex ways, especially when many elements are present. In liquids, however, individual ions may exist and move independently. Many minerals dissociate into ions, at least to some extent, when dissolved in water. Common salt (sodium chloride) dissolves easily in water, to give a solution of sodium ions and chloride ions, Na^+ and Cl^-. Individual ions may be taken *separately* out of solution, a process that happens all the time whenever organisms absorb mineral nutrients dissolved in water. Conversely, positive and negative ions may come out of solution *together* to form a solid precipitate, as occurs when you evaporate seawater, or hard tap water. (In hard water areas, a precipitate is visible on drinking glasses if you don't dry them off with a cloth after washing up.) The overall electrical charge of liquids and solids remains neutral during dissolution or precipitation, with the total number of cations and anions staying evenly balanced. The same is true of liquids and crystals during the melting of rocks or the crystallization of magma.

3.3.1 Chemical bonding

The bonding together of elements to form compounds can occur in two main ways. In **ionic bonding**, it is the electrical attraction between oppositely charged ions that keeps the compound together. In common salt (NaCl), for example, the elements sodium and chlorine are present as ions of opposite charge which mutually attract each other, holding the compound together. In **covalent bonding**, however, rather than electrons being lost by one element and gained by another, the atoms actually *share* electrons. In many compounds the bonding is partly ionic and partly covalent.

Ionic compounds like sodium chloride are relatively simple: there is only one cation, only one anion, and each ion consists of a single element. However, many ions, especially anions, are more complicated. For example, calcite ($CaCO_3$, calcium carbonate) is an ionic compound in which the cation is Ca^{2+} and the anion is CO_3^{2-}, the two positive charges of the calcium balancing the two negative charges of the carbonate ion. *Within* the carbonate ion, bonding of the carbon, C, to the three oxygens is largely covalent, although in this case the net result of these bonds is a negatively charged ion. The sulphate anion, SO_4^{2-}, like the carbonate anion, also has two negative charges, which can be balanced by one calcium cation (Ca^{2+}), giving a compound with the formula $CaSO_4$ (calcium sulphate, a mineral called anhydrite). If an anion involves more than one element, it is known as a *polyanion*; 'poly' simply means 'more than one'.

Why do elements behave as they do?

In an electrically neutral atom, the number of protons is matched by the same number of electrons, yet an electrically neutral atom may be highly reactive. Why should this be?

Most models for atoms have a nucleus (consisting of protons and neutrons), surrounded by clouds of electrons. The electrons are often depicted in a series of shells and subshells, like the skins of an onion (Figure 40). When full, each shell and subshell contains a fixed number of electrons, and the most stable configuration is for the outer shell to have its full quota of electrons. It is this tendency to attain a more stable state that leads atoms to bond with other atoms, and the type of chemical bond depends on how a full outer shell of electrons can be most easily achieved. The fundamental reason, then, for most of the variation in chemical properties of elements derives from differences in their number and arrangement of electrons, as well as in the number of protons in their nuclei.

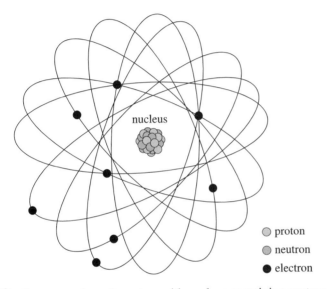

Figure 40   Representation of an atom with nucleus containing protons and neutrons, surrounded by clouds of orbiting electrons.

Elements show a periodic repetition of properties when placed in order of atomic number. Figure 41 presents a version of what is called the Periodic Table, which is an ordered list of elements that provides a framework within which to view systematic chemical features, though there is certainly no need to remember all the details. Reading the Table from left to right, starting at the top and working across row by row from top to bottom, each element has one more proton and one more electron than the element which precedes it. The atoms of elements at the bottom of the Table are bigger and heavier than those near the top. Most common gases (in ordinary room conditions) such as hydrogen, nitrogen and oxygen are near the top of the Table, while heavy elements such as lead and gold are nearer the bottom. In general, the Earth's most common elements are located in the top half of the Table.

As each element is characterized by the addition of one electron, there comes a stage when the outer electron shell has received its quota of electrons, and it becomes necessary to start putting electrons into the next major shell. Each row of the Periodic Table depicts the filling of each major shell. Different horizontal rows have different numbers of elements in them because of the variation in the quota of electrons which can reside in each outer shell. Elements are grouped into columns in the Periodic Table. The elements in

1 H hydrogen																	2 He helium
3 Li lithium	4 Be beryllium											5 B boron	6 C carbon	7 N nitrogen	8 O oxygen	9 F fluorine	10 Ne neon
11 Na sodium	12 Mg magnesium											13 Al aluminium	14 Si silicon	15 P phosphorus	16 S sulphur	17 Cl chlorine	18 Ar argon
19 K potassium	20 Ca calcium	21 Sc scandium	22 Ti titanium	23 V vanadium	24 Cr chromium	25 Mn manganese	26 Fe iron	27 Co cobalt	28 Ni nickel	29 Cu copper	30 Zn zinc	31 Ga gallium	32 Ge germanium	33 As arsenic	34 Se selenium	35 Br bromine	36 Kr krypton
37 Rb rubidium	38 Sr strontium	39 Y yttrium	40 Zr zirconium	41 Nb niobium	42 Mo molybdenum	43 Tc technetium	44 Ru ruthenium	45 Rh rhodium	46 Pd palladium	47 Ag silver	48 Cd cadmium	49 In indium	50 Sn tin	51 Sb antimony	52 Te tellurium	53 I iodine	54 Xe xenon
55 Cs caesium	56 Ba barium	57 La lanthanum	72 Hf hafnium	73 Ta tantalum	74 W tungsten	75 Re rhenium	76 Os osmium	77 Ir iridium	78 Pt platinum	79 Au gold	80 Hg mercury	81 Tl thallium	82 Pb lead	83 Bi bismuth	84 Po polonium	85 At astatine	86 Rn radon
87 Fr francium	88 Ra radium	89 Ac actinium	104 Db dubnium	105 Jl joliotium	106 Rf rutherfordium	107 Bh bohrium	108 Hn hahnium	109 Mt meitnerium									

58 Ce cerium	59 Pr praseodymium	60 Nd neodymium	61 Pm promethium	62 Sm samarium	63 Eu europium	64 Gd gadolinium	65 Tb terbium	66 Dy dysprosium	67 Ho holmium	68 Er erbium	69 Tm thulium	70 Yb ytterbium	71 Lu lutetium
90 Th thorium	91 Pa protactinium	92 U uranium	93 Np neptunium	94 Pu plutonium	95 Am americium	96 Cm curium	97 Bk berkelium	98 Cf californium	99 Es einsteinium	100 Fm fermium	101 Md mendelevium	102 No nobelium	103 Lr lawrencium

metals
metalloids
non-metals
all isotopes radioactive

Figure 41 The Periodic Table of elements. See text for discussion. Metalloids (semi-metals) have properties intermediate between metals and non-metals.

each vertical group have similar arrangements of electrons in their outer shells, so they tend to behave similarly, forming similar types of chemical bonds.

Look at the top row in the Periodic Table. It contains just two elements, hydrogen and helium, and after that we start a new row. Hydrogen contains one electron, and helium two: the implication is that once two electrons have been added, that particular shell is full, and electrons must be added to the next major shell, and so a new row is started over on the left of the Periodic Table.

● Using that logic, look at the Periodic Table, and decide how many electrons can be accommodated in the next shell of electrons (i.e. the elements in row 2).

○ Row 2 contains eight elements, and so we can reasonably conclude that the second shell of electrons can contain up to eight electrons.

Once the second shell is also full, another row must be started. The elements in row 3 may also accommodate eight electrons in the outer shells of their atoms, but at higher atomic numbers the atoms are bigger, and things get more complex. As atomic number increases, extra electrons are added to shells or subshells on or near the outside of the atom, so that what was an outer shell of electrons in elements with low atomic number becomes an inner shell of atoms with higher atomic number. As an inner shell it may contain more electrons than when it was the outermost shell. However, the complexities need not concern us, as our primary aim is to understand the kinds of chemical bonds favoured by different elements.

In *ionic* bonds, elements either *give up* or *take in* electrons, because to do so results in either an empty or a full outer shell of electrons. In *covalent* bonds, electrons are *shared* between two or more atoms, with the net result that each atom acquires a more stable configuration of electrons.

● Oxygen typically forms anions, O^{2-}. Can you explain this by virtue of the position of oxygen in the Periodic Table?

○ The oxygen atom takes in two negatively charged electrons to form O^{2-}. Oxygen occurs two positions away from the end of a row in the Periodic Table, and so its atoms contain two electrons fewer than can be accommodated in its outer shell. The acquisition of two extra electrons completes the preferred stable configuration.

● Where would you expect the most unreactive elements to be situated in the Table, and why?

○ The last column on the right. Here the outer electron shell of each element has its complete quota of electrons. In this stable state, there is no tendency to lose or gain any electrons, so these elements are unreactive. They are all gases — the **noble gases**. Being almost totally chemically inert, they are often called the *inert gases*: helium, neon, argon, krypton, xenon and radon.

● The elements fluorine, chlorine, bromine, iodine and the rare radioactive astatine are known as **halogens**, and their simple compounds, such as sodium chloride or calcium fluoride, are called halides. Find the halogens in the Periodic Table and, from their position, suggest whether they will form cations or anions, and what charge their ions will tend to have.

- The halogens occur in a column one position from the right-hand end of the Table. To form a stable electronic configuration, they need to *gain* only one electron, forming an anion with one negative charge. For this reason, the usual halogen ions are F^-, Cl^-, Br^-, and I^-.

- Find the metals sodium and potassium in the Periodic Table. From their position, suggest whether they are likely to form cations or anions, and what charge their ions will have.

- Sodium and potassium occur in a column at the left-hand end of the Table. To form a stable electronic configuration, they need to *lose* only one electron, forming a cation with one positive charge. For this reason, sodium forms the cation Na^+, and potassium forms the cation K^+.

- Given that ionic bonds involve the giving up of electrons by one element and the acquisition of them by another, can you predict where on the Periodic Table will elements occur whose atoms are most likely to form ionic bonds?

- Such elements occur towards either the left or right side of the Table.

If elements occur near the left-hand side they have perhaps only one or two electrons in their outer shells, and those can readily be lost. If elements occur near the right-hand side (but not of course, the extreme right end), they can achieve a full outer shell of electrons by gaining a relatively small number of electrons. Elements near the margins of the Periodic Table tend to form ionic bonds, with elements at the left-hand side usually giving up electrons to elements at the right-hand side. Hydrogen is rather anomalous because it can gain an electron or lose its only electron, and it may form covalent bonds as well as ionic bonds. Figure 42 depicts the chemical structure of two compounds, one ionic, involving Na and Cl, and the other covalent, involving C and H. Incidentally, the element chlorine itself also forms a covalently bonded molecule, Cl_2, in which one electron from each atom is held in common equally strongly by both atoms.

It is much harder to predict the typical behaviour of elements situated nearer the centre of the Periodic Table. For example, as we saw earlier, iron tends to form two cations, Fe^{2+} and Fe^{3+}, yet iron is more than three elements away from the left-hand end of the Periodic Table. Elements nearer the centre of the Table often form compounds with partly ionic and partly covalent bonding, and such elements may have a range of apparent ionic charges depending on which compounds they occur in. Even sulphur, which is only two positions to the left of the noble gases, can form a range of partly covalent, partly ionic compounds with different apparent ionic charges, including not only the more obvious S^{2-}, but even S^{6+}, in which it has, in effect, *lost* six electrons, forming the stable configuration at the right-hand end of the *previous* row.

The chemical behaviour of individual elements is not only influenced by variables such as temperature and pressure, but also by which elements are present and available for interaction in the immediate vicinity. Some elements show recurrent affinities for each other in rocks and minerals from a wide range of geological settings. As we will see later, many ore minerals are compounds involving sulphur, a trace element in the crust as a whole. Certain elements tend to bond *preferentially* with sulphur if sulphur is present in sufficient concentrations; these include copper, zinc, lead and silver.

(a)

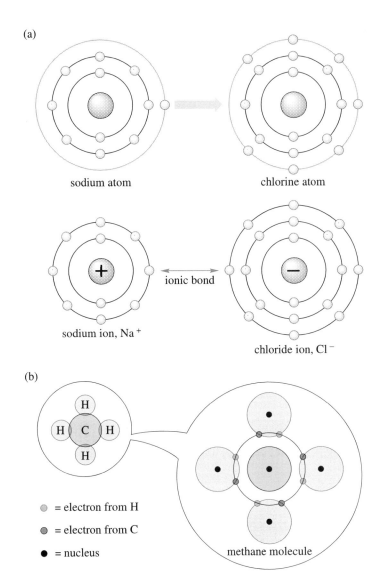

Figure 42 (a) The formation of sodium and chloride ions by transfer of an electron from the outermost shell of a sodium atom to the outermost shell of a chlorine atom, which results in a stable outer shell for each ion. (b) In methane, CH_4, a covalent compound, electrons belonging to carbon and hydrogen are shared.

Now listen to Audio Band 1: *Elements and the Periodic Table*, which reviews some of the points above and discusses how the chemical and physical properties of particular elements influence their uses.

Radioactivity

Although by definition all the atoms of a particular element have the same number of protons, the number of neutrons may differ, in which case each different version of the element is called an **isotope**. Lithium atoms, for instance, always have three protons in their nuclei, but can have either three or four neutrons (i.e. lithium has two isotopes). Most elements have several naturally occurring isotopes, and some have ten or more. The isotopes of some elements are **radioactive**: their nuclei are unstable, splitting up to give atoms with a different atomic number, thus forming different elements and emitting radiation in the process. Radioactivity is important in this Course for several reasons: radioactive decay can be harnessed as a major source of energy in nuclear power stations; the disposal of radioactive waste from nuclear power stations is an important environmental issue; radioactive decay is responsible for the internal heat of the Earth, and thus is the source of geothermal energy; and the natural decay of radioactive elements in minerals can be used to date rocks.

3.4 Mineral composition and structure

Every mineral has a chemical composition that varies within limits, and a specific internal structure, i.e. specific arrangement of atoms. All specimens of a particular mineral possess certain properties in common, regardless of when, where and how they were formed.

Under the right physical and chemical conditions, minerals can develop crystal forms that are among the most beautiful of natural objects (Plate 7). The flat external surfaces of crystals are called *crystal faces*, and their regular geometrical relationships to one another are determined by the arrangement of atoms within the mineral concerned. Although crystals of a given mineral may differ in size, and in the relative areas of crystal faces, the *angles* between the crystal faces are usually characteristic of that mineral. Different minerals that share similar internal structures have similar geometrical arrangements of crystal faces.

About 3500 minerals have been described and named, although relatively few are recognized as **rock-forming minerals**, i.e. minerals that are commonly found in rocks. Table 7 lists some of the better known and, in

The physical properties of minerals

René Haüy (1743–1822), a French mineralogist, accidentally dropped a large crystal of calcite and observed that it broke along three sets of planes only, with the result that all the fragments had a similar basic shape to each other (Figure 43). He then proceeded to break other calcite crystals in his own collection, and (presumably, after permission) many in the collections of his friends, and found that all the specimens broke in exactly the same manner. All the fragments, however small, had the shape of a rhombohedron (a three-dimensional form rather like a lop-sided cube), and to explain his observations, Haüy assumed that calcite is built of innumerable, almost infinitely small rhombohedra stacked alongside each other. His discovery remains an important advance in the understanding of crystals, and a pleasing example of how ideas in science can develop. Today we know that crystal shapes, and the shapes of the pieces of broken crystals, are related to the three-dimensional arrangement of atoms (or ions) in the solid.

All the physical properties of minerals reflect in some way their internal structure and chemical composition. Physical properties that often differ between one mineral and another, and which can be easily studied in crystal specimens larger than about a centimetre, include colour, degree of transparency, hardness, and density. Lustre, cleavage and fracture are also particularly useful when identifying minerals. *Lustre* is the way that light is reflected off a mineral's surface, e.g. the mineral may have a metallic sheen, or be vitreous like glass, or dull like chalk (but note that neither glass nor chalk are minerals as such). **Cleavage**

Figure 43 Broken crystals of calcite showing the characteristic rhombohedral shape of the fragments. Each fragment is bounded by similar sets of cleavage planes, none of which intersect at right-angles. The largest fragment is 2 cm long.

is the way that many minerals, like Haüy's calcite, tend to break along characteristic planes of weakness, e.g. they may split into thin sheets, rhombohedra or cubes. When a mineral breaks in a less regular way, the term **fracture** is used to describe the nature of the surface, e.g. like broken glass with a pattern of concentric ridges resembling the growth-lines of a shell. As with the arrangement of its crystal faces, the way that a mineral breaks is an indication of its internal structure. Minerals have many other different physical properties, including some that can only be observed with special equipment (such as an optical microscope or X-ray machine), and together they can be used to identify a mineral.

Table 7 The names and chemical formulae of some better known and, in most cases, more common minerals

1 Uncombined (native) elements	2 Simple ionic compounds	3 Simple polyanionic compounds	4 Silicates — mostly complex polyanionic compounds
gold Au silver Ag diamond C graphite C sulphur S	*Halides* halite NaCl sylvite KCl fluorite CaF_2 *Sulphides* galena PbS chalcopyrite $CuFeS_2$ pyrite FeS_2 *Oxides* rutile TiO_2 haematite Fe_2O_3 magnetite Fe_3O_4 ilmenite $FeTiO_3$ cassiterite SnO_2 wolframite $FeWO_4$ chromite $(Fe,Mg)Cr_2O_4$	*Carbonates* calcite $CaCO_3$ siderite $FeCO_3$ magnesite $MgCO_3$ dolomite $CaMg(CO_3)_2$ *Sulphates* gypsum $CaSO_4.2H_2O$ anhydrite $CaSO_4$ barite $BaSO_4$ *Hydroxides* goethite FeO.OH gibbsite $Al(OH)_3$ *Phosphates* apatite $Ca_5(PO_4)_3(F,Cl,OH)$	olivine $(Mg,Fe)_2SiO_4$ *Garnet group* pyrope $Mg_3Al_2(SiO_4)_3$ almandine $Fe_3Al_2(SiO_4)_3$ zircon $ZrSiO_4$ *Pyroxene group* augite $Ca(Mg,Fe)Si_2O_6$ enstatite $(Mg,Fe)SiO_3$ *Amphibole group* hornblende $Ca_2(Mg,Fe)_5Si_8O_{22}(OH)_2$ *Mica group* biotite $K(Fe,Mg)_3(AlSi_3O_{10})(OH)_2$ muscovite $KAl_2(AlSi_3O_{10})(OH)_2$ chlorite $(Mg,Fe,Al)_6(Si,Al)_4O_{10}(OH)_8$ *Clay minerals* kaolinite $Al_2Si_2O_5(OH)_4$ serpentine $Mg_6Si_4O_{10}(OH)_8$ *Feldspar group* orthoclase $KAlSi_3O_8$ albite $NaAlSi_3O_8$ anorthite $CaAl_2Si_2O_8$ quartz SiO_2

most cases, more common minerals, and their chemical formulae. (NB You don't need to learn all the mineral formulae.) The minerals are grouped into four main categories:

1 Uncombined (native) elements.

2 Simple ionic compounds which include the halides, sulphides, and oxides. These have compositions in which the anions consist of a single element (e.g. Cl^-, S^{2-}, O^{2-}). The structure of one mineral in this group, galena, and some galena crystals, are shown in Figure 44.

Figure 44 (a) The internal structure of galena (PbS) showing planes along which crystal faces, and between which cleavage planes, develop. (b) Crystals of galena, some broken to show the characteristic cleavage planes intersecting at right-angles. The largest specimen is 1 cm across.

(a)

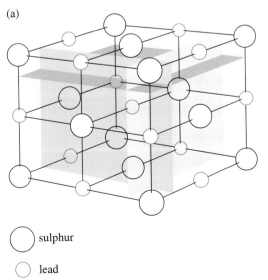

○ sulphur

○ lead

(b)

3 Minerals in which the anions are more complicated; they include the carbonates, sulphates, phosphates and hydroxides. In these simple polyanionic compounds, the cations often consist of a single element (e.g. Ca^{2+}, Ba^{2+}), but the anions are always more complex. They consist mainly of oxygen atoms which are covalently bonded, at least in part, to an atom of another element, with the whole anion having a net negative charge (e.g. CO_3^{2-}, SO_4^{2-}). Calcite, $CaCO_3$, is the main constituent of limestones, and is an important rock-forming mineral in the crust.

4 The **silicate** minerals, many of which are complex polyanionic compounds. About 95% of the Earth's crust is composed of silicates, reflecting the high abundance of silicon and oxygen in the crust. Most silicate minerals are complex structurally as well as chemically. Quartz is often regarded as a silicate, although it is actually a simple compound as far as its chemical formula is concerned. Quartz is the most common form of silica, i.e. silicon dioxide, SiO_2; rarer forms of silica occur at certain temperatures and pressures.

All silicates contain a basic 'building block' called the silicon–oxygen tetrahedron — a negatively charged unit of four oxygen atoms surrounding a silicon atom. In detail, this unit is a complex anion $(SiO_4)^{4-}$, in which four large oxygen ions (O^{2-}) are arranged to form a four-sided pyramid, called a tetrahedron, with a smaller silicon ion (Si^{4+}) fitted centrally into the cavity between them (Figure 45). Notice how the overall charge on the silicate anion is minus 4, because the four oxygens are each minus 2 (making their total minus 8) and the silicon is plus 4. Silicon is in the same vertical group in the Periodic Table as carbon, i.e. four columns away from the *left*-hand end. (In the carbonate anion, CO_3^{2-}, carbon is plus 4, with the oxygens each minus 2, making the total for the anion minus 2).

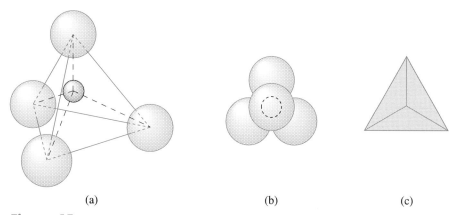

(a)   (b)   (c)

Figure 45 The silica tetrahedron. (a) Expanded view showing oxygen atoms at the corners of a tetrahedron and a small silicon atom at the centre. (b) A more realistic representation of the silica tetrahedron with the oxygen atoms touching. In this plan view the central silicon atom is hidden by the oxygen at the top of the tetrahedron. (c) The silica tetrahedron represented diagrammatically; the oxygen atoms have to be imagined as centred at the four points of the tetrahedron.

Although its formula is similar to other polyanions such as CO_3^{2-} and SO_4^{2-}, what makes the silicate anion so special is its ability to share oxygens covalently with other silicate anions, forming complex structures in which the silica tetrahedra take different arrangements. In the simplest combination, as in the mineral olivine, the oxygen ions of the tetrahedra form bonds with other elements, such as iron and magnesium. In most silicate minerals, however, oxygen ions are shared between adjacent tetrahedra, with the result that the tetrahedra form larger ionic units. The sharing of the oxygen ions by the silicon ions results in several fundamental configurations of tetrahedral groups: single chains, double chains, continuous two-dimensional sheets, and three-dimensional frameworks (Figure 46). These structures define several major groups of silicates: single chains — pyroxenes; double chains — amphiboles; sheets — micas, chlorite and clay minerals; and complex three-dimensional frameworks — feldspars and quartz.

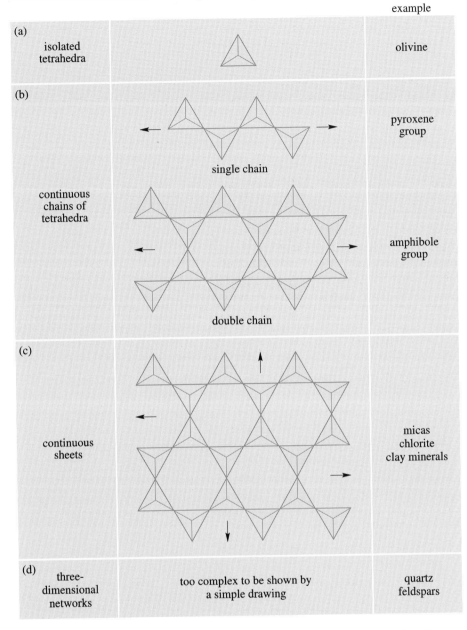

Figure 46 The main structural groups of silicate minerals shown by various arrangements of silica tetrahedra: (a) isolated tetrahedra; (b) continuous chains; (c) continuous sheets; and (d) three dimensional frameworks. The arrows adjacent to single chain, double chain, and sheet silicates indicate that these structures continue indefinitely in the directions shown.

As the mineral formulae in Table 7 show, the charges on what are, in effect, giant anion complexes are balanced by a combination of simple cations, mainly Na^+, K^+, Ca^{2+}, Mg^{2+}, Fe^{2+}, Fe^{3+} and Al^{3+}. Silicate minerals containing iron (*ferrum* in Latin) and magnesium are known collectively as **ferromagnesian minerals**; they tend to be dark in colour.

Question 21

Look at Table 7. Which of the following are ferromagnesian minerals: magnetite, pyrite, augite, hornblende, olivine, albite, biotite, chlorite?

Some minerals have chemical formulae such that they could be classified in more than one group. For instance, the bright green copper ore malachite has the formula $CuCO_3.Cu(OH)_2$, and is usually classified as a carbonate, although its formula shows that it could also be classified as a hydroxide, albeit a complex one.

● Write the name and formula of each of the following minerals into the appropriate place in Table 7: native copper, Cu; corundum, Al_2O_3; talc, $Mg_3Si_4O_{10}(OH)_2$; sphalerite, ZnS; celestine, $SrSO_4$.

○ Native copper, Cu, is a native element (first group); corundum, Al_2O_3 is an oxide (second group); talc, $Mg_3Si_4O_{10}(OH)_2$ is a silicate (fourth group); sphalerite, ZnS, is a sulphide (second group); celestine, $SrSO_4$ is a sulphate (third group).

Note that the term **ore mineral** may be applied to sought-after minerals from which metals may be obtained, irrespective of whether their concentration is sufficient for a rock they are in to be called an ore. For example, chalcopyrite is referred to as an ore mineral, wherever it occurs and in whatever amount. The term 'ore mineral' is not applied to minerals from which metals are not specifically extracted, such as fluorspar, common salt, mica and gypsum, even though all these compounds contain metals. These very important minerals are classified as **industrial minerals**: they either have useful properties in their own right (e.g. fluorspar is used as a flux; gypsum is used in plaster) *or* useful non-metallic elements can be extracted from them (e.g. fluorine from fluorspar; chlorine from common salt).

3.4.1 Ionic substitution

It is quite common for the ions of different elements to be able to occupy the same site in a crystal structure — the basis of a phenomenon called **ionic substitution**. The atoms and ions in crystalline compounds can be thought of as spheres of different sizes. Anions tend to be larger than cations; e.g. the common anions O^{2-}, Cl^-, and S^{2-} are all larger than Na^+, Ca^{2+}, Mg^{2+}, Al^{3+} and Si^{4+}. The more electrons an element loses to become a cation, the stronger the nucleus pulls in the remaining electrons. Most of the volume in a crystal tends to be occupied by anions, with cations fitting into the spaces between them. If two ions of different elements are of similar size (within about 10% of each other), and especially if they are also of similar charge, one can substitute for the other in a crystal structure. For example, the ions of magnesium and iron, Mg^{2+} and Fe^{2+}, have the same charge and are of similar size, so that one tends to replace the other fairly easily in lots of minerals. The overall balance of positive and negative charges in the whole structure must be maintained, however, so if the substituting ion has a different charge there has to be a balancing substitution elsewhere in the structure.

In addition to the ability of two or more ions to occupy a particular site, substitution may refer to the replacement of an existing ion already in a crystal by a different one — like a substitute footballer that comes on to the pitch to replace one that goes off. Just as the choice of footballer to go on the pitch at the start of a match (or later) might depend on the prevailing conditions (one player might be better on a wet pitch, or be more suited to play with a particular team combination or to tackle specific opponents), so the ion that fills a site in the crystal (either originally or later, by replacement substitution), is likely to depend on the precise conditions of temperature, pressure, its abundance and that of competing ions, and so on.

Substitution is shown by Mg and Fe in the mineral olivine. The formula of olivine is given in Table 7 as $(Mg,Fe)_2SiO_4$, i.e. with a comma between the two cations, because any natural olivine can have a composition that lies somewhere between two extremes. At one extreme is Mg-olivine (Mg_2SiO_4), and at the other is Fe-olivine (Fe_2SiO_4). A mineral like olivine that has a range of compositions between certain limits is said to show **solid solution**. (*Note:* Don't mistake this for a feature of liquids just because the term contains the word 'solution'.) A mineral displaying solid solution has the same crystal structure, whatever its precise chemical composition. The actual composition of an olivine crystal is determined to a major extent by temperature, which affects the size of the spaces into which the ions have to fit. Roughly speaking, the higher the temperature at which olivine crystallizes, the richer in magnesium it will be, even if both iron and magnesium are available in the surrounding magma.

In contrast to major elements, trace elements are only rarely present in sufficient quantities to form their own minerals. Economically important minerals in which a trace element is a principal component include tin in cassiterite (SnO_2), lead in galena (PbS), and fluorine in fluorite (CaF_2). In most geological circumstances, however, trace elements need to 'find' sites in the common rock-forming minerals normally occupied by more abundant elements. The trace elements usually have a different size and/or electrical charge, so they cannot enter rock-forming minerals in large amounts.

Some trace elements that substitute for major elements are listed below. The radius of each ion is given in picometres in brackets (1 pm = 10^{-12} m).

Ni^{2+} (77 pm) can replace Mg^{2+} (80 pm) (e.g. in olivine)

Ba^{2+} (144 pm) can replace K^+ (146 pm) (e.g. in feldspars)

Sr^{2+} (121 pm) can replace Ca^{2+} (108 pm) (e.g. in feldspars)

Ionic substitution is similarly important in understanding the effects of chemical pollution caused by human activities. The distance that chemical pollutants released into the environment will travel may be determined by the possibilities for substitution. The more readily pollutants become trapped by substitution in the materials they pass over, the shorter the distance they will spread.

3.5   Rocks and the rock cycle

In Sections 3.1 and 3.2 we briefly discussed the nature of rocks and minerals, and the overall structure of the Earth. In Sections 3.3 and 3.4 we looked at some basic chemical aspects of physical resources, especially the chemical properties of elements and compounds, and the composition and structure of naturally occurring minerals. In this Section we will consider in more detail the relationships between the three major rock types, which will enable us eventually to place physical resources in a wider geological context.

If you haven't done geology before, or would welcome a refresher, now would be a good time to have a first look at Video Band 3: Resource Geology. This will help you visualize some of the points in this Section. The main discussion and questions on the programme, which may require a second viewing, follow in Section 3.5.4.

3.5.1   Igneous rocks

Let's think more about the mineral grains — the crystals — in igneous rocks. Unless the freezing of magma occurs very quickly, crystals will develop and give a rock a characteristic igneous texture of interlocking and intergrown mineral grains, usually in random orientations. Generally speaking, the longer that the magma has taken to cool, the larger the crystals, and an igneous rock is described as coarse-grained if the crystals are over 2 mm across. In the case of granite, the crystals are often one or two centimetres long, but occasionally crystals can grow to be over a metre.

Figure 47 Obsidian. Width of specimen is 9 cm.

○ Look at the piece of black or very dark brown igneous rock called obsidian in Figure 47. From its appearance, would you expect it to have the same general chemical composition (i.e. similar percentages of different elements) as the granite in Plate 1?

○ The appearance of the two is so dissimilar that you would probably expect them to be of different composition. But, in fact, the percentages of the various elements in both the granite and the obsidian are very similar.

○ Can you suggest a simple explanation for the difference in appearance between the granite and the obsidian?

○ The obsidian has formed by very rapid cooling of magma. Had it cooled much more slowly, crystals like those in the granite would have formed.

○ In what kind of circumstances might magma cool very quickly?

○ When magma reaches the Earth's surface and is erupted onto relatively cold ground or into water. The lava then has no time to develop any large crystals; it may have microscopic crystals, or even none at all, as in the case of obsidian.

If a few crystals have already grown to a significant size before a magma is rapidly chilled, the resulting rock may have a few large crystals — *phenocrysts* — surrounded by tiny crystals or apparently no crystals at all; such a rock is called a porphyry and is said to have **porphyritic** texture (Figure 48 and Plate 1).

○ What very common manufactured material found in your home does the obsidian resemble most in general appearance?

○ Glass. Unless it's in very thin slivers, obsidian is not transparent like window glass, but is usually black or dark brown, like some bottles.

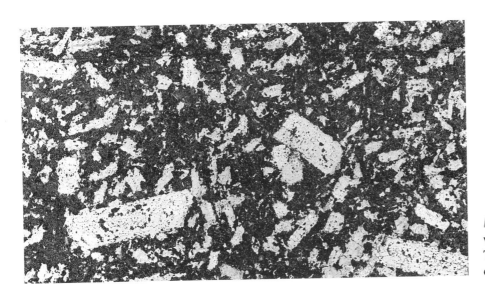

Figure 48   An igneous rock with porphyritic texture. The largest phenocryst on this cut surface is 7 cm long.

Like ordinary synthetic glass, volcanic glasses such as obsidian are supercooled liquids — frozen in physical circumstances that did not allow the chemical elements to sort themselves out into discrete crystals of different minerals. Eventually, however, after many years, glasses, whether synthetic or natural, may start to form spots or cloudy patches of tiny crystals. You probably noticed that the obsidian also looks rather like the broken piece of flint in Figure 15, having the same curved surfaces and no visible crystals. Indeed it is their close similarities in texture, splitting characteristics, and hardness that allowed both flint and volcanic glass (Figure 6) to be worked into useful implements in Prehistoric times.

You may well have got some igneous rock in your bathroom or kitchen. Pumice, which is used as an abrasive for removing skin that is hard or ink-stained, was once molten rock, and is similar in bulk composition to obsidian and granite. If you can, go and have a look at some. A piece is shown in Figure 49. Like obsidian, pumice has solidified on the Earth's surface: the difference is that at the moment it froze it was very frothy because a large amount of gas had been released from the magma. There are countless tiny holes in it — frozen bubbles — which is why its density is unusually low for a rock. Pumice, therefore, is a sort of frozen froth — mostly volcanic glass, but among the pale grey or white glass you may see small shiny crystals or dark fragments of other rock debris picked up during the eruption. You may also see thin streaks of slightly different colours, which are lava fragments streaked out during rapid flow of the magma.

Figure 49   A typical piece of carved pumice as bought in a chemists. Length 8 cm.

Figure 50 (a) Solidified surface of a basalt lava flow. (b) An exposure of granite.

Igneous rocks can also be classified on the basis of *where* they crystallized, irrespective of their chemical composition. **Extrusive** igneous rocks are those that have been extruded onto the surface of the Earth; another name for them is **volcanic** rocks. Volcanic rocks include ashes and other material ejected from volcanoes, as well as solidified lava flows (Figure 50a). Rocks that have crystallized *beneath* the surface are known as **intrusive** rocks, and the body of igneous rock itself is called an **intrusion**. **Plutonic** rocks have crystallized deep beneath the surface, and often form large intrusions many cubic kilometres in volume; they are exposed (Figure 50b) only after perhaps 5 or even 10 kilometres of overlying rocks have been removed by erosion. Plutonic rocks often make good decorative building stones.

Less extensive intrusions include dykes and sills which have generally cooled higher in the crust at shallower depths. **Dykes** are sheet-like intrusions that *cut across* pre-existing rocks, and are often steeply dipping, whereas **sills** are sheet-like bodies that have been intruded *between* layers or other planar structures of pre-existing rocks. A *magma chamber* is an underground 'reservoir' of magma from which dykes and sills may be intruded, and from which material may be supplied to volcanoes. If magma solidifies within a magma chamber, it will form an intrusive igneous rock. The relationships between these different types of igneous activity are summarized in Figure 51.

Figure 51 Block diagram illustrating various intrusive and extrusive igneous features.

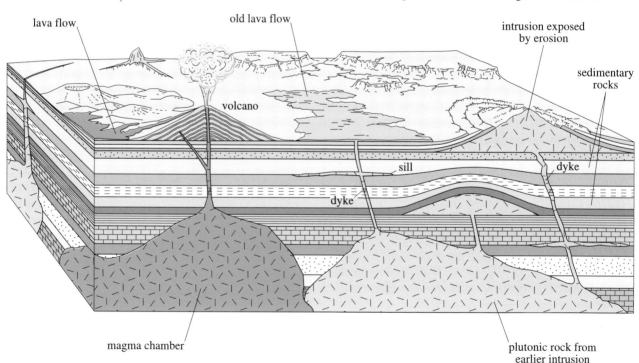

Like obsidian, some other igneous rocks lack a texture of interlocking, inter-grown crystals. Some volcanic eruptions break up and pulverize pre-existing rock, and fire-fountains spray showers of lava droplets into the air. The resulting fragments and ash accumulate in layers around the volcano, and form *pyroclastic* rocks, i.e. they are fragmental rocks which look like sediments but are in fact volcanic igneous rocks. Fast-moving flows of hot pyroclastic material are among the most lethal of volcanic hazards. During the eruption of Vesuvius in 79 AD, many of the citizens of Pompeii that had survived falling ash or noxious gases were overcome by flows of pyroclastic material.

The crystalline nature of most igneous rocks and their resulting toughness and resistance to weathering and erosion have made them much prized through the millennia for constructional and ornamental purposes, and in the case of volcanic glass, for tools and weapons. In addition, many ore deposits are found in association with igneous rocks.

3.5.2 Sedimentary rocks

Rocks of any type exposed at the Earth's surface are attacked and decomposed by the agents of physical and chemical decay, and the breakdown products are transported by water, wind or ice to be deposited elsewhere as sediment. Sedimentary rocks originate from the deposition of sediment that settles to the Earth's surface under gravity. With time, accumulations of sediment may eventually become compacted into roughly horizontal layers of sedimentary rock (Figure 52). The layers are called **beds** or **strata**, and the rocks are said to be *bedded* or *stratified*; *bedding planes* separate the layers.

Figure 52 Horizontally layered sedimentary rocks. Individual strata or beds (i.e. the layers) are separated by bedding planes. The beds are of harder (lighter) limestone, alternating with softer (darker) shales.

Weathering is the breakdown of rocks at the Earth's surface, whereas **erosion** is the mechanical removal of material, by the action of water, wind or ice. The two main types of weathering are physical weathering and chemical weathering. **Physical weathering** is the mechanical breakdown of rocks into smaller fragments, including individual mineral grains. The products of **chemical weathering** (the breakdown of rocks by chemical action, especially by water and aqueous solutions) include clays (see below) and soluble ions, especially Na^+, K^+, Ca^{2+}, Mg^{2+}, SO_4^{2-}, HCO_3^- and Cl^-, which are carried away in solution. Some of these soluble ions may become part of the bodies of organisms; some may be precipitated as salts by evaporation of water to form **evaporite** deposits, which are a source of common salt (halite, NaCl), anhydrite, gypsum ($CaSO_4.2H_2O$), and other valuable compounds.

○ Would you expect chemical weathering to be faster in dry, arctic regions or in wet, tropical regions?

○ Chemical weathering is much faster in wet, tropical regions, where both water and relatively high temperatures speed up the chemical reactions involved.

About 75% of all sedimentary rocks are fragmental or **clastic**. ('Clastic' comes from a Greek word meaning 'broken'; pyroclastic, for example, means 'broken by fire'.) Clastic sediments tend to be largely composed of two types of mineral: quartz — which is very resistant to chemical attack — and **clay minerals**. Clays are formed during the chemical weathering of a wide range of minerals present in igneous and metamorphic rocks. Minerals such as feldspars, micas, pyroxenes and amphiboles (Table 7) are chemically unstable in conditions that prevail at the Earth's surface and can break down by chemical reactions to form clays, especially in the presence of water. There are many clay minerals, and they all have very small crystals with a flat, sheet-like internal structure similar to that of the micas.

Clastic sedimentary rocks (and clastic sediments) can be classified according to the size of their fragments, which may range from boulders, down through cobbles, pebbles (as in conglomerate, Figure 34b), and granules, to sand, silt and clay. **Sandstones** (originally loose sand), tend to be composed mainly of quartz grains (Figure 53a); **siltstones** (originally loose silt) are composed mainly of fine-grained quartz and clay minerals; and **mudstones** are composed mainly of fine clay minerals. **Shales** are fine-grained rocks (usually of silt and clay) that split easily into thin layers (Figure 53b).

○ Sediments which have been transported by currents are generally deposited when the currents wane. Would you expect the finest grained sediments or the coarsest grained sediments to be deposited when a current starts to wane, and why?

○ Generally speaking, the faster the current, whether of water or air, the larger the particles it can carry. As soon as the current wanes, the largest and heaviest materials are deposited. Some large particles may not be picked up, but rolled or bounced along over the surface of, say, a river bed. The finest material is carried the furthest, perhaps beyond the mouth of a river and out to sea.

Figure 53 (a) Sandstone, to show its fragmental texture of (mainly) quartz grains. (b) Shale, to show the way in which it splits easily into thin beds because of the minute platy flakes of clay minerals that lie almost parallel to the bedding.

(a)

(b)

In addition to quartz, some sandstones and siltstones contain significant amounts of clays, feldspar, mica and other minerals, the relative proportions of which are determined by factors such as the composition of the parent rocks, the intensity of weathering and the distance over which the sediment is transported. The mineral composition of clastic sediments is influenced by the degree of **sorting**; i.e. the extent to which minerals of different grain size are separated from one another during transport. A well-sorted sediment contains grains of similar size: the hardness and density of the grains are often similar too. Sorting may enable certain minerals to accumulate in economic concentrations (see also Section 3.6).

Question 22

Imagine a mountain of granite from which sediment is being derived by weathering and erosion. Would you expect the ratio of feldspars and micas to clay minerals to increase or decrease the further away that the sediment is transported?

Clastic sediments become *lithified* (i.e. turned into rock) by the combined processes of compaction and **cementation**. Newly deposited sediments are full of water in the pores between the grains, and compaction by the weight of overlying sediments squeezes out the water. The increase of temperature with depth of burial often allows the water to dissolve some of the sediment, adding to any material already in solution. As water moves through the

Limestones

Limestones originate primarily not from the mechanical break-up and transport of rock fragments, but by direct precipitation of carbonate minerals from water or by the growth processes of organisms. Many species of marine animals and plants, including microscopic plankton, extract dissolved calcium ions and bicarbonate (also called hydrogencarbonate) ions (HCO_3^-) from seawater to make shells and skeletons of calcium carbonate ($CaCO_3$). **Plankton** are water-borne organisms that float or swim weakly, generally drifting with currents. The term includes both phytoplankton (plants, mainly microscopic algae) and zooplankton (animals, mostly microscopic).

Two calcium carbonate minerals are commonly secreted by calcareous organisms — calcite and aragonite. These minerals have the same chemical composition but different crystal structures: the less stable form, aragonite, converts to calcite over very long periods. When calcareous organisms die, their remains usually accumulate on the sea floor and become lithified to form limestones. If the water is very deep, however, dead calcareous plankton may partially dissolve before they reach the bottom.

Chalk is a well-known type of limestone that outcrops in southern England and elsewhere; it is almost pure calcite, and consists mostly of minute shells of countless billions of phytoplankton. Limestones are,

however, rarely so pure; usually some sand, silt or mud is deposited too. Limestones with abundant fossils of large organisms such as reef-building corals and shelly molluscs (e.g. snails, cockles, ammonites) can form attractive ornamental stones (Figure 54). Limestones are essential for the manufacture of cement, and are useful in countless other ways, such as the production of lime for the chemicals industry. Some planktonic organisms and sponges make use of the small amounts of silica (SiO_2) dissolved in seawater to form their skeletons, and when their concentrated remains are lithified, or dissolved and reprecipitated, the resulting hard rock is called *chert*, or *flint* when found in Chalk (see Section 1.4).

Figure 54 Fossiliferous limestone used for ornamental purposes. The sides of the cube are 6 cm long.

compacting sediment, dissolved material may be precipitated as cements, which in effect glue the grains together, filling up the spaces between them. Typical cements are silica (SiO_2) or calcium carbonate ($CaCO_3$). Whether or not a sedimentary rock is *porous* (having voids) or *permeable* (allowing fluids — i.e. liquids or gases — to move through it) is of immense importance to the oil, gas, and water extraction industries. The ability of sedimentary rocks to transmit a fluid, i.e. their permeability, is dependent not only on the size of the pore spaces but how well they are connected together: there may be a lot of pores but if they are sealed off (i.e. unconnected), a fluid will not be able to travel through them.

Sedimentary rocks are an immensely important source of building materials (Block 2), energy resources in fossil fuels (Block 4), and a variety of ore deposits (Block 5).

3.5.3 Metamorphic rocks

Metamorphic rocks are rocks of any type that have been altered mineralogically, *in the solid state*, by heat and/or pressure, possibly accompanied by the chemical activity of pore fluids.

When magmas rise into the crust and solidify below the surface they may be at temperatures well above 1000 °C. Hot bodies of magma may be in contact with cooler rocks for considerable amounts of time — perhaps hundreds of thousands of years — before they solidify completely. During this time they 'bake' the cooler rocks around them: the larger the igneous body, the greater the extent of baking, though rarely do the effects extend more than a few kilometres.

Another, more important process — **regional metamorphism** — affects huge volumes of rock, extending over tens of thousands of cubic kilometres. During plate collisions that form mountain belts such as the Alps and Himalayas, thickening of the crust causes huge volumes of sedimentary and igneous rocks to be buried to considerable depths and subjected to enormous pressures and high temperatures. Such rocks respond by deforming into huge and complex folds (Figure 55), and by recrystallizing into new minerals. Because of the enormous stresses involved, metamorphic rocks commonly show an alignment of platy and rod-like minerals, especially micas and amphiboles (Table 7). They are commonly banded too, with alternating layers of light and dark minerals.

Slate, schist and gneiss (pronounced 'nice') are the most common kinds of regionally metamorphosed rocks. **Slate** is a fine-grained metamorphic rock

Figure 55 Spectacularly folded metamorphic rocks in the Alps.

Figure 56 A piece of roofing slate, retaining evidence of original sedimentary bedding. The cleavage planes in this metamorphic rock are at a very different angle from the original bedding.

derived from fine-grained sediments. The sedimentary clay minerals have mostly changed into chlorite and micas, which become aligned in response to intense pressure applied during mountain-building periods in directions very different from that which compacted the original sediments. Consequently, slates usually split along planes quite different from the original sedimentary bedding planes (Figure 56). These new splitting planes in a metamorphic rock are called **cleavage** planes (not to be confused with the cleavage of a mineral crystal). More intense regional metamorphism at higher pressures and temperatures takes a rock beyond the stage of slate, giving **schist** (Figure 34c), a coarser grained rock with obvious alignment of minerals. Highly reflective flakes of mica are characteristic of schist, and unlike in slate, it is usually possible to see crystals of minerals like quartz and feldspar with the naked eye. Yet more intense metamorphism, at even higher pressures and temperatures, produces **gneiss** (Plate 6), in which the segregation of light and dark minerals into alternating bands is very obvious.

The metamorphism of limestone produces **marble** (Plate 5), which is made up mainly of recrystallized, interlocking crystals of calcite (Figure 57). Fossiliferous (sedimentary) limestones are often referred to as 'marbles' by quarry workers and those in the building trade. Geologists, however, restrict the term marble to metamorphic rocks composed primarily of calcite. The

0.5 mm

Figure 57 A thin-section of marble under the microscope showing recrystallized, interlocking calcite crystals.

regional metamorphism of quartz-rich sandstone produces **quartzite**, which consists of interlocking crystals of quartz. Both marble and quartzite tend not to show much alignment of their main constituent minerals, compared with rocks like schist and gneiss, because calcite and quartz do not form flat, sheet-like crystals.

The rearrangement of elements into new minerals during metamorphism is a process which happens in the solid state and *not* by crystallization from molten magma. Recrystallization in the solid state is not easy to envisage, but atoms and ions move from one site to another within and between crystals until they come to occupy the most stable overall configuration in new physical and chemical conditions. A similar process in fact happens every day in the manufacture of ceramic products and bricks. Bricks, for instance, may be thought of as 'artificial' metamorphic rocks, formed by heating clay at temperatures that are high enough for the constituent clay minerals to be metamorphosed into hard and brittle products composed of complex new silicates.

Metamorphism may also involve the interaction of minerals with fluids such as hot water, steam and carbon dioxide gas, which are powerful solvents at high pressures and temperatures. These fluids can add elements to rocks or remove elements from them, although usually in only small amounts.

3.5.4 Rocks and minerals—a recap

Geologists classify rocks into three general classes, according to how they were formed. Igneous rocks are formed from the molten state; sedimentary rocks are deposited at the Earth's surface from water, air, or ice; and metamorphic rocks are rocks of any origin that have been subsequently transformed (metamorphosed) by heat and/or pressure, often several kilometres down in the crust, possibly accompanied by chemical activity.

Rocks are generally either crystalline, i.e. formed of interlocking and intergrown mineral crystals, or fragmental, i.e. formed of mineral or rock fragments compacted and cemented together by later mineral growth. Crystalline rocks usually break along planes of weakness that pass through the interlocking crystals rather than between them. Fragmental rocks tend to break *between* the individual fragments or grains, rather than across them, a distinction illustrated in Figure 58. Most igneous and metamorphic rocks are crystalline, whereas most sedimentary rocks are fragmental. A few sedimentary rocks, including some limestones and evaporites, are more or less completely crystalline; most, however, possess fragmental (clastic) textures, though a microscope may be needed to detect fragments in very

(a)

(b)

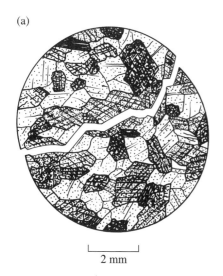

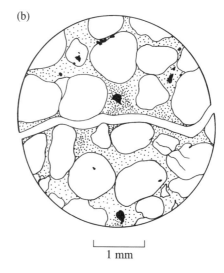

2 mm

1 mm

Figure 58 (a) Crystalline rock, showing how fracturing occurs mainly within the crystals, along their planes of weakness (mineral cleavage planes). (b) Fragmental rock, showing how fracturing normally occurs between the particles, along grain boundaries.

Folds, faults, joints and bedding planes

Rocks of any kind can be affected by tectonic movements within the crust and they respond by folding and faulting. Compressive forces cause folding, just like the folds you can get in a tablecloth pushed across a table. All sorts of **folds** may, however, occur in rocks, and they range from barely perceptible flexures to highly complicated structures, from the microscopic scale to features many kilometres across. Folds and faults are most easily detected in rocks that contain layers. Not all forces in the crust, though, are relieved by folding; rocks may also break in a brittle fashion. When this happens, bodies of rock move past one another along roughly planar surfaces called **faults**. Folds, rather than faults, tend to occur if rocks are deeply buried and heated up, causing them to behave in a more plastic fashion. **Joints**, in contrast to faults, are cracks — planar fractures — in rocks across which there has been *no* appreciable relative movement. Joints can occur in any type of rock. In sedimentary rocks, joints are usually perpendicular to bedding, and they often form two or three intersecting sets, with each set being a series of joints fairly evenly spaced and roughly parallel with each other. Joints are important when selecting stone for building or ornamental purposes. The study of geological structures such as folds, faults and joints, and their origins, is a major part of *structural geology*.

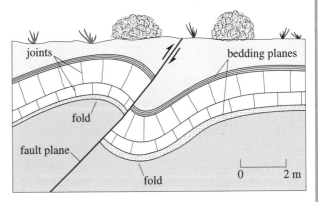

Figure 59   A section through strata, showing the distinction between folds, faults, joints and bedding planes.

fine-grained sediments. Most metamorphic rocks can be distinguished from most igneous rocks because they show a characteristic directional 'fabric' of banding or alignment of minerals. The presence of fossils usually indicates a sedimentary rock, though occasionally evidence of ancient life is still visible in metamorphic rocks such as marbles.

Look again at Table 7. Some generalizations can be made about the occurrence of some of the commonest minerals. Quartz is found in many igneous, sedimentary and metamorphic rocks. Nearly all the other silicates listed in Table 7 occur in various proportions in different igneous rocks. Chlorite and kaolinite occur in igneous rocks only where the original minerals have been chemically altered. Quartz and clay minerals are the main constituents of clastic sedimentary rocks, along with smaller amounts of mica, feldspars and other minerals derived from parent rocks. Calcite often occurs in sedimentary rocks, especially limestones, and is the dominant mineral in marbles. Metamorphic rocks formed by the recrystallization of clastic sediments typically consist of quartz, micas, and feldspars, possibly along with chlorite, amphiboles or garnets (see Table 7).

3.5.5   The rock cycle

Rocks are continually being formed and destroyed by geological processes which may be viewed within a large scale framework known as the **rock cycle** (Figure 60). Let's start with igneous rocks. Magma is less dense than solid rock, and tends to rise towards the Earth's surface until the temperature is low enough for it to crystallize. If igneous rocks (or any others) reach the surface they will then be broken down by weathering and erosion, and the soluble and insoluble debris will eventually accumulate elsewhere as sedimentary rocks. When igneous and sedimentary rocks are involved in powerful earth movements, especially the compressive forces associated with mountain building, they become buried and transformed into metamorphic rocks.

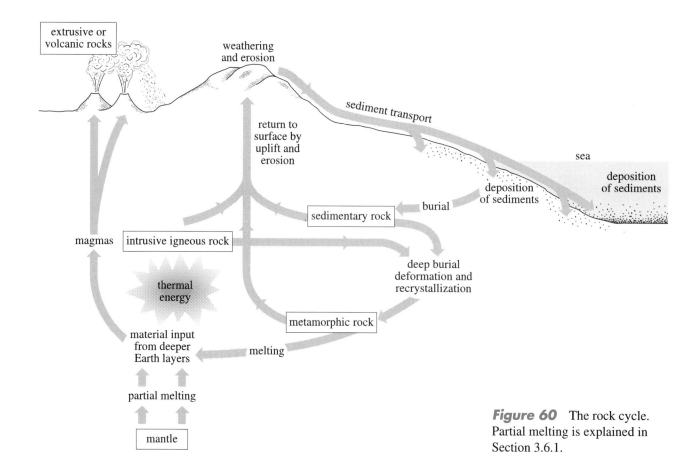

Figure 60 The rock cycle. Partial melting is explained in Section 3.6.1.

If metamorphic rocks are subjected to sufficiently high temperatures they will begin to melt, forming new magmas. Rocks of any origin in contact with hot magma may be metamorphosed. Some rocks, including a few sedimentary rocks, in contact with the intense heat of magmas may even melt directly, forming new magma which may cool to produce an igneous rock. In these ways material is continually, albeit slowly, moved around the rock cycle. In fact, given suitable geological conditions, any igneous, sedimentary or metamorphic rock can be melted to form an igneous rock, eroded to form a sedimentary rock, or metamorphosed to form a metamorphic rock.

Question 23

Match the following possibilities in the rock cycle (a) to (d) with the appropriate description of the process in (i) to (iv).

(a) a pyroclastic rock becoming a gneiss;

(b) a schist becoming a shale;

(c) a slate becoming a granite;

(d) a schist becoming a gneiss.

(i) a sedimentary process converting a metamorphic rock into a sediment;

(ii) a metamorphic process converting one metamorphic rock into another metamorphic rock;

(iii) an igneous process converting a metamorphic rock into an igneous rock;

(iv) a metamorphic process converting an igneous rock into a metamorphic rock.

We shall quite often return to the idea of cycles, and at this stage it is worth emphasizing a number of general points:

1   Natural cycles happen on all sorts of scales, involving many different materials.

2   Energy is required to move material around a cycle.

3   The rate at which material moves around cycles varies considerably, even within a single cycle. In fact, cycles of various kinds affect our use of resources in everyday life: those involving the home include the recycling of glass, paper, plastics and metal cans.

Another important cycle which interacts with the rock cycle is illustrated in Figure 61. This is the **water cycle** (also called the *hydrological cycle*) which represents the movement and availability of water. Water evaporates from the surface of the Earth, condenses to form clouds, and falls back to the Earth as rain, hail or snow. On land some of it is stored in lakes and as groundwater, and some is quickly transported back via rivers to the oceans as surface runoff. Water moves around different parts of the water cycle at different rates. Thus a drop of water falling into the sea remains there, on average, for about 4000 years, whereas a droplet of water in the atmosphere remains there, on average, for only about 11 days before falling as rain or snow. The driving source of energy for the water cycle is heat from the sun.

How does the water cycle interact with the rock cycle?

The water cycle interacts with the rock cycle most obviously in the weathering and erosion of rocks, and in the transport of material to the oceans (Figures 60 and 61).

An intriguing consequence of the existence of many complicated cycles on and within the Earth means that individual atoms may, over millions of years, form part of a huge variety of different substances — solids, liquids and gases of all sorts of chemical composition. Whether atoms are part of something inorganic or organic can readily change; a sodium atom in salt sprinkled on food today might be part of a nerve fibre tomorrow. And most of the individual atoms in your body are not the same as the ones there a few years ago; the body constantly rebuilds cells. The average period which an individual atom spends in your body varies somewhat from element to element, depending on the type of tissue containing it. For example, on average, a hydrogen atom spends 10 days in your body, and an oxygen atom

Figure 61   The water cycle (also called the hydrological cycle).

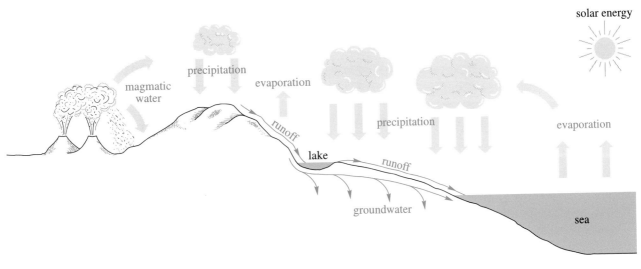

about 8 days. By contrast, calcium atoms, of which 99% are found in the skeleton, spend an average of about 11 years in your body, and a similar period is spent by the atoms of other metals absorbed into bone, like strontium, bismuth, lead and even the dangerously radioactive plutonium. These examples illustrate a useful general concept, called **residence time**, that may be applied to all sorts of geological phenomena, such as the average time that a water molecule spends in the atmosphere before falling to the ground as rain or snow (11 days), or the average time a copper ion carried to the sea by a river remains dissolved in the ocean before being precipitated in a solid mineral (30 000 years).

Activity 5

You can use the concept of residence time in your own home. Consider a few items such as a plastic bottle of fruit juice, a can of soft drink, and a bottle of washing-up liquid. How long, on average, do they stay in your possession between their purchase and going out to the refuse or recycling bin?

This would be a suitable time to watch, or watch again, Video Band 3: *Resource Geology*. Before you do, read through the following introduction and notes which provide a context for the programme. After watching, test your understanding of some of the most important points by answering Questions 24 and 25 (which will later serve as a summary). It will probably help you to read through the questions quickly and have them fresh in your mind before viewing the film.

Question 24

The following minerals (a) to (f) are mentioned in the film. Match them with their correct chemical formula chosen from (i) to (vi). (All six minerals are listed in Table 7.)

(a) pyrite; (b) gypsum; (c) anhydrite; (d) haematite; (e) galena; (f) barite.

(i) Fe_2O_3; (ii) $CaSO_4$; (iii) $BaSO_4$; (iv) $CaSO_4.2H_2O$; (v) FeS_2; (vi) PbS.

Question 25

Only four of the following thirteen items (a) to (m) are *in*correct. Which four are they, and why are they wrong?

(a) The plutonic rock granite contains a variety of trace elements, including some industrially useful metals, but their grade is usually far too low to permit economic extraction. The Shap granite is quarried for its bulk physical properties.

(b) The chemical composition of granite is not very different from that of the (upper) continental crust as a whole. The main minerals in the Shap granite are feldspar, quartz, and mica.

(c) The mineralization in the joints of the Shap granite originated when very hot and reactive watery fluids passed along joints in the granite while the granite was virtually solid but still very hot. The fluids altered the granite on either side of the joints, and dissolved various elements, including trace elements, out of the rock. As the fluids cooled, they precipitated some of the elements on joint planes as new minerals.

Video Band 3   Resource Geology

Speaker

John Wright   The Open University

The main aims of Video Band 3, which was made in 1983, are:

(a) To show how useful minerals and chemical elements can be concentrated to economic grades by natural processes in different parts of the rock cycle;

(b) To show that there are some predictable associations between different kinds of rocks and mineral deposits, but that even if the geological environment *is* favourable, concentration processes may not have reached the necessary grades for economic extraction.

(c) To help you become more familiar with the nature and appearance of some common types of rocks and minerals and a variety of geological features.

Seven localities in and around the Lake District are visited, at most of which you will see evidence of geological processes leading to the concentration of chemical elements to economic grades. They are:

1   Shap granite quarry.

2   Carrock Fell tungsten mine.

These demonstrate concentration processes related to the igneous part of the rock cycle.

3   Cliffs within a coal-bearing sequence, Whitehaven.

4   Kirkby Thore anhydrite and gypsum mine, near Appleby.

These demonstrate concentration processes associated with the formation of sedimentary rocks.

5   Egremont haematite mine.

6   Silverband barite and galena mine, Cross Fell.

These demonstrate concentration processes occurring in sedimentary rocks long after their formation.

7   Burlington slate quarry.

This demonstrates processes related to the metamorphic part of the rock cycle.

There is no need to be aware of the relative geographical position of the localities; they are fairly close to each other because it made the filming easier.

The following items or words, mentioned in the programme, need explanation:

Groundmass   The finer grained material of igneous rocks in which larger crystals are enclosed.

Nodules   Hard lumps in sedimentary rocks formed by the precipitation of minerals around a centre. They are often ovoid in shape, and are alternatively called concretions.

As mentioned in the programme, the veins in the Carrock Fell tungsten mine contain the ore minerals wolframite ($FeWO_4$) (Table 7) and scheelite ($CaWO_4$), as well as small amounts of arsenopyrite ($FeAsS$). (You are not expected to remember these last two minerals.)

(d) The 1% of tungsten present in the vein minerals of the tungsten mine represents a concentration factor of over a thousand times its average crustal abundance. By contrast, a grade of 60% iron in the haematite mine represents a concentration factor of only about 10.

(e) In weathered Shap granite, the quartz has decomposed to clay minerals, and of the main minerals, only feldspars and micas are chemically resistant.

(f) Only non-biological processes can concentrate elements in the rock cycle.

(g) The ironstone nodules in the coal-bearing sequence at Whitehaven are composed of iron carbonate; elsewhere, where they are thicker and more extensive, ironstones formed a valuable source of iron during the Industrial Revolution.

(h) In the absence of faulting or folding, sedimentary layers like those in the coal-bearing rocks at Whitehaven are laterally continuous, making it relatively easy to predict where they will occur under the Earth's surface.

(i) The evaporation of seawater in hot climatic conditions and the shell growth of marine organisms can each concentrate elements that are the soluble products of weathering.

(j) Under temperate climatic conditions, especially rainfall, the evaporite mineral anhydrite tends to become hydrated and transformed into gypsum, which is both softer and less dense.

(k) In the Silverband mine, the near-vertical veins of galena and barite do not pass upwards out of the shales because the mineralizing fluids were stopped by overlying limestones which are impermeable and relatively insoluble.

(l) The recrystallization of originally muddy sediments in response to pressure (and temperature), and the alignment of minute new mica crystals, gives a metamorphic rock with slaty cleavage.

(m) With high pressures and temperatures, some sedimentary rocks become metamorphosed into gneiss, a rock largely consisting of feldspar, mica and quartz, perhaps with some garnet. With even higher temperatures, gneiss can melt, giving granite.

3.6 Geological processes that concentrate physical resources

Having learned something about rocks and minerals, the structure of the Earth, and the rock cycle, we can look in more detail at how various geological processes can concentrate physical resources. As we saw in Section 1.2.1, many elements are distributed very sparsely in the crust. Except for common rocks quarried in their own right for building materials, for which chemical composition may not be relevant, it is only where natural processes have concentrated particular minerals that economically viable deposits exist. For example, as far as metals are concerned, a rock is only an ore if the metal has become concentrated in the rock to many times its average crustal abundance. Any understanding of the origin, nature and location of physical resources therefore requires an understanding of the processes of the rock cycle. Although the processes involved are not unusual, they may need to occur in particular combinations, and be carried locally to extremes, to form relatively rare concentrations — the 'currants in the bun'.

SADE—a scheme for understanding concentration processes

Economic deposits occur in a wide range of geological environments, but there are some universal aspects that make a useful checklist when considering any deposit. The formation of any economic deposit — using 'deposit' in the broadest sense for any natural concentration of a physical resource, whatever its position in the rock cycle — requires:

1   a SOURCE for the particular element, or elements, or other useful material;

2   an AGENT of transportation, such as magma, steam or running water, to scavenge and move the elements to the site of the deposit;

3   a reason why DEPOSITION or concentration took place where it did, such as a local change in the physical or chemical environment;

4   a form of ENERGY to drive the system, such as heat from a magma, solar energy, gravitational energy, and so on.

These aspects vary in interesting ways from one deposit to another. Although it is easier in some cases than others, attempting to apply this 'SADE' scheme will often help you to develop a better understanding of concentration processes.

3.6.1   Igneous processes

Look again at the porphyritic igneous rock illustrated in Figure 48. The larger crystals — the phenocrysts — crystallized first at greater depths where cooling was slower, and the much smaller groundmass crystals grew when cooling was faster, nearer the Earth's surface.

The phenocrysts are feldspars that have not only crystallized first but have a *different chemical composition* from the rest of the rock. How did this happen? When magmas cool slowly, the elements start sorting themselves out to form various minerals, but they do *not* crystallize all at once: different minerals crystallize at different temperatures. What happens to the magma? *As minerals crystallize, the composition of the remaining magma is changed.* This change is preserved if the minerals are separated from the liquid, especially when they have a different density, so that they sink or float (as shown in Figure 62a). This process is called **fractional crystallization**, because the initial magma has been separated into different fractions: the early-formed crystals and the remaining liquid, which are both compositionally different from the original magma. This is one way to form a variety of rock types from an initial parent magma, a more general phenomenon called **magmatic differentiation** (Figure 62).

The process of melting *to form* magmas is, in many ways, the reverse of crystallization *from* a magma. As a rock is heated up, different minerals melt at different temperatures, and so the composition of the first drop of liquid produced is very different from that of the rock as a whole. As more melting takes place, the composition of the liquid changes until, eventually, if all the

Figure 62   Magmatic differentiation. (a) In the first (chemical) stage of fractional crystallization, crystals form that are chemically different from the remaining magma; in the second (physical) stage, the crystals separate from the rest of the cooling liquid, and, being relatively dense in this case, sink to the floor of the magma chamber. (b) The liquid has migrated elsewhere, leaving only the earlier formed crystals behind.

(a)

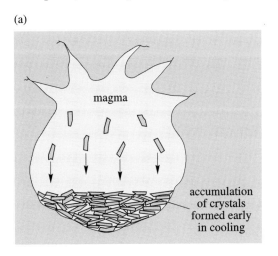

magma

accumulation of crystals formed early in cooling

(b)

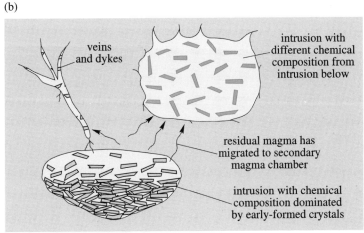

veins and dykes

intrusion with different chemical composition from intrusion below

residual magma has migrated to secondary magma chamber

intrusion with chemical composition dominated by early-formed crystals

rock were to be melted, the composition of the liquid would be the same as that of the initial source rock. However, the liquid or magma, being of relatively low density, is often able to escape and move upwards within the Earth before melting is complete. As a result, the magmas from which most igneous rocks crystallize are generated by **partial melting**, which is why their compositions are different from those of their source rocks.

Magmatic differentiation processes have two essential parts, one chemical and one physical. The first, chemical, part depends on establishing a *compositional difference* between different fractions of the magmatic system, e.g. between crystals and liquid. The second part is the *physical separation* that preserves the compositional differences between those fractions. Physical separation may involve the removal of a liquid from its partially molten source rock, or the separation of the crystals from a liquid during fractional crystallization, by crystal settling, for example, as in Figure 62(a).

The processes of partial melting followed by magmatic differentiation of the resulting liquid are responsible not only for the division of the outer Earth into mantle, oceanic crust and continental crust, but also for the generation of magmas that are the source of many valuable igneous ore deposits.

Table 8 shows typical chemical compositions for three common igneous rock types: peridotite, basalt and granite. The relative abundances of the major elements are conventionally expressed in terms of the percentage by weight of their *oxides*. It's crucial to realize that these chemical compositions do *not* indicate the presence of oxide *minerals*. For example, although the percentage of silica (SiO_2) in peridotite is 43.5% (Table 8), none of this is present as the mineral quartz. Peridotite has high FeO and MgO contents in its chemical analysis because it contains large amounts of the ferromagnesian minerals olivine and pyroxene, which also contain most of the 43.5% silica in the chemical analysis.

Table 8 Typical chemical compositions of some common rock types, expressed as weight percentages of the element oxides (see text for explanation)

Element	Peridotite	Basalt	Granite
SiO_2	43.5	50.8	72.3
TiO_2	0.8	2.0	0.3
Al_2O_3	4.0	14.1	14.0
Fe_2O_3	12.3	12.0	2.4
MnO	0.2	0.2	0.05
MgO	34.0	6.3	0.5
CaO	3.5	10.4	1.4
Na_2O	0.6	2.2	3.1
K_2O	0.2	0.8	5.1

Peridotite is the main rock type in the mantle, from which basaltic magma is generated by partial melting. Basalt, the main rock in oceanic crust, has more SiO_2 in its bulk composition and therefore contains minerals that, on average, have higher proportions of SiO_2, such as feldspar. Basalt also has lower MgO content than peridotite, and therefore has smaller amounts of magnesium-rich minerals. These relationships occur because ferromagnesian minerals like olivine tend to start crystallizing out from a cooling basaltic magma at higher temperatures, before other common igneous minerals such as feldspars. Conversely, during partial melting of peridotite mantle, ferromagnesian minerals tend to get left behind as residual minerals.

Granites have even higher SiO_2 contents and even lower MgO contents than basalts. Comparing it with basalt, would you expect a granite to contain larger or smaller amounts of (a) ferromagnesian minerals; (b) feldspars?

Granite has even smaller amounts of ferromagnesian minerals (in this case biotite rather than olivine and pyroxene) and even larger amounts of feldspar.

The amount of silica is actually so high in a granite that there are not enough metal cations to bond with all the silica tetrahedra to form complex silicates like feldspars and micas; as a result, the simple mineral quartz (SiO_2) crystallizes out, often late in the crystallization process. Quartz typically forms about 30% of granite, whereas in basalt there is usually not enough silica left over after crystallization of the complex silicates to form quartz itself; i.e. there are enough metal cations for virtually all the basalt to consist of complex silicates. Traditionally, igneous rocks can be described as fitting within a trend of increasing silica content, ranging from *ultrabasic* (with least silica) via *basic*, *intermediate*, to *acidic* (with most silica). Peridotite is thus a typical ultrabasic rock, basalt a typical basic rock, and granite a typical acidic rock.

As ferromagnesian minerals are dark in colour, most feldspars are white or pink, and most quartz is grey or transparent, the chemical change from basalt to granite is marked by a change from dark to light coloured rocks. A typical basalt has 40% dark ferromagnesian minerals, whereas a typical granite has 10% or less. The percentage of feldspar in a basalt is typically 60%, whereas in a typical granite the combined percentage of light coloured feldspar and quartz is about 90%.

Given what you now know about magmatic differentiation processes, how might a more siliceous magma approaching granitic composition be generated from (a) a basaltic magma; (b) solid basalt?

(a) During fractional crystallization of a basaltic magma, the early formation of ferromagnesian minerals leaves a liquid relatively *depleted* in iron and magnesium and *enriched* in silica; i.e. the *remaining* liquid becomes progressively more granitic.

(b) By partial melting of basalt; the ferromagnesian minerals remain solid because they have the highest melting points, whereas minerals like feldspar melt first, giving an *initial* liquid relatively rich in silica.

As a magma crystallizes, trace elements often substitute into sites in the common rock-forming minerals, but for some trace elements — the **incompatible elements** — there are no suitable sites. During fractional crystallization, these incompatible elements become more and more concentrated in the remaining liquid, and sooner or later *less* common minerals will start to crystallize. These are **accessory minerals** such as apatite and zircon; they normally occur in very small quantities (<1% volume), but they provide structures that can accommodate incompatible elements, and therefore many are important as ore minerals.

Question 26

Each of the following accessory minerals contains a useful element not found in common rock-forming minerals. What is it? Give its name, as well as its symbol. (a) Ilmenite; (b) cassiterite; (c) wolframite; (d) chromite; (e) zircon. (Table 7 gives the mineral formulae.)

Whereas chromite is a dense ore mineral that crystallizes at high temperatures, and is commonly found near the base of layered intrusions of *basaltic* composition, most accessory minerals bearing incompatible elements crystallize at relatively *low* temperatures, late in the cooling history of a *granitic* magma. They are often found in *pegmatite* veins associated with large granitic intrusions, and include apatite, cassiterite and wolframite.

In summary, partial melting and magmatic differentiation have been largely responsible for the chemical differentiation of the outer part of the Earth. The partial melting of peridotite rocks generates basaltic magmas, forming oceanic crust at ocean ridges, and the partial melting of basaltic crust can generate granitic magmas. When magmas are generated by partial melting, or differentiated by fractional crystallization, *chemical* processes differentiate elements between minerals and melts; *physical* processes then separate these fractions and preserve their different compositions. Fractional crystallization involves physical separation of chemically distinct, early-formed crystals, such as chromite and olivine, which sink and may accumulate as layers. The remaining liquids may be tapped off and further fractionated. Eventually the remaining liquid from a granitic magma may form pegmatite veins rich in valuable accessory minerals containing incompatible elements. The formation of ore minerals by these igneous processes are discussed further in Block 5.

3.6.2 Sedimentary processes

Any element concentrated by sedimentary processes ultimately requires a parent source for it: that source might be an igneous or metamorphic rock, or it could be a pre-existing sedimentary rock. Weathering, erosion, transport and deposition may separate minerals and concentrate elements, depending on their physical and chemical properties. Sedimentary processes are an integral part of the rock cycle around which elements are carried.

As explained in Section 3.5, sedimentary processes begin with the liberation and transport of rock fragments and mineral grains that resist chemical weathering, and with the chemical breakdown of less resistant minerals to clays and ions in solution. Soluble elements may be extracted by organisms and incorporated into rocks such as limestone when the organisms die. Other dissolved ions remain in solution until conditions are suitable for their direct precipitation, either through evaporation (giving evaporite minerals, e.g. halite and sylvite, Table 7) or through complex chemical reactions (e.g. forming iron and manganese ores).

Some elements are locked into minerals that are insoluble in water, and so may be transported only in mineral grains. Sediments deposited in river systems and shorelines may contain high concentrations of insoluble minerals, such as diamond, ilmenite and garnet. Dense resistant minerals (*heavy minerals*), such as cassiterite and zircon, are often rich in trace elements, or even composed entirely of them, hence the incentive to pan for native gold in certain streams and rivers (Figure 63). These heavy mineral sands are known as *placer deposits*.

Resistant grains and fragments can be sorted during transport: the movement of grains in water, or air, separates grains according to their size, shape and, often more important, their density. The grain size of clay minerals is very small, and their density rather low, so that they are usually transported much further than larger grains or the denser grains of many more resistant minerals; as a result, clay deposits tend to be relatively pure. Such sorting is clearly an important process in the formation of sediments and sedimentary rocks used for building materials (Block 2).

Figure 63   Panning for gold and heavy minerals in a British upland stream.

Weathering processes may leave behind insoluble *residual* deposits enriched in particular elements. The most widespread and important example is the residue of aluminium hydroxides that forms bauxite ore, the chief source of aluminium, but similar processes also result in enrichment of iron, manganese, copper and nickel.

Organic activity plays many roles in sedimentary processes. As far as physical resources are concerned, the most significant role of plants and animals is the fixing (i.e. incorporation into their bodies) of the elements carbon, hydrogen, oxygen and nitrogen. The soft parts of organisms normally decay after death, primarily because of oxidation and bacterial action, and organic chemicals are released into the surrounding sediment or water. Heat and pressure applied during burial within sedimentary basins may then gradually convert organic material into hydrocarbons (oil or natural gas) or coal (derived from land plants).

An important role played by plate movements in the formation of sedimentary mineral deposits is to determine the climatic belts through which plates pass. The overall distribution of climatic belts has, it seems, always been essentially the same as today — that is, coldest at the poles, warmest at the Equator, with gradational climatic belts in between. There have, however, been changes in the relative widths of climatic belts, especially between glacial and non-glacial periods of Earth's history.

○   How would you expect the relative widths of warm and cold climatic belts to vary between these two climatic extremes?

○   In warm, non-glacial periods, the warm equatorial belts expand and the cold polar belts contract; the reverse occurs during glacial periods. In fact, throughout most of geological time, the Earth has been without polar ice caps, and our present climatic regime is relatively rare in Earth's history.

While the overall distribution of climatic belts remains constant with respect to the poles (except for changes in relative width), plate movements cause plates to pass through different climatic belts. The UK, for instance, is now an area of continental crust at moderately high northern latitudes, but it has drifted there from a former position far south of the Equator. For example, in Ordovician times, about 500 Ma ago, Britain, which was then composed of two separate continental areas with an ocean in between, was at least 35° South — the latitude of Cape Town or Adelaide today. The main continental masses had merged by the Devonian and, continuing northwards, they crossed the Equator during the Carboniferous Period. Accordingly, it is possible to explain the age distribution of climatically influenced sedimentary mineral deposits, e.g. coal and bauxite typical of tropical settings, by the past positions of plates relative to the Earth's climatic belts.

Plate tectonics plays an initial role in the formation of oil and gas by determining whether or not the overall climatic setting is suitable for the appropriate planktonic life to thrive, from which nearly all petroleum is derived. The transformation from planktonic remains into petroleum requires not only a suitable sedimentary environment on the sea-bed, but also a subsequent history of burial that will ensure hydrocarbon generation. Plate tectonic processes influence whether or not there will be sufficient stretching of the crust to cause subsidence, allowing sedimentary basins to develop, and whether the local geothermal gradient (the rate of increase in temperature with depth) is adequate to generate oil and gas. Plate movements may not only create sedimentary basins by stretching the crust but destroy sedimentary basins by doming it up. Hydrocarbons tend to occur along continental margins (e.g. off the western side of Africa today), and where continental crust has been stretched and thinned because an incipient ocean was 'aborted', such as the North Sea, where continental break-up and sea-floor spreading started, and then ceased (Block 4 *Energy 1*).

In land areas remote from active plate boundaries, geological activity tends to be limited to erosion, and to the transportation and deposition of sediments (which may be useful, for example, as building aggregates). But if continental masses start to break up, subsidence and intermittent influxes of the sea may result in other valuable sedimentary deposits. Examples include evaporites (formed by the evaporation of shallow seas) and phosphates, both of which formed in basins along Africa's Atlantic coast when Africa separated from South America in the Cretaceous Period.

3.6.3 Metamorphic processes

Metamorphism can convert soft rocks like clays and shales into hard rocks useful for building purposes, and gentle metamorphism may improve the quality of coal, but may destroy oil.

Regional metamorphism usually involves little change in the bulk composition of a rock, so that a concentration that was sufficiently high to make an igneous or sedimentary rock an ore, for example, is normally carried over to the metamorphosed equivalent. The same elements will still be there, albeit in different minerals. The formation of new minerals from pre-existing ones (e.g. mica from clay minerals, hornblende from pyroxene), can expel trace elements into the hot, watery fluids that often exist between grains. This can happen when a mineral (e.g. pyroxene) that *can* contain a trace element (e.g. mercury) is transformed into a mineral that *cannot* contain that trace element (e.g. hornblende). If no other new mineral can contain the released trace elements, the hot watery solutions, now rich in trace elements, can migrate through the rocks along pathways between grains, and eventually form valuable deposits in regions of lower temperature and pressure. As hot water is involved, these deposits are normally recognized as a form of hydrothermal deposit (see below).

3.6.4 Hydrothermal processes

The cooling of magma bodies, the compaction of sediments and the formation of metamorphic rocks all involve the movement of water in the crust: water is often present in magmas, water can be squeezed out of sedimentary rocks, and during metamorphism water may be released from some minerals and from between mineral grains. Water temperatures of over 500 °C can be reached, and water as hot as this is a very powerful solvent. It can decompose minerals, leach elements, especially trace elements, from rocks it passes through, and transport significant quantities of elements in solution. After convection to favourable locations, where such hydrothermal solutions can cool and crystallize, **hydrothermal deposits** may form. Some of the world's most important deposits of lead, zinc and copper ores have formed in this way. The metal-rich solutions themselves are often rich in common salt (sodium chloride), in which case they are called *brines*.

Spectacular effects occur on the ocean floor, when basaltic lava at temperatures of around 1300 °C comes into contact with seawater at about 2 °C. There is a vigorous interaction between hot rock and cold water.

Question 27

In which of the following plate tectonic settings would you expect this interaction to happen most often? (a) A passive continental margin, (b) a constructive plate margin, (c) a destructive plate margin.

As the rocks of the new oceanic crust cool and contract, cracks form. Seawater penetrates them and boils, forming steam and causing further cracks to develop. The lavas often solidify in the form of rounded though mis-shapen pillows — in which case they are known as *pillow lavas* (Figure 64). Seawater penetrates deep into the hot pile of basalt, and the water begins to circulate. The circulating hot water causes minerals in the hot basalt that lack water in their chemical structure (i.e. the *anhydrous* minerals such as pyroxene) to be transformed to *hydrous* minerals such as chlorite and serpentine.

Figure 64 Recently erupted basaltic pillow lavas on the ocean floor. They were photographed in the central valley of the Mid-Atlantic Ridge at a depth of about 4000 m. The largest 'pillows' are nearly 1 m across.

As you can see from Table 7, the presence of water in complex hydrous minerals is usually indicated by the presence of hydrogen in the chemical formulae — not as H_2O itself, but as (OH) which, for instance, chlorite, serpentine, amphibole and biotite all have in their formulae. Common elements in seawater, such as sodium, may be added to the rock as it is altered, but more importantly, some elements from the basalt, such as copper and zinc, are dissolved in the circulating hot water. Ore minerals may then be precipitated in rocks of the ocean floor. If the fluids reach the surface, they emerge as metal-rich brines and precipitate their metal content on the ocean floor as dark-coloured deposits, especially around vents known as 'black smokers' (Figure 65). Ore deposits of this kind are described in Block 5.

Figure 65
Metal-rich hydrothermal fluids being discharged from a vent on the ocean floor known as a 'black smoker'. On leaving the vent the fluids immediately precipitate sulphides and other minerals to give a smoky appearance.

⬤ Consider the deposition of ore minerals containing Cu and Zn on the ocean floor as outlined above; what can you say about the source, agent, deposition and energy (SADE) of that system?

◗ The *S*ource of the Cu and Zn is the hot basalt rock; the *A*gent which leached the metals and transported them to the site of deposition started out as seawater; the reasons for *D*eposition on the ocean floor are the change in chemical conditions, and the fall in temperature, when the hot brines meet the cold seawater; and the source of *E*nergy is the heat from the hot basaltic magmas derived from the mantle, and the heat in the mantle is ultimately derived from radioactive decay.

As a result of hydrothermal activity, the top kilometre or so of oceanic crust contains major concentrations of metal sulphides, especially of copper and zinc, along with other metals in lesser amounts. In addition, the overlying seawater is supplied with manganese and other elements by these hydrothermal solutions, and, as a result, crusts and nodules of manganese oxides, which also contain copper, cobalt and nickel, are widespread on the ocean floor.

Ore deposits on and under the sea bed are, of course, hard to find and difficult to exploit, mostly being beneath 3 or 4 kilometres of seawater in the open ocean. (A possible future exception to this generalization could be manganese-rich nodules that might prove practicable to remove from the deep sea bed.) The 'conveyor belt' of sea-floor spreading slowly brings the various metal concentrations towards subduction zones. In rare cases, remnants of oceanic crust called **ophiolites** escape subduction at an active plate boundary, and are scraped up and tectonically emplaced onto continental edges (Figure 66). Where ophiolites are exposed on land their ore deposits are relatively easy to exploit. The copper ores of Cyprus, mined since pre-Roman times, are of this type, as are copper ores in Newfoundland; and several major chromite mines in Turkey and Pakistan are also in ophiolites, caught up in the Alpine–Himalayan collision zone.

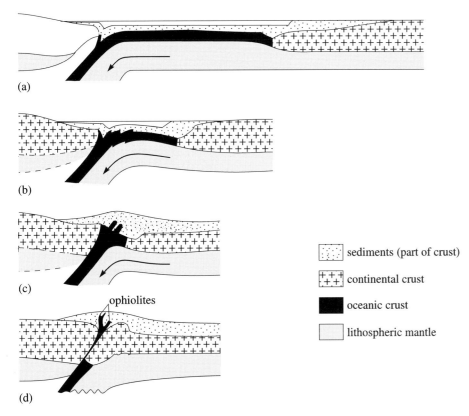

sediments (part of crust)

continental crust

oceanic crust

lithospheric mantle

Figure 66 Ophiolites are remnants of oceanic crust that have escaped subduction and been scraped up on to the edges of continents. The sequence (a) to (d) shows the progressive contraction of an ocean basin caused by subduction and the ultimate collision of two continents, with ophiolites emplaced at their junction.

Normally, however, the oceanic lithosphere simply descends into the asthenosphere along subduction zones where it undergoes dehydration (and perhaps partial melting). The dehydration produces hydrothermal fluids in which metals and other elements may become concentrated. Metals that have already been concentrated at *constructive* plate boundaries can thus be redistributed into new ore deposits associated with magmatism above *destructive* plate boundaries. Many of the world's largest copper and molybdenum deposits occur in these locations, e.g. in western North and South America and in the southwestern Pacific.

Away from plate boundaries it is harder to relate mineral deposits of igneous or hydrothermal origin to the workings of plate tectonics. Such deposits may result from slight deformations of the plates themselves, especially doming up or stretching, rather than lateral plate movements. Examples include the hydrothermal lead, zinc and fluorite veins in Carboniferous limestones in Europe and North America, discussed in Block 5.

3.7 Overview

All the concentration processes mentioned above operate within the rock cycle. Elements become concentrated into various minerals at different stages in the cycle, depending on their individual properties, chemical affinities, and prevailing conditions. Similar processes may be involved in the formation of quite different resources, depending on the available elements. For instance, the chemical processes in sediment needed for coal formation are similar to those required for the precipitation of iron as a carbonate; the physical processes required for the concentration of dense materials, such as gold, can also accumulate resistant low-density minerals, such as quartz, to produce pure sands used in glass-making. The movement of fluids, which can carry metals and form valuable vein deposits, may also alter feldspars in a granite, producing clays, especially kaolin or china clay.

Local enrichments of useful elements only become reserves if they make up a high enough proportion of their host rocks for economic extraction. For instance, a seam of coal may be pure, perhaps suitable for burning in a power station, but if it is only one or two centimetres thick it cannot be worked economically. Many granites contain the radioactive mineral uraninite, often as isolated grains; but these occurrences will not be ores of uranium if the costs of extraction are excessive compared with the uranium market price. You may be familiar with the many old mines in the Mendips, North Wales, the Peak District and southern Scotland, and may perhaps have collected lumps of the dense, shiny grey ore mineral, galena (PbS), from spoil heaps or even exposed veins. These deposits still contain lead but are no longer ore bodies, largely because the price of lead failed to keep pace with the cost of mining them.

Many physical resources are associated only with particular rock types, which is one of the best guides to exploration. There's no point in searching for oil in the metamorphic rocks of the Scottish Highlands (any oil would have been eliminated long ago by very high temperatures and pressures) or for tin in the Chalk (it is almost entirely calcium carbonate, and lacks the appropriate tin-bearing minerals).

We have seen how plate tectonics and continental drift may influence the generation of physical resources. The three types of plate boundary each display characteristic forms of geological activity. Being able to recognize these geological characteristics in ancient rock sequences can enable us to work out the approximate original position of *former* plate boundaries. In turn, knowledge of ancient plate settings can help us to predict the *general* location of economically significant deposits. As we will see, however, in Block 5, exploration involves a variety of methods from high-tech, high-resolution remote sensing and sophisticated geophysical techniques, to classical smaller scale field investigations.

If we stand back from the details of different plate boundaries, we can see that one consequence of plate tectonics is the *plate tectonic cycle* (Figure 67). On the large scale, the outer portions of the Earth are continually on the move. Oceanic crust is generated and then destroyed where it sinks back into the upper mantle. This happens comparatively rapidly on geological timescales: the oldest portions of the ocean floor at the present time are nowhere more than about 200 Ma old. In contrast, continental crust is generated above destructive plate boundaries, but because it is much less dense it is not dragged back down into the mantle. Rather it is 'destroyed' only by the very slow processes of weathering and erosion, by which some material from the continents is washed down into the oceans, and hence may be returned in part to the mantle via subduction zones. As with the 'destruction' of oceanic crust, the component atoms themselves are recycled. The rock sequences of the continents are very much older and more complex than those in the oceans, and the oldest rocks on Earth so far sampled were formed about 3900 Ma ago. The Earth itself formed even earlier, about 4600 Ma ago.

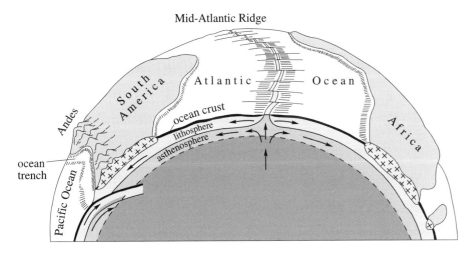

Figure 67   The plate tectonic cycle can be seen in this cut-away diagram showing the relationships between the plates carrying Africa, South America, and the east Pacific Ocean. Movement within convection cells carries heat to the surface primarily in ocean ridges whereas cooled oceanic lithosphere eventually descends to the mantle down subduction zones. The thicknesses of the layers are not to scale.

The workings of the rock cycle and of plate tectonics through geological time have ensured that the global distribution of mineral deposits is very uneven. The 'currants' are not spread uniformly through the 'bun'. Similarly, certain types of mineral deposit are not spread uniformly through the stratigraphic column, but formed preferentially during certain periods of Earth's history. For example, coal and hydrocarbons are not found in economic quantities in rocks older than about 400 Ma. The reason in the case of coal is that plants did not colonize land areas to any extent until about 400 Ma ago, and in the case of hydrocarbons it is mainly because they are fluid and volatile and have been driven out of older rocks by the heat and pressure associated with metamorphism — the older the rocks, the greater the chance, on average, that they will have been affected by metamorphism.

Stand back further, and we can see that the Earth as a whole is an immense object in which processes are happening on all sorts of scales from the movements of subatomic particles or microbes, to the slow grinding of lithospheric plates. Things are continually changing over the vastness of geological time. The interactions between the component parts of this whole Earth are exceedingly complex. It is difficult to grasp details of the Earth on a global scale; so, to investigate it, and to make judgements scientifically, we have to break it down into smaller parts. Those parts are dynamic — as opposed to static — and are called *systems*. A system is an ensemble of objects, substances or even ideas that are linked together by actions and mutual interdependence. Familiar examples are the Solar System, the nervous system and the circulation system of the body, and a transport system like the London Underground. There are usually systems within systems: for example, the whole Earth is itself a system within the Solar System.

Every physical resource is the product of a dynamic system. We often attempt to describe a system using a model, i.e. a simplified representation of a real system that, although omitting many details, describes its essential features. A good model must behave sufficiently like the real system to allow fairly accurate predictions about that system's behaviour.

○ Looking back to earlier parts of this Section, what rather obvious large-scale geological systems can you identify?

○ The three most obvious ones are the rock cycle, the water cycle, and the plate tectonic cycle. Each cycle may be regarded as a system in its own right and, as we have seen, each interacts with one another on different scales.

Question 28

(a) Which of the two types of crust generally has far greater structural complexity, often resulting from several quite different episodes of folding, faulting, igneous activity and metamorphism — and why?

(b) What percentage of the age of the Earth are the oldest portions of oceanic crust?

Question 29

Which part of the rock cycle (igneous, sedimentary or metamorphic processes) is most closely associated with each of the following physical resources: (a) table salt; (b) ornamental marble; (c) basalt used for road surfacing; (d) oil and gas.

3.8 Geological time and the ages of rocks

There is a natural tendency to think of rocks as something solid and indestructible. This is largely because our observational timescales, like our lifespans, are very short compared with the rates of most geological processes, such as the rate at which material moves around the rock cycle. By 1850, scientists were suggesting that the Earth was as much as 40 Ma old.

○ How many times older than this estimate is the age of the Earth now known to be?

○ Over a hundred times older (about 112 times). As stated earlier, we now know that the age of the Earth is about 4.6 billion years.

An appreciation of time is important in this Course for several reasons.

1   First and foremost, we should be familiar with the rates at which physical resources are produced, as well as the rates at which we consume them. In most societies, a wide variety of physical resources are being consumed at rates thousands or even millions of times faster than they are generated by geological processes.

2   History, whether it be of peoples, species, or the Earth itself, is characterized by changes that are both cyclical and directional (i.e. irreversible in the long term). These two characteristics of time are very evident in our own lives. On the one hand there is a cyclical element as night follows day, and as seasons reappear year after year; on the other hand, we get older and cannot reverse the arrow of time. In effect, we age through a series of cycles, and the history of the Earth is somewhat similar. Rocks and minerals are continually being created and destroyed in the rock cycle, but many features of the Earth are directional too.

For example, compared with early in its history, the Earth's interior is cooler today, with a quite different atmosphere, and life thrives on what was once a lifeless planet.

3   In general, the longer the time interval encompassed, the greater the opportunity for more unusual, more intense and influential natural events to occur. Events of greatest intensity are expected to be the least frequent, as is true with natural phenomena such as floods, droughts, hurricanes, earthquakes, volcanic eruptions, and meteorite impacts.

4   If we cause damage to the environment, it can take a long time for the scars to heal. As a simple example, vehicle tracks in some deserts are expected to last for hundreds of years before being obliterated by wind or rain. Chemical pollution is often less visible but far more serious. For example, some synthetic pesticides and detergents are transported by rivers to the sea where they are known to persist for decades without showing any sign of altering to less harmful compounds.

Unravelling the *correct sequence of events* that led to a particular set of circumstances is a crucial step in understanding those circumstances; imagine a detective trying to solve a complex 'whodunnit' without trying to piece together events in the order that they happened. The detective uses the order of events to shed light, for example, on motive, opportunity and means. Similarly, establishing the order of geological events is an important step in understanding the reasons why physical resources occur where they do, in the concentrations they do. Knowledge of past events can be immensely useful for making *predictions* about where further resources can be found, and sometimes just as importantly, where they cannot be found.

Two aspects of age may be ascertained from rocks: **relative age** and **absolute age**. Consider the statement: 'this newspaper is more recent than that one'. It is a clear indication of relative age, but says nothing about the actual age of each newspaper, nor the time difference between them. The same is often true of rocks.

Imagine a pile of old daily newspapers accumulating at home in a recycling bin. Unless the order of newspapers has been disturbed for some reason, the oldest newspaper will be at the bottom of the bin, and the youngest at the top. The same is also true of sediments accumulating under gravity; generally, the deeper you go in a sedimentary sequence, the older the layers of sediment are. Unless they have been overturned (which may happen during plate collisions and mountain-building), the arrow of time will be upwards through a set of strata. In fact, sedimentary rocks provide such an important key to the past that they are sometimes said to be the diaries of Earth's history.

Imagine you had, say, thirty newspapers in the recycling pile, and you only knew the date of the top one, say 10 October 1994 — could you be sure of the date of the bottom one? To get it right, you would have to be completely certain of the rate of newspaper accumulation. Did you buy just one newspaper per day, every day, and did they always end up in the bin in the right order, or did they get jumbled up after the dog tipped the bin over, and so on? To be sure of the true age of the newspaper at the bottom, you would really have to look at the date on it — its *absolute* date. The same general sort of uncertainties apply when trying to sort out the ages of rocks that have been folded, faulted, and intruded by magma, and some problematic age relationships can only be resolved by radiometric dating.

Radiometric dating is the name of a general technique for determining the absolute ages of rocks. There are now over a dozen separate methods, based on the decay of elements with naturally occurring radioactive isotopes, such as uranium, thorium and rubidium. Although the details need not concern us here, the principle uses the fact that radioactive isotopes break down with time to produce something different, usually another element altogether, but sometimes a different isotope of the same element. If we know the rate of radioactive decay, and can measure the precise amounts of radioactive isotopes and their decay products, we can work out for how long the process has been going on. It's a little like going into a bathroom, finding the bath running, and trying to estimate roughly how long it's been filling up. If you know the volume of water in the bath, the rate at which water was running out of the tap, and assume that it had always been running out at the same rate and that no water had leaked out or evaporated, you would be able to say for how long the bath had been running. The same is true for the radiometric dating of rocks — you have to be able to measure rates and the amounts of materials concerned (which are often tiny), and you have to make several assumptions. There are all sorts of uncertainties involved, and so radiometric ages are always associated with a margin of error. It is rather like finding a torn scrap of newspaper paper in the attic with the words '… March 1985' where the date would be. Just as we can express the most accurate date for that newspaper fragment as 16 March 1985, ± 15 days, because we only know it is some day in March, the age at which a granite crystallized from molten rock might be given as 393 ± 5 Ma. Normally, the older the rock, the greater the margin of error. Many radiometric dating techniques are most effectively applied to igneous rocks, but metamorphic rocks and some sedimentary rocks can also be dated.

The study of sequences of strata is called **stratigraphy**, and such sequences have long been used to establish a geological time chart. Initially this only told us the relative ages of rocks, but many key levels, such as those at the boundaries between geological periods, have been assigned absolute dates. Figure 68 is a summary of the stratigraphic column, showing the main divisions of geological time. There are two major but unequal subdivisions: the **Precambrian**, which comprises the first seven-eighths or so of Earth's geological past, and the **Phanerozoic** which covers the remainder. 'Phanerozoic' means 'visible life', and reflects the fact that, although the oldest known fossils are about 3800 Ma old, fossils are only abundant from the start of the Cambrian Period, about 540 Ma ago, when a wide range of organisms first evolved hard parts. Many Phanerozoic sedimentary rocks contain abundant fossils, and evolutionary change has led to different fossils occurring in rocks of different ages. Fossils are therefore extremely useful for correlating, i.e. matching up, rocks of the same age from one area to another. Once it is established that strata in a new area have fossils characteristic of a particular geological period, it is easy to assign an approximate absolute age to the strata by referring to a recently published stratigraphic column showing absolute ages.

By the end of the Course, you should be familiar with the names and the order of the geological periods, but for the moment you should at least know the age ranges of the Precambrian, and of the Palaeozoic, Mesozoic and Cenozoic Eras.

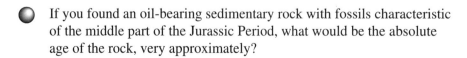

If you found an oil-bearing sedimentary rock with fossils characteristic of the middle part of the Jurassic Period, what would be the absolute age of the rock, very approximately?

Looking at Figure 68, the Jurassic Period is dated as between 210 and 150 Ma, so the rock was deposited approximately 180 Ma ago.

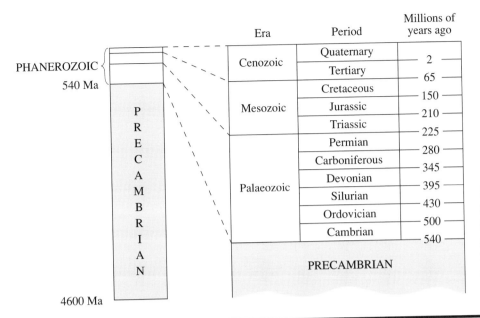

Figure 68 A summary of the stratigraphic column, showing the main divisions of geological time. Subdivisions of the Phanerozoic are not drawn to scale, and absolute dates are approximate.

The relative ages of rocks

There are some simple criteria for determining the relative ages of rocks, and geologists use them all the time when making geological maps. Here are some important ones, based mostly on field relationships:

1 *Superposition* Sedimentary strata and lava flows are laid down layer upon layer, and so layers higher in the sequence must be younger than those lower down. ('Super-' just means 'above'.) This assumes that the rocks are still the 'right way up', i.e. that they have not been turned upside down by subsequent folding and faulting. Usually, there are sufficient indicators in the rock for the original 'way up' to be recognized.

2 *Horizontality* Sediments are typically deposited in nearly horizontal layers. If the layers are observed to be tilted or folded, then the tilting must have taken place after they were laid down.

3 *Cross-cutting relationships* When sedimentary strata have been cut by a feature such as a fault or an igneous intrusion (e.g. a dyke, in black in Figure 69), the cross-cutting feature must be younger than the rocks it cuts through.

4 *Included fragments* Any rock that contains fragments of another rock must be younger than the rock from which the fragments were derived.

5 *Faunal succession* Over geological time, organisms have evolved, and become extinct, and assemblages of species have succeeded one another in a particular order. In other words, there has been a succession of faunas (animals) and floras (plants). Sedimentary rocks that contain the same assemblage of species may be inferred to be of similar ages, even though they may be on opposite sides of the world.

1.
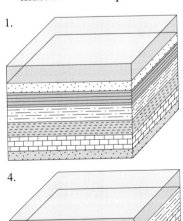

2.

3.
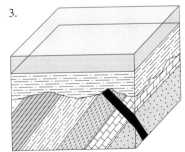

4.

5.
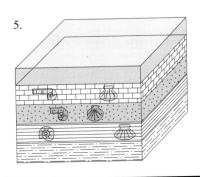

Figure 69 Diagrams to illustrate the five criteria used for determining the relative ages of rocks.

3.9 Summary of Section 3

1 A mineral, geologically defined, is any naturally occurring substance that has a definite crystalline structure and a chemical composition that may vary within certain limits. A rock is any naturally occurring assemblage of mineral grains.

2 Igneous rocks are formed when magmas solidify; sedimentary rocks are formed from sediments deposited at the Earth's surface; and metamorphic rocks are rocks of any type that have been changed by heat and/or pressure, possibly accompanied by chemical activity.

3 The Earth has a rigid outer skin of mobile lithospheric plates, each composed of crust and topmost mantle. There are two types of crust: continental and oceanic. Of the two, oceanic crust is thinner, denser, simpler in structure, and generally far younger, being nowhere older than about 200 Ma. Oceanic crust is generally basaltic in composition, whereas continental crust is richer in silica, having a composition between that of basalt and granite. Some plates include regions of both continental and oceanic crust, which merge at a passive continental margin.

4 New oceanic crust is produced by sea-floor spreading at constructive plate boundaries, marked by ocean ridges. Oceanic crust is destroyed at destructive plate boundaries, where it disappears slowly down subduction zones marked by deep ocean trenches. At conservative boundaries, plates grind alongside each other, with crust neither being created nor destroyed. Continents may collide at collision zones, forming mountain ranges. Radiogenic heat is the main cause of convection in the less rigid asthenosphere layer over which plates move, causing continental drift. Most deformation (including folding and faulting), igneous activity and metamorphism generally take place at plate boundaries.

5 Every chemical element contains a specific number of protons in its atoms. Neutral atoms contain equal numbers of protons and electrons. Elements may form ions with stable electronic configurations — either positive cations (by losing electrons) or negative anions (by gaining electrons). In ionic bonding, the attraction between oppositely charged ions keeps a compound together, whereas in covalent bonding, atoms share electrons. The chemical behaviour of elements can be predicted to some extent by their position in the Periodic Table. Elements near the side margins of the Table tend to form ionic bonds, with elements at the left-hand side usually giving up electrons to elements at the right-hand side. The extreme right-hand column is occupied by the chemically stable noble gases.

6 Elements can be grouped into major elements and trace elements. Major elements each form more than 0.5% of common rocks, and together they make up about 95% of the crust. Rock-forming minerals are dominated by the complex silicates, but other mineral groups important as physical resources include native elements, halides, sulphides, oxides, sulphates, carbonates, and phosphates. Ions of different elements that have a similar size and electrical charge may substitute for each other in a crystal structure.

7 Rocks are continually being created and destroyed within the rock cycle. Given suitable physical conditions, any igneous, sedimentary or metamorphic rock can be melted to form an igneous rock, eroded to form a sedimentary rock, or metamorphosed to form a metamorphic rock.

The water cycle interacts with the rock cycle mainly in weathering, erosion and transport of material to the oceans. The plate tectonic cycle involves repeated creation and destruction of oceanic crust.

8   The formation of a variety of igneous rock types from an initial parent magma (by fractional crystallization, for example) is called magmatic differentiation. Partial melting and magmatic differentiation processes are responsible for dividing the Earth into mantle, oceanic crust and continental crust. Partial melting of mantle peridotite generates basaltic magmas, forming oceanic crust at ocean ridges, and partial melting of basaltic crust can generate granitic magmas. When magmas are generated by partial melting, chemical differentiation divides elements between melts and residual minerals; and as minerals crystallize from a magma, chemically distinct, early-formed crystals may accumulate separately, preserving the changed composition of the remaining liquid. The last remaining liquids from granitic magmas often form pegmatite veins which may be rich in valuable accessory minerals containing incompatible trace elements.

9   Sedimentary processes begin with the liberation and transportation of rock fragments and mineral grains that resist chemical weathering, and with the chemical breakdown of less resistant minerals to clays and ions in solution. The soluble products of chemical weathering may eventually be precipitated as evaporite minerals or deposited in sediments via organic materials, such as shells. Resistant grains and solid breakdown products can be sorted during transport: the movement of grains in water, or air, separates grains according to their size, shape and density. Dense resistant minerals, often rich in trace elements, can be concentrated in river systems as placer deposits. Weathering processes may leave behind residual deposits enriched in insoluble minerals.

10   Plate tectonics and continental drift play an important role in the formation of physical resources found in sedimentary rocks, especially in determining: whether the overall climatic setting is suitable for the appropriate life to thrive (in the case of coal, oil and gas) or for deposits such as evaporites to form; whether there is sufficient stretching of the crust to cause subsidence, allowing sedimentary basins to develop; and, in the case of hydrocarbons, whether the local geothermal gradient is adequate to generate oil and gas.

11   Hydrothermal processes involve the movement of hot watery fluids, which can react with and alter rocks through which they pass. The fluids may dissolve trace elements and deposit them elsewhere as hydrothermal minerals.

12   The formation of any economic deposit requires a *Source* of the useful elements, an *Agent* of transportation, a reason why *Deposition* or concentration took place where it did, and a form of *Energy* to drive the system.

13   There are recurrent associations between different kinds of rocks and particular resources in different parts of the rock cycle, but even if the geological environment is favourable, concentration processes may not have reached the necessary grades for economic extraction.

14   The relative age of rocks may be deduced from their field relationships, and, in the case of sediments, from their fossil content. An absolute age can be obtained by radiometric dating, based on the decay of naturally occurring radioactive isotopes.

4 PHYSICAL RESOURCES AND SUSTAINABLE DEVELOPMENT

4.1 Renewability of physical resources

In Section 3 we learned that several important natural cycles are involved in the generation of physical resources, including the rock cycle, the plate tectonic cycle, and the water cycle. The rate at which material is moved around these cycles by natural processes is very variable, and, except for the water cycle, is generally extremely slow by the standards of a human lifetime. Many types of physical resource have taken millions of years to form in sufficient quantities and concentrations to be worth exploitation. It may take tens of thousands of years for an exposed igneous rock like a granite to weather into a significant accumulation of sand, and another million years for those grains of sand to be cemented together to form a hard sandstone suitable as a building stone.

A resource that is exploited faster than it is replenished by natural processes is said to be **non-renewable**. The term 'non-renewable' doesn't mean that a resource will *never* be renewed, but that renewal by Earth's natural processes would take such a long time that it is non-renewable on human timescales. For example, coal probably takes at least a million years to form (and most of the coal in UK rocks was formed over 250 Ma ago). Peat — a precursor of coal on the borderline between a physical and a biological resource — is, however, more quickly renewed, usually taking hundreds of years or a few thousand years to form from rotting vegetation. But, in practice, peat cannot be regarded as a renewable resource because we're consuming it more quickly than it's being produced. By contrast, timber grown in well-managed forests is a renewable resource, and other *biological* examples are easy to find because their timescales of regeneration are relatively short.

Soil is a product of Earth's surface processes, and is an exceedingly valuable resource with both physical and biological components. Rudimentary soils may form in as little as 50 years, but, depending on various factors, rich fertile soils may take many hundreds of years to develop. Soils may not form at all where weathered debris is eroded as rapidly as it forms, or where floodwaters regularly dump transported sediment over alluvial plains.

Renewable energy resources are supplies of energy on Earth from internal and external processes that are continuously available, whether they are used or not. They include solar, tidal, wind, and heat from volcanic areas (geothermal energy) (Block 4 *Energy 2*). We cannot change the rate at which these sources make available energy (much of it radiated into the atmosphere from the Earth's surface), although we may use part of the energy from the total available. These continuous energy resources thus contrast with non-renewable coal, oil and natural gas ('fossil fuels'), the accumulated energy of which is much more under our control: we can generally choose to spend it or save it. (Actually, even in the absence of humans, some solar energy stored in fossil fuels is dissipated naturally by combustion, seepage or chemical reaction.) Although coal and oil, for example, are beginning to form somewhere today, they won't be available in economic quantities for several million years. Oil is being consumed at least a million times faster than it is being generated. And resources such as oil, gas and coal, once burnt, cannot be recycled in the same way as can, for example, metals; once the energy of fuels is spent (i.e. converted), it cannot, in practice, be retrieved.

There is no magic borderline between renewable and non-renewable; where the line is drawn will change according to the rate at which a resource is consumed: the greater the rate of consumption, the less likely that replenishment will keep up. Rates of geological processes vary, and the rate of an individual process may vary from place to place and over time in a single place. Just how long a process takes to produce a given result will depend on the history and nature of the setting. Other than water and certain forms of energy discussed above, it's very difficult to find examples of physical resources that are replenished as fast as we consume them. As we'll see shortly in Section 4.4, the concept of renewability is linked to that of *sustainability*, and in particular to *sustainable development*.

4.2 Physical resources in everyday life

Let's briefly remind ourselves of the extent to which we use physical resources in everyday life. What about the paper this is printed on? The main resource is biological, of course (cellulose fibres from sugarcane and wood pulp), but non-renewable physical resources give essential properties to paper, such as its ability to take ink without spreading, to reflect light, to resist tear, to minimize 'show-through', and so on. Clays of various kinds are commonly used as fillers and as coatings (up to 35% clay in the glossiest papers), and other common additives are limestone or chalk, titanium dioxide for whiteness, and barium sulphate (barite) for weight. And at least 15 tonnes of water are needed for every tonne of paper manufactured.

Perhaps you're using a highlighter pen as you read this. The bodies of highlighters are mainly polystyrene or polypropylene, the fibre part holding the ink is polyester or nylon — all of which, like other plastics, are derived essentially from hydrocarbons, especially oil. The inks are based on water or, if 'permanent', an organic solvent such as alcohol. Most of the dyes are complex organic compounds derived mainly from oil, and some require tiny amounts of metals in their chemical formula. Safety regulations impose upper limits on metal concentrations in inks; e.g. barium 500 ppm, lead 90 ppm, and arsenic 25 ppm. Many inks contain no metals at all; for example, the fluorescent dye used in pink highlighters, rhodamine, contains just carbon, hydrogen, oxygen, nitrogen and chlorine.

You can extend your appreciation of the ways we use physical resources by looking at everyday purchases, including food and drink, in a new light. For example, next time you're drinking a can of cola, look at its contents. The

Coins: composition, substitution and recycling

Before you read much further, jot down the different denominations of UK coins and get an example of each one in front of you.

The £1 coin is nickel–brass: proportions in the alloy (by weight) are 70% copper, 24.5% zinc, 5.5% nickel. The 50p, 20p, 10p, and 5p, are cupro-nickel: 75% Cu, 25% Ni. Until September 1992, the 2p and 1p pieces were bronze: 97% Cu, 2.5% Zn, 0.5% Sn. The new 2p and 1p pieces are copper-plated steel: by weight 7% Cu, 93% steel (2p), and 9% Cu, 91% steel (1p). This substitution represented a considerable saving on metal costs, especially with such a reduction in copper and the elimination of tin.

In 1992, there were 16 000 million (1.6×10^{10}) coins in circulation in the UK ; equivalent to an average of about 290 coins for every individual. The total number of coins issued by the Royal Mint varies much from year to year, e.g. 2281 million in 1990–91 and 722 million in 1991–92. Re-specification of coin weight and size may reduce resource use; for example, the weight of the new 10p coin issued in 1992 was reduced from the 11.31 g of the old coin to 6.50 g. Old 5p pieces (reclaimed when the new and smaller 5p coins were issued in 1990) were recycled to make the new 10p pieces; the old 10p pieces were similarly recycled whenever cupro-nickel was required.

Glass

There's probably glass in every room of your home, if not on your wrist or immediately in front of your eyes. It's obtained by melting together several compounds based on common physical resources: silica (SiO_2) from quartz sand; soda ash (sodium carbonate, Na_2CO_3) obtained artificially by reaction of common salt (NaCl) with limestone; limestone ($CaCO_3$); and dolomite ($CaMg(CO_3)_2$). The fused materials are cooled at a rate fast enough to prevent crystallization — glass is therefore a supercooled liquid. Glass may eventually start to crystallize, becoming cloudy ('devitrified'). Some Egyptian glass, however, remains uncrystallized after 4000 years, and the natural glass obsidian may still be clear after hundreds of thousands of years.

Most forms of glass in the home, e.g. drinking glasses, bottles, windows, fibreglass insulation, etc., have a rather similar chemical composition (expressed as oxides by convention, just like the chemical composition of igneous rocks, and not indicating the presence of these specific compounds): SiO_2 70–74%, Na_2O 12–16%, CaO 5–11%, MgO 1–3%, Al_2O_3 1–3%. Between 0.1% and 1.0% each of iron, potassium, and sulphur oxides are also usually present from impurities, and minute amounts of other compounds may be added for particular properties such as colour. This ordinary glass is known as 'soda-lime glass'. Its major disadvantage is its great expansion when heated: that's why it's dangerous to pour boiling water into a cold milk bottle or drinking glass. In borosilicate glasses, all the calcium and much of the sodium is replaced by boron, an element obtained from the evaporite mineral borax; this makes the glass extremely resistant to chemicals, and fairly resistant to sudden heat. Pyrex™ ovenware is a familiar example. More recently, cooker hobs, cooking ware and windows for gas or coal fires, which need to be extremely resistant to thermal shock, have become made of 'glass ceramics', in which lithium, aluminium and titanium are important constituents. Some glass ceramics do not expand at all on heating, and many are resistant to fracturing. Tin plays a crucial part in the manufacture of most windows; they are made so flat by floating the molten glass on a layer of molten tin.

A complete spectrum of glass colours can be obtained with precisely controlled additives: for example, manganese (Mn) for purple, selenium (Se) for pink or red. The colour often varies according to the specific cation: for example, Cu^{2+} gives blue-green, Cu^+ gives red. Sand containing even as little as one part per thousand of iron oxide will give ordinary soda-lime glass a greenish tint. However, to avoid using expensive high-purity raw materials, manufacturers often decolourize glass by adding minute amounts of colorants that produce complementary colours to green so that the finished articles appear colourless.

A television tube in normal operation produces X-rays that need to be absorbed by various glass components. The funnel and neck of the tube commonly use lead glass, while barium glass is used for the front plate. Lead crystal drinking glasses contain over 24% of lead oxide (PbO), giving a glass that is heavy and easily cut to allow the light to be internally reflected with maximum brilliance. Spectacle glass that reacts reversibly by darkening in bright light and then returning to its original state in gloomier conditions contains minute crystals of silver halides. The tiny crystals actually convert to metallic silver in sunshine, darkening the spectacles. Mirrors are traditionally produced by precipitating a layer of pure silver on an extremely clean glass surface. A layer of copper is deposited on top of the silver to prevent it from oxidizing. Both layers are then protected by a layer of enamel. Alternatively, the reflective layer may be aluminium rather than silver.

'carbonated water' contains carbon dioxide usually derived (in the UK) from combustion of North Sea gas (methane). Very dilute phosphoric acid (a traditional constituent of colas) is obtained by dissolving sedimentary rock containing phosphates in sulphuric acid. And if you're eating crisps, the chances are that common salt has been used as flavouring and preservative, and that the packet includes a thin layer of aluminium to seal in moisture.

Question 30

In March 1992, 1007 million £1 coins were in circulation in the UK. Given the composition of the £1 coin (see Box) and that its weight is 9.5 g, calculate the number of tonnes of copper, zinc, and nickel required for all those pound coins.

4.3 The recycling of physical resources

Recycling is a universal aspect of the living world; without it life would soon grind to a halt. When an organism dies, or perhaps simply produces waste products, its atoms of carbon, nitrogen, and hydrogen, for example, move on to another part of the complex cycle involving each element, and sooner or later they may be incorporated into the body of another organism. And, as we saw in Section 3, even elements within rocks are slowly moved around the rock cycle and the plate tectonic cycle.

Recycling the materials we use is an important method of conserving any resource, especially non-renewable resources, and is a way of short-circuiting the immensely long natural cycles that would otherwise be the only means to generate the resources concerned. **Recycling** can be defined as reusing a substance, not necessarily in its original form, that might otherwise be left as waste. **Reclamation** describes the actual collection of materials separated from waste, while recycling involves rather more — the collection and separation of materials from waste to which subsequent processing usually takes place to produce a marketable product. Humans, incidentally, are not the only species to recycle useful materials such as building materials that are not part of their bodies. For example, birds often rebuild nests with twigs and grass from previous nests (sometimes incorporating small pieces of plastic and other synthetic materials), and beavers reuse logs when building their dams. A nice example of the recycling of building materials by humans is that of the concrete in the Berlin Wall, pulled down in 1989, having separated East and West Germany for 28 years: some was used as souvenirs, and some as hard core for construction.

(Note: the data given below are mostly for 1993, and are likely to change rapidly.)

About 20 million tonnes of waste are produced by households in the UK — about one tonne per year for every household. However, only 5% of this is recycled; 86% is buried in landfill sites and the remaining 9% is incinerated. In most cases the energy that could be generated from landfill and incineration is not harnessed. Domestic wastes obviously vary very much from household to household, but a fairly typical analysis is presented in Figure 70. Most of the remaining 380 million tonnes of waste disposed of in the UK comes from agriculture, mining and quarrying, manufacturing industries, demolition and construction, and food processing.

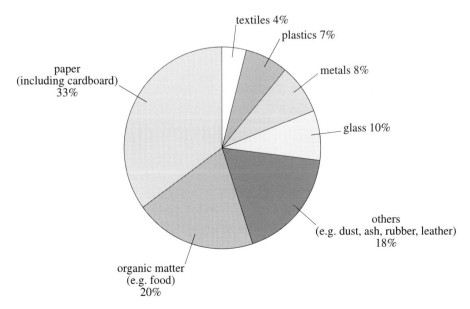

Figure 70 A typical analysis of household waste in the UK (percentage by weight).

Recycling of domestic waste can offer the potential for considerable savings without major sacrifices by the consumer. The main benefits and incentives are to: (a) conserve raw materials and energy; (b) minimize pollution and waste; and (c) save money. In particular, recycling can:

- save materials that can be used to make new products;
- reduce energy costs of extraction and manufacturing;
- slow down the consumption of non-renewable resources;
- reduce the amount of waste and requirement for landfill sites;
- make incineration more efficient by removing non-combustible material;
- reduce imports of expensive raw materials;
- reduce the various forms of pollution associated with extractive industries;
- increase general awareness of environmental issues.

Recycling domestic waste, however, has limitations and obstacles, including the following:

- Collecting waste for recycling is only worthwhile if there is a market for it.
- Kerb-side collection schemes from individual homes can be very expensive. Some local authorities attempting to meet government recycling directives are nevertheless prepared for a recycling scheme to lose money initially, and believe that financial and political benefits will eventually result from changing 'throw-away attitudes'.
- There are often technical difficulties with collecting, sorting, cleaning or reprocessing.
- True calculations of resource saving, energy saving and reduced environmental impact must be based on complete analysis from raw materials, production, distribution, recycling and final disposal; without this, benefits may be underestimated or overestimated.
- Special trips to collection points (e.g. bottle banks) may use far more energy than is saved by recycling the materials concerned.
- A widespread glut of recycled materials on the market may push down prices and threaten the viability of individual schemes.
- Manufacturers may entice the environmentally conscious purchaser with misleading labels that imply recycling is possible when the appropriate facilities don't exist locally.

Despite these various factors, the percentages of domestic waste materials recycled in the UK are increasing rapidly as recycling schemes and centres start up, sorting methods improve, environmental awareness spreads, people discover that recycling is a satisfying activity, new uses are found for recycled materials, legislation enforces action and subsidies provide incentives — all interrelated factors. The Government has set local authorities a target of recycling 25% of domestic waste by the year 2000; in 1993 the level was only about 5%. It's estimated that at least 60% of domestic waste could be recycled. In many ways, waste, including some already buried in landfill, is a resource awaiting development (see Block 2).

There are three main categories of recycling:

1   *Direct reuse*   Typical examples are the returnable and refillable milk bottle or beer bottle, compressed gas cylinders, and standard 45-gallon drums for chemicals, oil, etc. The average milk bottle is returned 24 times for cleaning and refilling before someone fails to return it; very few break in use. Bottles collected from pubs are reused about 18 times. In Germany, the different manufacturers of mineral waters use identical bottles to make reuse easier; the same is also true of some types of wine bottles. Of the three categories, direct reuse involves the least energy and

processing complexity in getting the material back into use. However, refillable containers are not always associated with a saving of energy and a reduction of environmental impact. Refillables have to be strong to withstand repeated transport, handling and filling, so more energy and materials go into their manufacture, and there are additional energy costs in cleaning and redistribution. Retailers tend to dislike returnable bottles because valuable space has to be used for storing empties.

2   *Direct recycling*   The materials that are unfit for reuse or simply discarded are cleaned and reprocessed in some way before being put to the same general purpose again. For example, glass from a bottle bank may be broken down to *cullet* at a glassworks and remelted to make more bottles. Currently most direct recycling occurs during manufacture, e.g. misshapen or broken bottles formed during glass making are fed back to the melting chamber. Although industry calls this recycling, it is not to be confused with the recycling of post-use material from homes and offices, public collection points, or waste disposal sites. Recycling of domestic refuse can only be remotely economic if very specific materials are selected for recycling, with efficient sorting to avoid contaminants. Sorting equipment is becoming increasingly sophisticated: aluminium cans, for example, can be lifted off a conveyor belt by applying an electrical charge; X-ray machines can separate out PVC from other plastics by identifying the chlorine present.

3   *Indirect recycling*   The materials are used again, usually after some processing, but for a quite different purpose. For example, some glass is too difficult to sort and clean for cullet use; instead it may be ground up and used for a skid-resistant and durable road-surfacing material. Similarly, plastic containers unsuitable for direct recycling may be ground up, remelted or compacted and used for objects where detailed appearance and structure are unimportant — such as refuse sacks and traffic cones. Other forms of indirect recycling are the conversion of organic refuse to combustible gases, and the use of heat from the combustion of refuse for local heating systems.

Let's look at the recycling of some common products made from physical resources, and requiring physical resources during their manufacture.

Glass

The average UK family discards 10 bottles per fortnight, though only about 25% are recycled. But the raw materials from which glass is made (see Box above) are plentiful and fairly cheap, so are there other reasons to recycle it? Yes, there are several; for example, recycling saves further destruction of land by quarrying, saves space in landfill sites, saves energy at the glass works (recycled glass melts at a lower temperature than the raw materials), and reduces pollution. Glass is infinitely recyclable, unlike paper. Glass that melts at low temperatures is the most suitable for recycling. A common problem is people putting 'glass ceramics' from electric cooking hobs and saucepans in glass recycling banks, assuming they are ordinary glass. The ceramics have a much higher melting point, remaining as lumps in the new glass, and hence weakening the whole batch, which has to be rejected. Mixing recycled glass of different colours produces a green colour (due to the presence of iron compounds). Thus green glass is made with 80% recycled material, clear glass with only 20%. We use about a billion green bottles each year, mostly imported wine bottles. However, although 50% of glass taken to bottle banks is green, less than 20% of UK-made glass is green, and, unless preferences change, there could come a time when there won't be a UK market for green recycled glass. Transport costs mean it's inefficient to export it, so new uses for recycled coloured glass may have to be found.

Drink cans

On average, each person in the UK discards 125 drink cans per year; that's over 7 billion cans for the whole population. Nearly all food cans are made of tin-plated steel, whereas about 70% of drink can bodies are aluminium, 30% are steel, and most have aluminium ends. The aluminium is alloyed with manganese and magnesium to enhance strength and malleability, and can design is occasionally improved so that the weight is reduced. Aluminium drink cans are worth between £550 and £650 per tonne (depending on whether they're flattened and baled). Twenty cans can be remade from recycled aluminium for the same energy required to make one from new aluminium ore, a 95% saving. (Note that aluminium ore itself is not scarce; it is the saving of energy required for production of the metal that is the chief benefit from aluminium recycling.) About 20% of UK aluminium drink cans were being recycled in 1993 but the percentage is increasing rapidly. The thin layer of tin on steel cans is removed, cast into ingots, and sold; the steel is fully recycled too. (About two-thirds of all cans, whether food, drink, paint, aerosols, etc., are steel; 11.5 billion are used each year, of which 1.5 billion are recycled.) In general, producing steel from scrap as opposed to new raw materials saves 50–75% of the energy used in the steel-making process.

Figure 71 Imaginative recycling of drink cans used to make goat pens in Damaraland, Namibia, Africa.

Activity 6

(a) What proportion of cans in your household are steel as opposed to aluminium? When cans are being recycled, steel ones are separated out from aluminium ones using magnets. If you have a magnet, try this with unused cans in your kitchen, or with cans you've collected for recycling.

(b) If you have some kitchen scales, weigh a few empty aluminium drink cans, establish their average weight, and work out how many you would have to collect for a tonne.

(c) As a tonne is worth about £600, how much is each can worth?

Plastics

In UK domestic refuse, plastics form about 20% by volume and 7% by weight. The main plastics group, *thermoplastics* (which soften when warmed and harden when cooled), includes some types that are currently unsuitable for recycling, but the number of uses for the range of recycled thermoplastics is already great and fast increasing. The enormous diversity of plastics, and inadequate labelling, create a problem at the sorting stage. Some plastic containers are now made from a sandwich of greyish recycled plastic between thin layers of new plastic of the appropriate colour. Less than 1% of plastic refuse is *thermosetting* plastics (as, for example, used in melamine tabletops and light switches); these cannot be recycled like thermoplastics because once set they can never be melted and reformed. Some *biodegradable* plastics are made using micro-organisms that convert carbohydrates formed from carbon dioxide and water during photosynthesis into plastics; in landfill sites the plastic simply degrades back to carbon dioxide and water by the action of soil bacteria. These are a costly but potentially important alternative to hydrocarbon-based plastics. Unless well screened out they can cause problems in recycling processes, and litter may increase if people believe discarded plastics will simply disappear. Bottles are the easiest form of plastic to recycle. Thin plastic wrapping films (which are expensive to sort and clean) are probably best recycled indirectly by incineration with energy recovery.

Question 31

Only about 0.25% by weight of the plastic in domestic refuse was being recycled in the UK in 1993. Roughly, (a) how many tonnes of plastic were being recycled that year; (b) how many tonnes were *not* being recycled?

Paper

About 33% of waste paper in the UK is recycled, although the profit margin is very low. The fibres weaken with repeated recycling, and new fibres must be added to maintain quality. As well as the physical resources incorporated into the paper itself (see above), those used in the manufacture and recycling of paper include water, caustic soda (NaOH), sulphur, and chlorine-based compounds. Recycling saves some of these resources, but further chemicals are required for de-inking during recycling.

Activity 7

What recycling schemes does the local authority operate in your area for glass, plastics and metals? For example, is there a kerb-side collection scheme? If so, what percentage of households take part? What percentage of domestic waste is locally recycled? Are there deposit banks for glass, plastics and metals nearby? If you take pre-sorted glass, plastics and metals wastes to the local refuse site, can they be recycled from there? (The easiest way to answer these questions may be to phone the local authority recycling or refuse-collecting department.)

How does recycling of domestic refuse in the UK compare with other countries? For various reasons, the impact of recycling is difficult to assess from simple statistics of the percentage of domestic refuse recycled. For example, in very poor nations virtually all domestic refuse goes for landfill or incineration (without energy retrieval), but recyclable materials like plastics and metals (which may form relatively low proportions of household purchases compared with developed nations) are discarded far less readily, and may have been reused many more times than in the UK before being thrown away. In Denmark, 20% of household waste is recycled, and 60% is burnt in incinerators that generate local heating and electricity. Other countries with relatively high recycling figures include Holland, Germany, and Austria, whereas France, like the UK, recycles only about 5%.

4.4 Physical resources, environment and sustainable development

For most of history, humans have regarded their potential to influence or even harm their wider environment as negligible compared with that of natural processes such as floods, volcanoes, and earthquakes. But in the early 1970s, concerns with human-induced environmental problems, including the depletion of resources, began to move from the periphery to the centre of debate. The first United Nations Conference on the Environment took place in 1972 in Stockholm. In 1987 an important report, known as the Brundtland Report, by the United Nations World Commission on Environment and Development, chaired by Gro Harlem Brundtland (later Norwegian prime minister), contained the most widely accepted definition of **sustainable development**:

> Development that meets the needs of the present without compromising the ability of future generations to meet their own needs.

At the Earth Summit held in Rio de Janeiro in 1992, 150 heads of government put issues of development and environment at the top of the political agenda. Among the outcomes was Agenda 21, a comprehensive programme of action to achieve a more sustainable pattern of development for the twenty-first century. The problem, of course, is how to translate the desirable notion of sustainable development into practice, how to measure it, and how to assess progress towards its achievement.

Humans are becoming aware that their activities can threaten the balance of the **global commons**, i.e. resources such as the atmosphere and the oceans that are beyond national ownership. We may be the first generation to perceive clearly some of the major drawbacks of the Industrial Revolution. Pollution arising from the use of physical resources has been documented around the world, and is even detectable in the Antarctic ice sheet. The excessive burning of fossil fuels by a small part of the world's population emits greenhouse gases that may cause global warming and degrade the atmosphere (Block 4 *Energy 1*). The less 'visual' (i.e. less readily perceived) environmental impacts are now regarded as often the most potentially serious for future generations; e.g. compare the emission of ozone-destroying gases from some aerosol sprays with noise and dust from local quarry operations. The opportunities of future generations should not be adversely affected by the activities of the present generation, a principle called *intergenerational equity*. Similarly, the lives of people in one region of the Earth should not be adversely affected by the activities of people in another region: *inter-regional equity*.

To sustain most industries based on a *renewable* resource (let alone a non-renewable one), laws or self-imposed restraint are essential; overuse or overkill is a short-term strategy. Fisheries, for example, are often in the news because sustainability is threatened. It's no good catching more and more fish because eventually there are none to reproduce a future population; extinction follows, locally at first and then globally. Sustainable fishing always leaves sufficient numbers of young to grow and reproduce the next generation. Note that the term 'sustainability' can be used simply to refer to maintenance of the status quo, whereas sustainable *development* implies aspects of growth and increase.

If the rate of exploitation of any system exceeds the 'maximum sustainable yield', the system gives ever-diminishing returns. Long-term management requires a good understanding of the resource system. For example, although water is generally a renewable resource, successful provision of fresh water year after year requires understanding of the rates of individual steps in the water cycle (Block 3). For non-renewable resources such as oil, coal, metals and industrial minerals, their use by future generations depends on the amount being added to the reserves category keeping up with the amounts lost by consumption. This may be possible for a few generations, but the amounts, for example, of oil and natural gas buried in rocks are finite, no matter how effective new exploration and extraction methods may be. To avoid compromising the ability of future generations to meet their own needs, alternatives — i.e. substitutes — that fulfil all the uses of such resources will have to be developed well ahead of their final depletion.

As far as physical resources are concerned, the general principles of sustainable development require us to:

- extract and use all non-renewable resources (i.e. the vast majority of physical resources) sensibly and sparingly, in ways that provide long-term benefits and which do not restrict the options of future generations;

- use renewable resources within the limits of their capacity for regeneration;

- develop ways to recycle materials and thereby minimize the use of virgin physical resources;

- develop ways to manufacture and package products with smaller amounts of materials without loss of quality;

- develop longer-life products;

- develop substitutes for non-renewable resources;

- ensure that other species are not harmed (e.g. by pollution), and that biodiversity (the total number of species and the richness of ecosystems) is maintained;

- attempt to understand as fully as possible the Earth's natural systems, and human interaction with them, in order to limit the potential environmental impacts of any proposed development, and to redress existing environmental problems.

The **precautionary principle** holds that lack of scientific certainty should not be used as a reason for postponing measures to prevent threatened environmental damage. The UK government, for example, embraced this in a 1990 White Paper: 'Where there are significant risks of damage to the environment, the Government will be prepared to take precautionary action to limit the use of potentially dangerous materials or the spread of potentially dangerous pollutants, *even where scientific knowledge is not conclusive*, if the balance of likely costs and benefits justifies it'.

Of course, such statements sound good, but who assesses what constitutes a *significant* risk, and how? Is the understanding of science by the public, and especially politicians, sufficient to assess scientific messages? How exactly are the costs and benefits accounted: are the benefits viewed only in financial

Thinking globally, acting locally

'Think globally, act locally' expresses the philosophy of many environmental organizations. The principle of *shared responsibility* means that everyone —from international organizations through national governments to local authorities and individuals— has a role in delivering sustainable development. Individuals who wish to be involved in developing a more sustainable world can act in a variety of settings: for example, *at work*, by supporting drives for energy saving, 'green purchasing' and recycling; *as parents or others involved with children*, by developing their interest in the environment or responding to their concern; *as aware citizens*, by becoming active in political parties, voluntary organizations and local affairs, and by voting or simply exchanging views.

⬤ For those who wish to reduce the consumption of physical resources in everyday life at home, recycling is not the only option. What other ways can you think of, which can ultimately save you money too?

◯ Among the examples you may come up with are:

- *Saving energy in the home*
  Install effective insulation; ensure the heating system is properly controlled with a thermostat to operate at the lowest comfortable temperature; turn off electrical appliances when not required.

- *Choosing products carefully*
  Don't buy things you aren't going to use or don't really need; cut down on throw-away products and those with unnecessary packaging; buy energy-efficient appliances such as energy-saving light bulbs; buy some products second-hand.

- *Saving energy and materials used for transport*
  Walk or cycle if possible; consider public transport for longer journeys; organize a car-sharing scheme for regular journeys; when driving, avoid very high speeds, fast starts and sudden braking; keep your engine well tuned.

- *Saving water*
  Avoid dripping taps and leaks; clean bottles, etc. for recycling only with used water (e.g. after washing-up); collect rainwater in a butt for use in the garden; reuse relatively clean water from the house in the garden.

terms? What kinds of precautionary action can be taken in practice? The costs of inaction can outweigh the costs of implementing precautionary measures, and narrow the choices of future generations. The prevention of groundwater pollution, for example, is usually far easier than its cure. Generally, the more global a problem, the more entrenched its hold and the more difficult it is to solve. How long will the global reverberations of nuclear waste disposal, climate warming, and atmospheric pollution last? Do catastrophes have to occur, either when some global threshold is reached (e.g. loss of the ozone layer), or by a sudden disaster (e.g. explosion of a nuclear reactor), before action is taken?

For the first half of the twentieth century, applied geology courses and companies were almost exclusively devoted to the acquisition of resources: how to find and extract them. There was a gradual shift away from the dominance of metallic minerals and coal, towards petroleum, industrial minerals and water. Between 1985 and 1990, over half of new UK graduates employed in geology joined the petroleum industry or the companies and consultancies that serve their exploration effort. Only since the 1970s have textbooks and courses shown any significant mention of the environmental impacts of the extraction and use of physical resources. Concern for these environmental issues has started to offset the geologist's traditional preoccupation with *supplying* physical resources. The focus is now not just on the inputs to society but its *outputs*: solid wastes, liquid effluents and gaseous emissions. And, increasingly, earth scientists are being funded to offer perspectives on environmental change that are only available from the record in the rocks: to gather data, for example, on the rate of change of ancient climates, past levels of carbon dioxide in the atmosphere, and trace elements in seawater. For many people, 'the environment' seems only to exist at and above the Earth's surface; whereas with a geological perspective it extends below the ground and back through time. The speed and severity of human impacts on the environment can only be appreciated with a grasp of the immensity of geological time.

Sir Crispin Tickell (formerly UK ambassador to the UN), who helped to initiate the 1992 Earth Summit, wrote (in 1994):

> Most governments are concerned with short-term issues. Some find it difficult to look beyond the end of the month or even the end of the week. Once the pressure for change is off, they tend to revert to business as usual, and — worse — the same tired agenda in which crude notions of economic growth come out top.

Progress tends to be seen as synonymous with economic growth, indicated at least partly by increased throughputs of resources and energy. There are, however, some positive indications, although most of these are restricted as yet to just a few countries and settings:

- 'The environment means business'. Employment connected with the environment is increasing and is set to become a profitable growth industry, affecting companies, small businesses, scientific consultancies, legal firms, educational institutions, etc.

- The positive link between environmental performance and competitiveness means that the financial community is increasingly taking account of environmental concerns in investment decisions.

- Some leading companies, national and international, are already *voluntarily* adopting environmental policies and targets.

- A very small but growing number of firms are evaluating the environmental performance of their suppliers.

- Many universities are perceiving that taking on board the 'environmental agenda' is both a challenge and an opportunity, essential for their future in recruiting students, in finding them jobs, and in opening up avenues in research, consultancy and training.

- Regulations governing extraction and use of physical resources at local, national and international level are increasing.

- Identifying and eliminating sources of pollution often leads to the most cost-efficient use of resources, and the 'polluter pays' principle is becoming established.

- There is some evidence that continued economic growth is not necessarily incompatible with high levels of environmental quality.

Question 32

Referring back to Section 1.3, and allowing 20 years for each human generation, calculate roughly how many generations there have been since (a) the origin of our genus *Homo*; (b) the origin of modern humans, *Homo sapiens sapiens*; (c) the earliest known mine.

Sustainable development concerns future generations. Yet it's very rare for any organization — whether an industrial company, political party or government department — to attempt to plan ahead more than about 20–25 years, i.e. about one generation. For many reasons, including the unpredictability of technological innovations, forecasting over such timescales is notoriously difficult, and becoming more so. Yet if there is to be a future for even a tiny fraction of the number of generations that have existed before us, long-term strategies are essential.

Opinion polls show that the public, and especially young people, tend to be more concerned about the environment and sustainability than most political and business leaders and media editors. Politicians who seek election or re-election will increasingly have to take environmental issues more seriously. There are a few signs that this is happening. In the UK, for example, by 1994 Government transport policy was influenced by the threat of global warming to the extent that planning authorities were being asked to bring houses and employment centres close to each other to reduce carbon dioxide emissions from cars, and out-of-town shopping centres were being discouraged for a similar reason. In general, however, global environmental problems will not be solved without concentrated efforts by all nations, sooner rather than later.

Before you move on to Block 2, you might like to consider how you would answer the following questions:

- If people realized the extent to which they were dependent on physical resources for their existence, would they be so quick to criticize the opening up of a new quarry or mine near them?
- Should heavy taxes or levies be imposed on the extraction of virgin materials in order to encourage recycling and use of substitutes made from recycled materials?
- Will the governments of every country eventually have to impose stringent regulations on resource management and offer large financial incentives to ensure sustainable development?
- Should industrialized nations expect developing nations to remain relatively poor, foregoing economic growth and consuming few physical resources in order to protect the environment?
- Does the onus for action and example rest with the industrialized nations?
- Do governments and individuals have the will to face difficult and potentially painful choices?
- Do the important choices have to be painful?
- What are the important choices?

4.5 Summary of Section 4

1   Non-renewable resources are those that are exploited faster than they are replenished by natural processes, e.g. fossil fuels, metal ores and industrial minerals. In contrast, water is generally a renewable resource, and renewable energy resources are those that are continuously available, whether they are harnessed or not, e.g. solar, tidal, wind and geothermal energy sources.

2   Recycling is reusing a substance, not necessarily in its original form, that might otherwise be left as waste. It includes direct reuse, and direct and indirect recycling. Among the benefits of recycling are the conservation of raw materials and energy, the minimization of pollution and waste, and the saving of money. Current limitations include the high cost and scarcity of reclamation schemes, and technical difficulties with sorting and reprocessing.

3   Of the 20 million tonnes of household waste produced in the UK, only about 5% is recycled; 86% is buried in landfill sites and 9% is burnt. The

Government has set a national target of 25% recycling of household waste by the year 2000.

4   Sustainable development is development that meets the needs of the present without compromising the ability of future generations to meet their own needs. A sustainable approach to physical resources includes using them sensibly and sparingly; recycling; developing longer life products and substitutes; minimizing the environmental impacts of extraction, processing, manufacture, use and disposal; and ensuring that biodiversity is maintained. Environmental issues are here to stay, and employment connected with maintaining or improving the environment is increasing.

OPTIONAL FURTHER READING AND SOURCES OF DATA

Press, F. and Siever, R. (1994) *Understanding Earth*, W.H. Freeman and Co, New York. An excellent, clearly written introduction to earth sciences with many colour illustrations.

The Open University (1983) S236 *Geology*, Milton Keynes, The Open University. A second level Open University course covering a wide range of basic geology.

Woodcock, N. (1994) *Geology and Environment in Britain and Ireland*, UCL Press, London. A well-illustrated and clear account ranging across the spectrum of resources, including interesting sections on geological influences on society and human impacts on the Earth. Although concentrating on the British Isles, each major resource is placed in a global perspective.

Metals and Minerals Annual Review. A comprehensive review of metals, industrial minerals and energy minerals published mid-year by Mining Journal Limited, London.

Mineral Commodity Summaries, United States Department of the Interior, Bureau of Mines. An annual summary of about 80 elements and minerals, giving not only US data but also world production and reserves, with brief though useful sections on events, trends and issues, and substitutes.

Mining Annual Review. A comprehensive country-by-country review of mining, exploration, production, etc., published mid-year by Mining Journal Limited, London.

World Mineral Statistics, British Geological Survey/NERC. An annual publication of statistical data spanning the last five years, but lacks discussion. In two volumes: Volume 1: Metals and energy; Volume 2: Industrial minerals.

OBJECTIVES FOR BLOCK 1

Now that you have completed Block 1, you should be able to do the following.

1 Explain in your own words, and use correctly, all the terms in the *Glossary* relating to Block 1 (in bold).

Section 1

2 Discuss the meaning of the terms 'physical resources' and 'environment'.

3 Describe the variation in quantities of chemical elements required globally each year as physical resources, giving examples, and summarize the factors that influence the relative use of particular elements.

4 Explain the difference between elements and compounds, giving examples, and outline the range of materials, including energy sources, used as physical resources.

5 Outline key developments in the history of human use of physical resources, and give examples of, and reasons for, the substitution of physical resources.

6 Describe the process and outline the history of making iron and steel.

7 Express numbers in scientific notation, and do simple calculations involving numbers expressed in this way.

Section 2

8 Explain the difference between the real and nominal price of a physical resource, and discuss the typical patterns of changes in price since 1900, giving examples.

9 Discuss the probable influences on future patterns of global production and consumption, including the disparities in both population growth and the consumption of physical resources between industrialized and developing regions.

10 Explain in qualitative terms, using simple diagrams, or interpret from diagrams, the economic concepts of supply and demand and their relationship to the price of a physical resource and price-elasticity.

11 Explain how reserves and resources are defined, including the main categories of resources, and describe the influences that may alter their classification.

12 Outline the main stages in the activities of an extractive industry, and the factors that tend to dominate industries based on large-scale extraction, especially of high-value resources.

13 Summarize the main cost and revenue factors influencing whether or not a resource is exploited, including the significance of place value.

14 Explain and discuss the concept of reserves lifetime, giving examples.

Section 3

15 Describe the rock cycle, and the ways in which material is moved around it by geological processes, and account for the difference in nature and origin of igneous, sedimentary and metamorphic rocks, giving examples.

16 Describe the main structural features of the Earth, including its lithospheric plates and the main types of plate boundaries, and account for the principal differences between oceanic and continental crust.

17 Describe, using examples, the difference between ionic and covalent bonding, referring to internal atomic structure and the general position of elements in the Periodic Table.

18 Outline the main groups of common rock-forming minerals, and give examples of the types of rocks in which they occur.

19 Summarize the main processes by which physical resources are concentrated in different parts of the rock cycle; i.e. the igneous, sedimentary, metamorphic, and hydrothermal concentration processes.

20 Outline the role of plate tectonics and continental drift in the generation of physical resources.

21 Apply the SADE scheme (*Source, Agent, Deposition, Energy*) when attempting to understand or explain the formation of a particular physical resource.

22 Explain the difference between the relative and absolute ages of rocks, and outline in simple terms the ways in which such ages are obtained.

Section 4

23 Explain the difference between renewable and non-renewable resources.

24 Summarize the main categories in the recycling of physical resources, and outline the benefits of, and the current limitations to, this process.

25 Define sustainable development and outline how a sustainable approach can be applied to physical resources.

ANSWERS TO QUESTIONS

Question 1

(a) Get lucky — send the unicorn salt in a waste bin.

(b) Ge germanium, Tl thallium, U uranium, C carbon, K potassium, Y yttrium, Se selenium, Nd neodymium, Th thorium, Eu europium, Ni nickel, Co cobalt, Rn radon, S sulphur, Al aluminium, Ti titanium, Na sodium, W tungsten, As arsenic, Te tellurium, B boron, In indium. In terms of the amounts we use, the relative importance of these elements varies greatly, as revealed by the rest of Section 1.2.

(c) The only element that is not a solid is radon (Rn), a gas.

Question 2

About 4×10^9 tonnes of water $(2/1000 \times 365 \times 5.5 \times 10^9 \, t)$ — a figure that is, of course, growing every year as the population increases.

Question 3

(a) Cs, Ga, Ge, Mg, Rb, V, Y. (b) Au, C, Cl.

Question 4

Iron production in the Weald eventually ceased because local supplies of wood, needed for charcoal, became exhausted.

Question 5

During the process called 'puddling', *cast* iron is remelted and agitated to *oxidize* out remaining impurities such as carbon, silicon and phosphorus. After running off some slag, and driving out further slag with a steam hammer, minute strands of slag still remain, resulting in a fibrous texture which *increases* the iron's strength and resistance to fracture. Iron produced in this way is called *wrought* iron.

Question 6

(a) Incorrect. Girders of wrought iron are *less* susceptible than those of cast iron to brittle fracture of the kind that caused the Tay Bridge Disaster.

(b) Correct.

(c) Incorrect. In the nineteenth century, it was the local availability of *coal* that determined where industry expanded far more than the proximity to high-quality iron ore.

(d) Incorrect. The ability to use scrap iron and steel, and iron ores relatively rich in phosphorus, are some of the advantages of the *Siemens 'open hearth'* process over the *Bessemer* process.

(e) Incorrect. It is true that in the 1930s, Britain introduced tariff barriers that boosted its iron and steel making industries. However, the extract from 1934 footage in the programme spoke in a favourable tone about the belching of smoke from chimneys that had been smokeless for years and made no reference to any detrimental effect on the local environment.

(f) Correct.

(g) Incorrect. The steel makers began to import ore from places as far afield as Australia not because reserves of the Northamptonshire Ironstone and Frodingham Ironstone were exhausted but because importing foreign ores became more economic and more efficient.

(h) Correct.

Question 7

In chemical terms, the job of the blast furnace is to get enough *carbon* and enough energy close to the iron *oxide* so that it can *reduce* it from iron *oxide* to iron.

Question 8

The coke must be quenched quickly with water to prevent its oxidation in air. The higher its temperature, the more likely that the carbon will react with oxygen in the air.

Question 9

The response of the British Steel Corporation, formed in 1967, to slackening demand, was to imitate the style of successful industries abroad, notably *Japan*. Even the smallest blast furnace in that country made about *four* times the tonnage of Britain's largest blast furnace. In 1973, BSC proposed that steel-making be rationalized into *five* major works, the largest of which would be built at Redcar, on *Teesside*. Deep water harbours were built to receive the cheapest ore from anywhere in the world. Steel works were constructed with everything on site, raw materials were bought in as needed, reducing stockpiling and wastage, and at least some recycling was built into the design — improvements that were all part of the process of *rationalization*.

Question 10

(a) About 500 years (250 million in 1000 AD and 500 million in about 1500);

(b) a little less than 100 years (1200 million in 1850 and 2500 million in 1950);

(c) a little less than 40 years (2500 million in 1950 and 5300 million in 1990). The figures given in the text show that since about 1750, the rate of increase has itself been increasing, i.e. the doubling time (see Box on the term 'exponential') has been *decreasing* steadily.

Question 11

Your completed table should look like Table 9.

Table 9

	Weight of materials in 1980 car/kg	Weight of materials in 1990 car/kg	Change in percentage contribution: % of 1980 value	Change in weight of materials: % of 1980 value
steel	810	633	+2	−22
cast iron	240	113	−6	−53
plastics	90	136	+6	+51
aluminium	60	90	+4	+50
others	300	158	−6	−47
Total	1500	1130	n/a	−25*

(a) The average total weight decreased by 25%. (1130/1500 ≈ 75%.) There is an asterisk (*) against −25 in the far right column to alert you to an important point about percentages in general. The figure of 25% is obtained by calculating what percentage of the earlier total weight is the new total weight, and subtracting from the original 100%. The correct answer (−25%) is *not* the same as adding up all the percentage changes in the far right column. (That total would be −21, not −25.) The reason is that the percentages in that column are not percentages of the same total, but each is a percentage of the weights of each separate material in 1980, and those weights are not equal. The point is that you cannot use a set of percentages as a basis for calculations about absolute amounts, averages and so on, unless all the percentages are based on the same total. The percentages in column three ('Change in percentage contribution') actually add up to zero (though n/a, meaning not applicable, is shown), because each one relates to percentages of the same totals (i.e. 100%, representing each whole car in 1980 and 1990).

The typical car in 1990 was smaller in size than in 1980, which itself led to a reduction in weight. The reduction in average weight of a typical car achieved not only a saving of certain materials, but, other things being equal, should have reduced the amount of fuel consumed when moving that car on the road. But there are many limitations in interpreting such a small amount of data. Even if the average total weight of a car diminished by 25%, the number of newly produced cars may have gone up by over 25%, increasing the total weight of physical resources required for all new cars. And what happened in the years between 1980 and 1990? Do these findings indicate a real, sustained trend or just a chance blip? Is there an overall saving in the amount of energy needed to produce materials for the car? For example, the typical 1990 car is lighter but contains 30 kg more aluminium, a metal that requires a great deal of energy to produce. We would need to be given far more information before such questions could be answered.

(b) *Less* steel was needed for the typical car in 1990 than in 1980. Although there was a 2% increase in steel relative to other materials, the average weight of the whole car decreased by 25%, and the weight of steel went down by 177 kg — a saving of 22%.

(c) The weight of cast iron dropped by 53%, from 240 to 113 kg.

(d) The weight of plastics increased the most, up by 51%, only just more than aluminium, which increased by 50%. Note that, although the percentage contribution of plastics doubled from 6% to 12% (i.e. increased by 100%), the weight increased by less because the total weight of the car decreased by 25%. The weight of cast iron decreased the most, down by 53%. Given that plastics and aluminium are far less dense than steel and cast iron, the *volume* of materials used will not have gone down by the same percentage as did weight. Depending on the precise densities of all the materials concerned, it is conceivable that, with a greater proportion of far lighter materials, the total volume of materials actually *increased* despite a 25% reduction in weight.

Question 12

Production reached 6×10^6 tonnes in 1963 (after another 9 years) and 12×10^6 tonnes about 1972 (after nearly another 9 years). The doubling time over that period was therefore about 9 years, so the average percentage rate of increase per year was 70/9, i.e. about 8%.

Question 13

To answer this question, you need to know the total amount of aluminium produced in 1950 and 1990. From Figure 18, the amounts are 1.5×10^6 t (1950) and 1.8×10^7 t (1990). The amount consumed by the developing world in 1950 was 2% of 1.5×10^6 t = 3.0×10^4 t; in 1990 it was 19% of 1.8×10^7 t = 3.4×10^6 t. The percentage increase is therefore $(3.4 \times 10^6/3.0 \times 10^4) \times 100 = (1.13 \times 10^2) \times 100 = 113 \times 100 = 11\,300\%$; i.e. the weight of aluminium used by developing countries increased by a factor of 113.

Question 14

The six missing numbers are: **10**; **113**; **6.7**; **105**; **15** and **7**.

The relevant calculations are as follows. The amount of aluminium consumed by the industrialized world in 1950 was 98% of 1.5×10^6 t = 1.47×10^6 t; in 1990 it was 81% of 1.8×10^7 t = 1.46×10^7 t. The percentage change is therefore $(1.46 \times 10^7/1.47 \times 10^6) \times 100 \approx (1.0 \times 10^1) \times 100 = 10 \times 100 = 1000\%$ increase; i.e. the total weight of aluminium used by industrialized countries increased by a factor of **10**. The value of **113** for developing countries was calculated earlier.

As the population in industrialized countries rose by a factor of 1.5 (i.e. $1.2 \times 10^9/0.8 \times 10^9$), you have to divide 10 by 1.5, giving **6.7** as the factor by which the average amount of aluminium used by an individual in the industrialized world had increased. The average amount of aluminium used per person in the industrialized world in 1950 was 1.47×10^6 t $/0.8 \times 10^9 = 1.84 \times 10^{-3}$ t = 1.84 kg, i.e. about **105** times more than someone in the developing world. ($1.84 \, kg/0.0176 \, kg \approx 105$)

In 1990, the average amount used per person in the industrialized world was, we know from the above, 6.7 times higher than in 1950, i.e. 12.3 kg (6.7×1.84 kg). (To check this, divide the total amount consumed in the industrialized world by its population, i.e. $1.46 \times 10^7/1.2 \times 10^9 \approx 1.22 \times 10^{-2}$ t = 12.2 kg). This amount is therefore about **15** times more than for someone in the developing world ($12.2 \, kg/0.83 \, kg \approx 15$)

The average amount of aluminium consumed by an individual in the developing world increased by 47 times (calculated earlier), as opposed to 6.7 times for someone from the industrialized world. This means that, over this period, the average consumption of aluminium per person in the developing world increased **7** times faster than for someone in the industrialized world ($47/6.7 \approx 7$).

Question 15

The demand curve shifts to the left, and the new equilibrium price and equilibrium quantity will both be lower than the original.

Question 16

The mercury has to be concentrated by a factor of $0.2\%/8 \times 10^{-6}\%$, i.e. by 25 000.

Question 17

Items (a), (c), (d), (e) (h), (j) and (k) are correct. Items (b), (f), (g) and (i) were incorrect, as explained below:

(b) The Parys Mountain mines were *re*-discovered in 1768; they had probably been worked by the Romans, and possibly even by the Phoenicians before them.

(f) Generally, cut-off grades have *fallen* with increased global production.

(g) During recession, demand curves generally shift to the *left*.

(i) Only if the projected *price to cost* ratio is very high will a mine venture even be considered today.

Question 18

The consumption figures include a significant amount of recycled copper, which was mined in earlier years.

Question 19

In 1992, the reserves lifetime for the elements, in years, was: lead 20; mercury 43; nickel 51; rhenium 78; silver 19; sulphur 26; tin 39.

Question 20

As, Ba, Be, Cu, Mo, and Sr are trace elements; Al, Ca, Fe, K, Mg, and Si are major elements.

Question 21

Augite (a member of the pyroxene group); hornblende (a member of the amphibole group); olivine; biotite (a mica); and chlorite. All these ferromagnesian minerals are silicates containing iron and magnesium.

Question 22

The ratio would generally decrease with increasing distance from the granite mountain because the feldspars and micas would have had more chance to break down chemically to clay minerals, and, in addition, the fine clay minerals are more easily transported than other mineral grains.

Question 23

(a) = (iv); (b) = (i); (c) = (iii); (d) = (ii).

Question 24

(a) = (v); (b) = (iv); (c) = (ii); (d) = (i); (e) = (vi); (f) = (iii).

Question 25

Items (a) to (d), (g), (i), (j), (l) and (m) are correct. Items (e), (f), (h) and (k) were incorrect, as explained below:

(e) In the weathered Shap granite, the *feldspars* and *micas* have decomposed to clay minerals, and of the main minerals, only *quartz* is chemically resistant.

(f) Biological processes *can* concentrate elements in the rock cycle. Coal, for example, contains carbon concentrated by plants.

(h) Sedimentary layers like those in the coal-bearing rocks at Whitehaven are not necessarily laterally continuous; they may thicken or thin laterally over short distances, perhaps forming isolated lenses, making it difficult to predict their subsurface location.

(k) In the Silverband mine, the near-vertical veins of galena and barite do not pass upwards out of the *limestone* because the mineralizing fluids were stopped by the overlying *shales* which are impermeable and relatively insoluble. The greater solubility of limestone, and the numerous fractures within it, allow the relatively easy passage of mineralizing fluids; consequently, ore minerals tend to replace limestone more readily than shales.

Question 26

(a) titanium Ti; (b) tin Sn; (c) tungsten W; (d) chromium Cr; (e) zirconium Zr.

Question 27

(b) a constructive plate margin, i.e. the site of sea-floor spreading along an ocean ridge.

Question 28

(a) Continental crust, unlike oceanic crust, is not dense enough to be subducted into the mantle at destructive plate boundaries; it is therefore generally very much older, and is far more likely to have been subject to episodes of structural deformation, igneous activity and metamorphism.

(b) About 4% of the age of the Earth (200 Ma/4600 Ma).

Question 29

(a) sedimentary processes; (b) metamorphic processes; (c) igneous processes; (d) sedimentary processes.

Question 30

Copper: 6696 t, i.e. $(70\% \times 1.007 \times 10^9 \times 9.5)/10^6$; zinc: 2344 t; nickel: 526 t.

Question 31

(a) Only about 3500 tonnes were being recycled (0.25% of 7% of the 20 million tonnes total of domestic waste);

(b) about 1.4 million tonnes were *not* being recycled.

Question 32

(a) 120 000 generations;

(b) 10 000 generations (taking the origin of modern humans as 200 000 years ago);

(c) 2150 generations.

COMMENTS ON ACTIVITIES

Activity 1

In the writer's kitchen were: sea salt from the French Mediterranean (in a plastic bottle); a limestone chopping board from Portugal; a cup made in the USA; a wine glass made in Venezuela; a stainless steel cheese knife with a handle made of Connemara marble from Ireland. All these are based on physical resources. Some biological resources included nutmeg from the West Indies, coriander from Morocco, peppercorns from Malaysia — each in a glass container of unknown provenance. It's often hard to find out where the raw materials came from for a particular object, e.g. where did oil come from for the plastic bottle, or iron for the knife blade? In every case, though, it's obvious that a huge number of physical resources must have been involved at some stage, such as in the manufacture of the rock-cutting equipment to shape the limestone chopping board, in making the vehicle to transport it, in obtaining the variety of fuels used, and so on.

Activity 2

Figure 72 shows the completed graph.

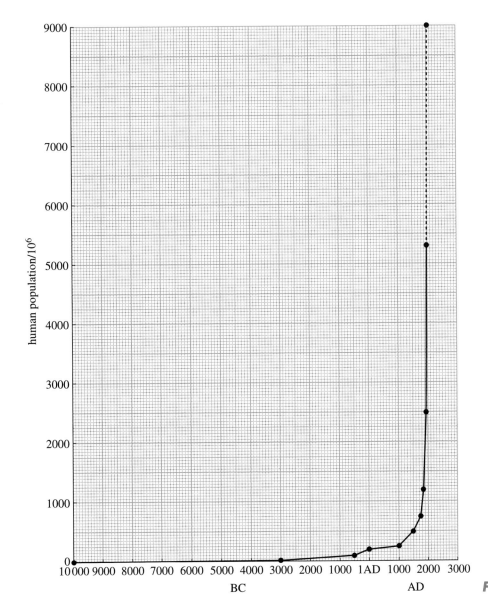

Figure 72

Activity 3

Your answer will vary, of course, with your house, especially with its age and location. In the writer's previous house in Cardiff, built about 1900, a roof of natural slate had been replaced by artificial tiles that simulated slate; all the window frames were still wood, but two crumbling limestone window lintels had been replaced by concrete ones; the hot water pipes were copper, but had once been lead; the fireplaces had been bricked up, and in effect, replaced by storage heaters. Cast iron guttering had been replaced by plastic guttering. The writer's present house in Milton Keynes was built in 1979 and, apart from the replacement of a glass front door with a wooden one, no significant substitution has yet taken place.

You probably know examples of substitution where the more typical pattern of replacement has been reversed for aesthetic or other reasons, such as the replacement of a ceramic tile fireplace by natural stone; a plastic or aluminium window frame by wood; or a plastic bath by a cast-iron one.

Activity 4

(a) When the cost of rail travel went up sharply, I spent more on petrol.

(b) On buying a house, I had to buy paint, paintbrushes, wallpaper, an aluminium ladder, plastic dustsheets, plastic brooms, nails, screws, screwdrivers, and a great many other products, all bought together *in parallel* as a result of a single purchase (the house). Not surprisingly, changes in house prices are considered to be of great economic significance because so many complementary goods are affected.

Activity 5

In my household, the residence time for a 1 litre plastic bottle of fresh orange juice is 2 days; for a can of soft drink, about 10 days; and for a bottle of washing-up liquid about 6 weeks.

Activity 6

(a) In my household, 95% of cans were aluminium (unmagnetic), reflecting a high proportion of soft-drink cans of a particular brand; the remaining 5% were steel food cans.

(b) The average aluminium drink can weighed just under 17 g, so I would have to collect nearly 60 000 cans for 1 tonne (£600).

(c) Each can is therefore worth about 1p.

Activity 7

Living in Milton Keynes, I can use a weekly kerb-side collection scheme to which 70% of households currently belong (*c.* 54 000). About 170 tonnes are collected each week, representing nearly 25% recycling of domestic refuse.

Figure 73 The weekly kerb-side recycling collection scheme operating in Milton Keynes. (a) Bins for paper (right) and plastic, glass and metal (left). (b) Contents of the left bin in (a) are placed into the appropriate containers in the recycling collection vehicle.

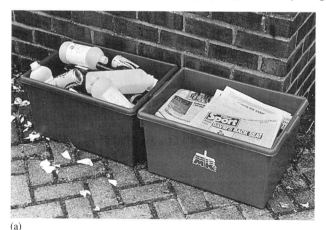
(a)

(b)

Paper (collected from a red bin kept by the household) forms the bulk (89 t per week), and the remaining 81 t of mainly glass, metal cans and plastics are collected from a blue bin, and partially sorted by the operators of a purpose-built collection vehicle. There are also bottle banks (for plastic and glass) and can banks near supermarkets, and pre-sorted materials can also be recycled via local refuse sites.

Acknowledgements

The author would like to thank the Block Assessor, Geoff Browning, of Staffordshire University, for his helpful comments and suggestions.

The following student readers are thanked for their comments on an early draft: Julia Adamson, Tom Denne and Iris Rowbotham.

Grateful acknowledgement is made to the following sources for permission to reproduce material in this text:

Figures

Cover: Satellite composite view of Earth, copyright © 1990 Tom Van Sant/ The GeoSphere® Project, Santa Monica, California, with assistance from NOAA, NASA, EYES ON EARTH, technical direction Lloyd Van Warren, source data derived from NOAA/TIROS-N Series Satellites. All rights reserved; *Figure 4(a):* Peter Sheldon; *Figure 4(b):* BAS/88/34, British Antarctic Survey; *Figure 5:* Tioxide Europe Limited; *Figure 6:* Dr O. Williams-Thorpe; *Figure 8:* The National Museum of Science and Industry; *Figures 9(a), (b):* Steve Drury; *Figure 12:* courtesy of the BBC; *Figure 13:* by courtesy of the Roman Baths Museum, Bath; *Figures 14(a), (b):* Thames Water Utilities Limited; *Figure 15(a):* Department of the Environment (London), © Crown copyright, reproduced by permission of the Controller of Her Majesty's Stationery Office; *Figure 15(d): The Macmillan Encyclopedia,* 1981 edition, Macmillan Reference Books; *Figures 16–21: Episodes,* September 1992, International Union of Geological Sciences; *Figure 27:* Peter Sheldon; *Figure 33:* RTZ Limited; *Figure 37:* from *Earthquakes Newly Revised And Expanded,* by Bruce Bolt. Copyright © 1993 by W. H. Freeman and Company. Used with permission; *Figure 39:* United States Geological Survey; *Figure 46:* Reprinted by permission from *Physical Geology* by J. Monroe and R. Wicander. Copyright © 1992 by West Publishing Company. All rights reserved; *Figure 47:* Reproduced by permission of the Director, British Geological Survey: NERC copyright reserved; *Figure 51:* Reprinted with the permission of Simon & Schuster, from the Macmillan College text *Essentials of Geology* 2/e by Frederick K. Lutgens and Edward J. Tarbuck. Copyright © 1986 by Charles E. Merrill Publishing Company; *Figure 52:* Reproduced by permission of the Director, British Geological Survey: NERC copyright reserved; *Figure 55:* Chris Hawkesworth; *Figure 63:* Reproduced by permission of the Director, British Geological Survey: NERC copyright reserved; *Figure 64:* Prof. Roger Searle, University of Durham; *Figure 65:* Robert D. Ballard, Woods Hole Oceanographic Institution; *Figure 67:* Wyllie, P. J., *The Way The Earth Works,* Copyright © 1976 John Wiley & Sons, Inc. Publishers. Reprinted by permission of John Wiley & Sons, Inc.; *Figure 71:* Martin Wright, Still Pictures, London; *Figure 73:* Peter Sheldon.

Physical Resources and Environment